A Writer's Eye

BOOKS BY EUDORA WELTY

A Curtain of Green and Other Stories 1941
The Robber Bridegroom 1942
The Wide Net and Other Stories 1943
Delta Wedding 1946
The Golden Apples 1949
The Ponder Heart 1954
The Bride of Innisfallen and Other Stories 1955
The Shoe Bird 1964
Losing Battles 1970
One Time, One Place 1971
The Optimist's Daughter 1972
The Eye of the Story: Selected Essays and Reviews 1978
The Collected Stories 1980
One Writer's Beginnings 1984
Photographs 1989

EUDORA WELTY

A Writer's Eye

Collected Book Reviews

EDITED, WITH AN INTRODUCTION, BY

PEARL AMELIA McHANEY

UNIVERSITY PRESS OF MISSISSIPPI   JACKSON

Grateful acknowledgment is made to the following:
The New York Times Copyright 1943, 1944, 1945, 1946, 1948, 1951,
1952, 1953, 1956, 1957, 1958, 1961, 1963, 1965, 1970, 1971, 1972, 1973,
1974, 1975, 1976, 1977, 1978, 1981, 1984.
The Hudson Review Copyright 1949.
New York Post Copyright 1949, 1950, 1951.
Saturday Review of Literature Copyright 1942, 1950.
Sewanee Review Copyright 1967.
Tomorrow Copyright 1943, 1945.

97 96 95 94   4 3 2 1

The paper in this book meets the guidelines for permanence and
durability of the Committee on Production Guidelines for Book
Longevity of the Council on Library Resources.

Library of Congress Cataloging-in-Publication Data

Welty, Eudora, 1909–
    A writer's eye : collected book reviews / Eudora Welty : edited,
with an introduction, by Pearl Amelia McHaney.
        p.   cm.
    Includes bibliographical references (p.   ) and index.
    ISBN 0-87805-683-1 (alk. paper)
    1. Books—Reviews.   I. McHaney, Pearl Amelia.   II. Title.
PS3545.E6M66   1994
028.1—dc20   93-33643
                                                     CIP

British Library Cataloging-in-Publication data available

For
NONA BALAKIAN
who initiated me into my richly rewarding experience
on the staff of the *New York Times Book Review*
in the summer of 1944

Contents

Contents

Contents

Contents

Acknowledgments

I wish to thank Eudora Welty for the opportunity to prepare this edition. I also wish to thank Nash K. Burger, Noel Polk, and Dabney Hart for their personal and professional encouragement and generosity. Jane Hobson, Marjorie Patterson, and Matt Stinson of the Interlibrary Loan Department of Georgia State's Pullen Library were always helpful and inventive. I am grateful for research support from the Department of English and the Research Office of Georgia State University. The Mississippi Department of Archives and History proved as usual to be an excellent and cooperative source for Welty scholars; Hank Holmes, Anne Lipscomb, and Nancy Lipscomb were particularly helpful. I thank Lorna Stark for support beyond the call of sisterhood and Lothar Hönnighausen and LeAnne Benfield for their generous assistance. Meredith, Emily, and Gretchen Schmidt, who have learned at an early age to live with the making of a book, are thanked for their honesty, industry, and personal responsibility. I am especially thankful to Tom McHaney for his loving friendship, his enthusiasm for research, his honesty in criticism, and his creativity with words.

Introduction

The best introduction this collection could have would be a six-column review by Eudora Welty. She could quickly appraise the sixty-seven reviews written over forty-two years, mostly for the *New York Times Book Review*. She could tell a literary anecdote about Robert Van Gelder, her mentor and friend at the *Book Review*, and how exciting it was to work in New York during the summer of 1944. She could pick out quotations from the reviews to show the humor, the painterly eye, the astuteness of the reader-reviewer as quickly as she could isolate the weaknesses of the merely chronological arrangement and the awkwardness of the collection's scholarly garb. She would doubtless say that some of the reviews are but mayflies, and that some are butterflies worthy of stretching under a glass, but that, as she said of Virginia Woolf's reviews in *Granite and Rainbow*, "writing them earned her the time to write her novels, and the least of them is a graceful and imperturbable monument to interruption." Best of all, a review by Eudora Welty would give us once again her delightful wit and mindful words about a subject we all adore—books.

It is not news that Eudora Welty wrote book reviews, but it may come as news that she wrote so many.[1] Preparing the nonfiction collection *The Eye of the Story* (1978), Welty originally gathered eighteen reviews. Reviews of two books (*A Haunted House and Other Stories* by Virginia Woolf and *Henry Green: Nine Novels and an Unpacked Bag*, a critical study) had to be cut so everything else could be put in.[2] The sixteen remaining reviews show the range of Welty's reviewing career though they focus chiefly on major writers: Virginia Woolf, Elizabeth Bowen, William Faulkner, E. M. Forster, Ford Madox Ford, Isak Dinesen, S. J. Perelman, and E. B. White. Among the lesser-known subjects for the reviews reprinted in *The Eye of the Story*, but equally important in the world of *belles lettres*, are Washington Irving (journals), novelist and nonfictionist George R. Stewart, Australian Nobel winner Patrick White, and detective fiction author Ross Macdonald. The reviews in *Eye* are often quoted in Welty scholarship and have been the primary subject of three critical essays.[3] Together, these reviews show a range that does not surprise us, but they represent less than one-fourth of Welty's work as a reviewer, work she took seriously and enjoyed.

This edition collects all sixty-seven of Welty's reviews of seventy-four books. Seen together, the reviews reveal the delightful variety of books sent to Welty for comment: first novels, best-sellers, southern novels, translations, short story volumes, collected stories, essays, histories, criticism, biographies, memoirs, travel books, journals and letters, photography, children's books and fairy tale collections, even a book on growing healthy house plants. The subjects of the books vary also: World War II (European fronts, London air raids, Pacific maneuvers), Ireland, England, the South, ghost stories, detective mysteries, and humor. Welty says that when she was first a regular reviewer, she liked best the surprise of what would next be offered for her to read.

Having all of Welty's reviews available in one gathering fills in numerous gaps, some, of course, that we didn't even recognize until we came up to the precipice. The review of Virginia Woolf's posthumously collected stories, *A Haunted House and Other Stories* (1944), deleted from *The Eye of the Story*, her first review of a significant writer, can now be read in the context of her other comments about Woolf and writing. Two more Perelman titles—*Crazy Like a Fox* (1944) and *Westward Ha! Around the World in 80 Clichés* (1948)—that were not included in *The Eye of the Story* are reprinted. Reviews of *The Collected Stories of Elizabeth Bowen* (1981), and *Essays of E. B. White* (1977), written after *The Eye of the Story* was published, complement her praise and recommendation of Bowen and White.

In addition to reviewing Isak Dinesen's *Last Tales*, which she included in *The Eye of the Story*, Welty also reviewed two critical analyses of Dinesen's writing. It is interesting to read her assessment of other critics: Each book was moderately successful, she said, but neither showed well-enough that its author had been "stirred, delighted, touched, bored, maddened, even baffled" by Dinesen's genius. In both reviews, Welty advises the reader not to follow the critics but to read the fiction itself. "I suspect," Welty writes about Robert Langbaum, author of the study she liked better, "that his own first response to her stories was 'That's beautiful!'—before it was 'That's important.' He has demonstrated that they are important, and also acclaimed them for being marvelous. 'Marvelous' is the relevant and better word, is it not?"

Welty's review of *Henry Green: Nine Novels and an Unpacked Bag* (1961) fills out her appraisal of one of her favorite writers in a similar fashion. Shortly after completing her essay "Henry Green: Novelist of the Imagination," Welty was asked to review English professor John Russell's analysis of Green's writings. Russell passes Welty's litmus test, for, in her view, he "has been seized by the delight that Henry Green's extraordinary prose can give, for delight I think does open the door to this writer whose work does then become so moving." Welty was often on the frontier of recognizing genius in writing (witness her early and continued praise of Faulkner, before Cowley's Viking Portable and before the Nobel Prize). When Henry Green's autobiography *Pack My Bag* had its first American printing in the United States in June 1993, reviewers quoted Welty's early essay.

William Sansom is another writer whom Welty reviewed from the beginning of his career, though her earliest review of his work was until recently not well known. Sansom was a British contemporary of Green's, and like Green, he fought in the London Fire Fighters and used the experience in his first collection of stories, *Fireman Flower* (1945). Welty's review of this book was discovered by Suzanne Marrs as a typescript among the papers that Welty donated to the Mississippi Department of Archives and History. Published in 1944 by Hogarth Press in England, the collection was brought out in the United States by Vanguard Press the next year. Welty, perhaps at the suggestion of Diarmuid Russell, read the book for Vanguard and provided a comment that is excerpted on the book's dust jacket. The review itself was published in a small, avant-garde monthly titled *Tomorrow* (1941–51), owned and edited by New Yorker Eileen Garrett and published by Creative Age Press for whom Welty's childhood friend, Jacksonian Hubert Creekmore, had worked after World War II. Other Welty friends who reviewed for *Tomorrow* included *New York Times Book Review* people Nona Balakian and Nash Burger, the latter also a Jackson native.

Welty reviewed a later volume of Sansom's stories about Italy, *South*, for the *Saturday Review*, and then for the *New York Times Book Review*, *The Stories of William Sansom* which she said included "an excellent appreciation by exactly the right fellow-writer, Elizabeth Bowen." "Sansom's talent," Welty wrote in her first review, "is an exciting matter for the new American readers. . . . Along with their fantastic or dreamlike quality, the stories are extraordinarily vital—perhaps, for one thing, because they are visually concrete and startling." Then of the stories in *South*, she wrote, his "descriptive power is a steady fireworks." In her third review of Sansom fiction, she delights in being reminded that "the very act and mystery of writing a story is central to his work." The reviews of Sansom are interesting in another light also, for each was written for a different publication.

Welty's very first book review was published in September of 1942 in the *Saturday Review of Literature*'s special "Deep South" issue, edited by Mississippian David Cohn. Cohn wrote to Welty's agent, Diarmuid Russell, asking for a "short story or sketch of 2,000–2,500 words."[4] Nothing of that description was readily available, so Russell sent *The Robber Bridegroom*, Welty's fairy tale novella of the Natchez Trace, to be excerpted. Cohn returned it and published no fiction in the issue because, as he says in his introduction, many of the Deep South writers "were so busy writing books that they could not turn aside" from their projects to send him contributions (*Saturday Review* 19 September 1942: 3).

Russell's ambition for his client to be a part of the special issue nonetheless resulted in Welty's first review. She was assigned *But You'll Be Back*, a first novel by Marguerite Steedman from Georgia. The Deep South issue (other special issues in the 1940s series focused on the Southwest and the Old or Upper South) included several essays of particular interest in the context of Welty's developing career, especially "Patterns of Regionalism in the Deep South" by Chapel Hill regional sociologist Howard W. Odum and "What Deep South Literature Needs" by Cleanth Brooks, one of the editors, with Robert Penn Warren, of the *Southern Review* (Odum, 5–7; Brooks, 8–9, 29–30).

Brooks, in fact, begins his essay remarking about a review of Welty's first book, *A Curtain of Green and Other Stories*. Louise Bogan, he notes, had written that the stories were representative of the "Gothic South," leading Brooks to lament that the "country's intense interest in and ignorance of the South . . . is in part the result of the decay of our ability to read, and of our current confusions about the nature of literature" (8; Bogan, *Nation* 6 December 1941: 572). Welty, he asserts, has given the southern subject a form that is "remarkable for the variety of styles which she has mastered" (29–30). Brooks concludes that the region needs "more intelligent readers" and "a group of critics and reviewers more sensitive and more intelligent than it presently has" (30). Welty takes up this problem in her review by noting that the dust jacket of Steedman's novel says Steedman's characters are "'Normal Southern' people." Welty writes that this "is a jolting phrase, and one hopes does not indicate that hereafter southern people are to be subdivided from the rest of the country" (22).

In the same issue, Jennie Gardner, book review editor for the *Memphis Commercial Appeal*, points out that few of the South's writers review for the regional papers. "There's little market for any deep criticism in the Deep South, and consequently, as criticism, our reviews are vastly unimportant" ("Book Reviewing in the Deep South," 15). Five of the eight book reviews and two of the essays in the Deep South issue are indeed written by southern novelists. Welty's first book review thus appears alongside the work of novelists and literary critics Harry Harrison Kroll, Roark Bradford, Robert Penn Warren, and Cleanth Brooks. *A Curtain of Green* and her forthcoming novella that Cohn did not excerpt, *The Robber Bridegroom*, are advertised next to her review. Faulkner's *Go Down, Moses* and novels by six of the contributors to the issue are also advertised.

Welty's astute review of Marguerite Steedman's novel is an appropriate response to the call made in the issue for criticism of southern writing by distinctive southern writers. Her first review begins in the way that became Welty's pattern, a description of the book itself. Certainly, this is an obvious and sensible approach, called for by the very nature of book reviewing, but Welty does it with flair and her personal style. *But You'll Be Back*, she writes, is the story of the small Georgia town of Thessaly, "its threatened life, its death by ruin and fire, and its dramatic renascence" (22). Steedman "knows her little towns," Welty observes, but she creates only "stock sentimental characters" and "contents herself with an old cliche" to represent emotional involvement. She does this, Welty suggests, because "the author herself has not been emotionally affected by her ethical ideas" (22–23): "When the time comes, as it should, to look through the outside of this life to the inside, she backs away" (22). The plot and characters are manipulated; "there is no interplay of character, only a one-way effect of an omnipotent Aunt Cora on the others" (22). The subject of the novel is interesting, but in Welty's view the author does not allow the characters to live their own lives.

Welty's concerns in her 1942 review reflect her own practice in the making of fiction, ideas she has articulated many times over her fifty-year writing career. In an uncollected essay about her first story "Death of a Traveling Salesman" (1936), Welty said,

I faced the serious hazard of imagining myself inside characters whom I had no way of really knowing. . . . I never doubted, then or now, that imagining yourself into other people's lives is exactly what writing fiction is. . . . Imagining yourself inside the skin, body, heart, and mind of any other person is the primary feat, but also the absolute necessity. (755)[5]

Characters who speak for themselves, who motivate and control the actions of the story, are essential to Welty's notion of what it takes for a story to succeed.

Ultimately, Steedman's writing lacks "passion," a term Welty uses critically in a majority of her reviews. Steedman "has not been emotionally affected by her ethical ideas. . . . She is sure of them, often enthusiastic, sometimes sentimental, but not possessed. She is actuated by something less and something lighter than emotion, the development of a bright idea" (23). Steedman writes well enough, Welty says, but her "ease has permitted carelessness at times, and there are smudgy traces of journalism in an occasional absurdity of phrase and now and then a veil of sheerest hokum falls over the page." Although Welty had not yet published a novel of her own, she unhesitatingly decides that Steedman's first novel is a failure and clearly identifies its problems. The rationale for the judgments Welty so competently and confidently articulates in this initial review does not change throughout her career of writing and reviewing.

Shortly before this first book review was published, Robert Van Gelder, editor of *The New York Times Book Review*, had interviewed Welty for the *Book Review* where he wrote of the young short story writer, "She writes easily, perfectly naturally, enjoying the job and lost in it" (Prenshaw 3).[6] Soon, he invited her to review *Sweet Beulah Land*, a southern novel by Bernice Kelly Harris (*NYTBR* 7 March 1943: 9). That was the auspicious beginning to the relationship: between 1943 and 1984, Welty wrote fifty-nine of her sixty-seven book reviews for the *New York Times Book Review*, twenty-six of them in the 1940s, mostly during the editorship of Van Gelder.

Van Gelder's high regard for the young Mississippi writer led him, in 1944, to invite Welty to come to New York for a summer internship as a copy reader for the *Book Review*. It was Van Gelder's idea to invite "someone who was not a professional" for their input.[7] (As Welty remembers it, she thought it intriguing that the previous intern had been a psychologist.) Welty was responsible to Van Gelder, but everyone had to have an interview with Lester Markel, the tyrannical editor of the Sunday edition of the *New*

York Times. In his gruff manner, Markel asked Welty for her qualifications, for "I hear you have applied for a job with our Sunday *Book Review.*" She remembers replying "nakedly" with " 'No, I was invited to work on it and I'm already working.' It was the truth—I had no other thing to say. And he said it was very very irregular." She settled into her job—copy editing and writing. Welty says she was also "responsible for thinking up fresh reviewers for the paper." Nash K. Burger, a University of the South- and University of Virginia-educated childhood friend from Jackson, was one of the first that she recommended. When the then unknown Burger's very first review appeared on page one, the intemperate Markel demanded to know "who in the hell is Nash K. Burger?" Van Gelder calmly replied, "Nash K. Burger is the author of the book review on the front page." Van Gelder won the round, and Burger reviewed more than one book a month during the following year before joining the *Book Review* staff for a thirty-year career starting in 1945.

Welty enjoyed New York city life, the hard work at the copy desk, and she says she learned a great deal about writing, but not necessarily about fiction. "You wouldn't write a very good review if you kept applying it to what you could learn to write fiction. You can't mix them," she says. In a 1978 interview with writer Reynolds Price, she likened writing essays and stories to going in "two different directions—upstream and downstream. I can't work on them simultaneously. I like both. I think it's more natural to me to write stories, but I like writing essays. I'm not a born critic, but I may be a born appreciator. I like to write about things I like" (Prenshaw 230). When the summer internship was over, Welty returned to Jackson where she concentrated on writing fiction and an occasional book review.

The most curious commodity shared by Welty and Burger (in addition to Jackson childhoods, the same school teachers, a southern humor, and the ambition to write) is the pseudonym *Michael Ravenna.* While Welty was in New York in 1944, her two brothers and many close friends were in Europe fighting. Working at the *Times* kept her in close touch with the "real war" as well as the growing literature about or from the war. Although *Book Review* policy discouraged staff—Welty's status—from writing reviews, occasionally someone had to write a quick review to meet a missed deadline, to fill space, or to cover a last minute book of importance. Reviews by staff members were printed with pseudonymous bylines. Welty's first such review, of *Artist at War* (16 July 1944), appeared under the name Michael Ravenna. A month later "Ravenna" reviewed a war novel written by an Austrian ex-

Nazi, Franz Hoellering, entitled *Furlough* (20 August 1944: 5). A third review by "Ravenna"—*I Got a Country*, another war novel, about allied soldiers stationed in Alaska—was published on 27 August 1944 (page 5). It has long been assumed that Welty wrote the second and third Ravenna reviews, but they are now acknowledged as the work of Nash Burger. Burger was reviewing from Mississippi, and it had already been decided to run his review of *Invasion Diary* by Richard Tregaskis on the 20th and of *Cluny Brown*, a novel by Margery Sharp, on the 27th, so when there was space for other short reviews by Burger, they were printed under the pseudonym that Welty had already used for a book about the war. When asked why the staff used "her" pseudonym, Michael Ravenna, Welty quipped, "I probably couldn't think of another name."

For Burger, the enterprising Michael Ravenna took on a life of his own, and much later Burger recalled fan letters and requests for more Ravenna reviews.[8] Ravenna went underground when Burger joined the *Book Review* staff the next year, and Burger fashioned new pennames when necessary, until Ravenna surfaced to review the first novel of fellow-Mississippian Shelby Foote (25 September 1949: 30). The quixotic Ravenna made a point of mentioning recent Southern writers who had come before Foote, including Eudora Welty, as well as congratulating the excellent first novel, *Tournament*.

Those who have known about the Michael Ravenna reviews have speculated variously about Welty's choice of pseudonym. Was it because women weren't expected to review war novels as Burger suggested in his 1969 essay? Welty says, "Being a woman had nothing to do with it. After all, Van Gelder had hired a woman hadn't he?" (Correspondence to editor 1991). Multiple reviews by one writer in the same issue were discouraged, but Welty says this was not the case in the instances of her use of the pseudonym. Certainly, she recalls, the name alludes to Ravenna, Italy, locale of various war maneuvers, and the war was exceedingly on everyone's mind. Nash Burger, interviewed in Charlottesville, Virginia, where he still writes, claims to know what Michael Ravenna looks like. But Welty, who talks to Burger often, will say only, "Well, he ought to; he's the only one who does." Her final word on the matter is that it was, "Just a name that came to me. Why not Michael Ravenna?"

Before, during, and after her summer at the *Times*, Welty wrote the most concentrated number of book reviews, all for Van Gelder: six in 1943, twelve in 1944, and six in 1945. As editor of the *Book Review*, Van Gelder favored issues that included a fair amount of fiction, and he was most interested in having fine writers review for him, rather than seeking out an expert in the book's subject. Welty was perfectly suited for this. When she wrote her first review for Van Gelder, she had published *A Curtain of Green*, *The Robber Bridegroom*, and all of the stories to be gathered in *The Wide Net*. With that considerable labor of fiction behind her, Welty recalls that the journalism that she wrote during 1943—in addition to the reviews, there were two essays ("Pageant of Birds" for *New Republic* and "Some Notes on River Country" for *Harper's Bazaar*)—was satisfying in its quick turnaround time.[9] By autumn, she had started "Delta Cousins," the germ of *Delta Wedding* (Kreyling 99–105).

Writing book reviews had several advantages. Stories were more demanding and speculative, needing to be shopped to the right editor. Straight deadlines were relatively simple by comparison. Rarely was a review subject to further criticism; the work went in, editors shaped it a bit, and it appeared in print. Also, there was money to be earned, promptly paid. Burger recalls that his page-one review in 1944 earned him forty dollars. After working her way from obscure literary journals into lucrative national magazines, Welty still appreciated the extra payments for the reviews.

Though Welty has said in many ways that reviewing and writing fiction were very separate jobs, she still benefited as a writer from her literary journalism. As Michael Kreyling describes in *Author and Agent*, the review that Welty wrote of Virginia Woolf's *A Haunted House and Other Stories* significantly helped Welty to focus on her own fiction. She wrote to her agent, Diarmuid Russell, "I had to review Virginia Woolf's last book of stories and if they print my review as written (they never do) I would be interested to see if you agree" (11 April 1944, quoted in Kreyling 108). Making the aesthetic shift to long fiction as she rewrote her story "Delta Cousins" as a novel, Welty could draw on the experience and confidence earned by the chance to survey recent fiction as reviewer and as copy editor of many other reviews.

The work for the *Times* had another plus. Welty admired Van Gelder (the integrity of Welty's reviews were, to this point, maintained—editorial changes were made mostly to shorten the reviews) and this, she said in an interview recently, made reviewing pleasant work. The months in New York put her in the middle of all that was happening in the war, in the country's largest cultural center, and gave her a nine-to-five office job for the first (and last) time in her career. She recalls that it was hard work, but satisfying.

After she returned to Jackson, she continued to review a varied selection of books for the Sunday *Times*: *Six Novels of the Supernatural*; *The Western Journals of Washington Irving*; *Apartment in Athens* by Glenway Wescott; *Names on the Land: A Historical Account of Place-Names in the United States* by novelist George R. Stewart (both page-one reviews); three fairy tale books; and *Gumbo Ya-Ya, A Collection of Louisiana Folk Tales*.

The smorgasbord ended when Van Gelder moved to Crown Publishers in 1946, partly frustrated by Markel's interference with his autonomy as *Book Review* editor. Editorial duties at the *Book Review* during the next three years were handled, chaotically at best, by a variety of editors working under Markel's sharp scrutiny. John K. Hutchens managed for a year or two before he was driven out by Markel, moving to the *Times*'s rival, the *New York Herald Tribune*. Staff editor William DuBois and Markel's Sunday Magazine editor Herbert Lyons took frustrated turns before editor Francis Brown took over in 1950.[10] An additional deterrent from writing reviews, after Van Gelder left the *Book Review*, was Welty's work on the stories of *The Golden Apples*, her first lecture on writing, and her critical essay derived from the lecture, "The Reading and Writing of Short Stories."[11]

In the late summer of 1948, concurrent with the writing of the final story of *The Golden Apples* cycle and concerted efforts on her agent's part to sell the completed stories, Welty wrote three reviews. Of the three books, only one was completely successful, in her judgment. *Westward Ha!* lacked Perelman's usual sharpness because it was artificially generated as a *Holiday* magazine commission. The plot of Dorothy Baker's *Our Gifted Son* was unnaturally controlled by the author. But, Hollis Summers, the author of the third book reviewed, *City Limit*, Welty wrote, had "compassion, a good eye not conditioned by anything, a good ear conditioned by some worthwhile anger, and a view of youth and innocence that is fresh, dignified, and rewarding" (*NYTBR* 19 September 1948: 18). These three reviews, written at the peak of Welty's short-story career, represent a significant crossroads of journalism, craft in fiction, and Welty's developing aesthetic in criticism.

After the review of *City Limit* in the *Book Review*, Welty reviewed a few volumes for three other publications before settling into a rhythm of one or two books reviewed in most years for the *Book Review*. She reviewed Faulkner's *Intruder in the Dust* for the *Hudson Review* in its inaugural year (1949). She did three book reviews for the *New York Post*. And for the *Saturday Review of Literature*, where she had started reviewing, she praised a William Sansom collection of stories. From 1952 until her final review in 1984, only one review (of *Martha Graham: Portrait of the Lady as Artist* for the *Sewanee Review*) is not published in the *Book Review*. These thirty-one reviews represent the second half of Welty's reviewing "career"; and of them, thirteen are collected in *The Eye of the Story*.

Welty has always said that she's never written anything she did not want to write. Her reviews show her engagement. No book or review is simply thrown off, and Welty writes from the reader's point of view. For reviews, she does not take the role of fiction writer, but assumes instead the duties of the literary journalist, reading, assessing, and reporting. Her wonderful facility with words and her honesty as a reader and writer make her reviews themselves brilliant moments of reading matter. When she tells the plot— and only briefly—it is with newly-created metaphors, often with allusions to painters and paintings, and the authors' best lines. Even when Welty encounters what an academic might call a subgenre, something not readily categorized in the canon of literature, or even something that is ephemeral, she reads carefully. Ghost story collections are a case in point: She asks what must happen in a story so that the reader will *Sleep No More*, as one book was titled (1944). One requirement is the delicious *frisson* of scariness. The stories in *The Great Fog, and Other Weird Tales*, for example, "raise only the intellectual hair, not the pulling kind" (3 September 1944: 5). Reviewing detective fiction, Welty explains just what makes Ross Macdonald's *The Underground Man* (1971) and its hero Lew Archer not only better than the average, but as successful and well-crafted as any mainstream fiction.

Of special interest are the reviews of books about World War II. She reviewed three books of art depicting the war at first hand: *Artist at War* by George Biddle (brother of Franklin Roosevelt's Attorney General, Francis Biddle), sketches made at several Mediterranean and African fronts; *Men and Battle*, sketches by artist David Fredenthal drawn during the attack on Arawa, New Britain, in 1943; and *G. I. Sketch Book*, a small pocket-sized Infantry Journal edition of *Art in the Armed Forces* edited by Aimee Crane. Welty comments not only on the subject matter that is brought fresh to the reader back home, but also on the artistic merit of the pictures and the arrangement of the volume. Biddle compares his effort to Goya's depiction of the Napoleonic invasions of Spain, so Welty continues the comparison saying, "Where Goya drew disaster in the act—falling bodies, the thrust of violence in its present moment—George Biddle draws the aftermath of disaster, the sprawling pattern in its wake" (*NYTBR* 16 July 1944: 3). Welty writes that Biddle is a "competent artist, but a good writer" (24). The review of *Artist at War* is lengthy enough to allow Welty room, beyond description of the book, to discuss the dignity of the soldiers being drawn, the issue of truth in art, and censorship. Even though the government has withdrawn the program that sent artists like Biddle to the front, she observes, Welty is encouraged that the idea itself is such a "hopeful example of a new, a human and subjective attitude of a country toward war, that may be a sign in itself that we can never tolerate another one" (24).

In all her reviews, Welty is vigilant for the truths and passions that are central to humanity, wherever they occur. The books she recommends most highly use the topical and the specific to reveal underlying connections among all people, the very threads of life that were, for example, challenged by the dissolution of democracy under Hitler's rule. Welty writes with the same emphasis upon vigor and passion from the first to the last books that she reviewed. If a pattern or a style in the writing of the reviews can be detected, it is a felicitous habit of eye and mind that works throughout the forty-year span of the reviews. "This book," she begins—and then unravels tapestries of her own words to retell the scenes that delight her most. From among her own passions and interests, she repeatedly alludes to painters and fairy tales. In epic fashion, she includes in nearly every review a list— places, scenes, or characters—with strings of gerunds and participles. If no catalogue can be extracted, she builds one from adjectives of praise. She concludes with "What this reader loves . . ." about the book under review.

Unlike many writer-reviewers, Welty never strikes the virtuoso's pose. She keeps the voice of the book's author in the foreground of the review. In fact, as her own fiction writing merited her a reputation of the highest regard, she appears to quote more and more from the books under review, so that her reviews in the 1970s and 80s are mostly ingenious weavings of the language and plots of the books. One might guess that the novice reviewer would be the one to quote extended passages, but the reverse is true for Welty. In the forties, she confidently analyzed the writing and wisely chose the author's words to illustrate her judgment. She let the books defend or condemn themselves.

Her review of Annie Dillard's *Pilgrim at Tinker Creek* is a prime example. Welty writes that, "A reader's heart must go out to a young writer with a sense of wonder so fearless and unbridled." Such headlong passion and emotion are exactly what Welty requires, but in the next paragraph, after several more lines of praise, Welty writes, "I am not quite sure that in writing this book she wholly accomplished" her ambition. Welty quotes scenes that show both Dillard's unbridled exuberance and her consequent failure to go beyond enthusiastic solipsism. Yet, even in this, which is one of Welty's most devastating reviews (and there are several), Welty concludes with encouragement: "But how much better, in any case, to wonder than not to wonder, to dance with astonishment and go spinning in praise, than not to know enough to dance or praise at all . . ." (*NYTBR* 24 March 1974: 5).

Her first review of S. J. Perelman (*Crazy Like a Fox* 2 July 1944) illustrates how she can praise the writer using her own words. She quotes Perelman's humor for more than half of the review, weaving in her own Perelmanesque tricks with words: "With his Dyak-like tread he has crept up on the movies, on Corn, on Jitterbugging, Bee-keeping . . . and with a maniacal glitter in his eye has done his deadly work" (6). Even as she is obviously enjoying her work, she stops to explain how Perelman manages "that sudden materializing of figures of speech, calculated to throw the bystander, or the reader, over the head of the sentence and press a little nerve at the back of his ear" (6).

Though they are, in her own view, a minor chapter in her life's work, Welty's reviews are as sensory-laden, as thoughtful, and as well-crafted as her stories. She says she never reviewed as a fiction writer thinking to learn something of her craft, but always with the hope to enjoy the reading of the book. When the book is successful, Welty reveals for the next reader why it is so. Is there heartfelt passion or compassion? Is the description particular and sensory? Are the dialogue, plot, and characters believable? Is there an honesty, a truth behind the writing? If, on the other hand, the reader—that is, the reviewer—stumbles, what is it in the path that slows the reading? Does the author keep the characters bound by some outside motive, refusing to let them act from their hearts? Does the author restrain her own feelings? Does the author (or publisher) have an ulterior purpose that bars the natural drive of the book?

It may well be true that Welty only reviewed the books that she thought she would like, but it is not true that she indiscriminately praised every book that she reviewed. If she sometimes spared the author—as with Dillard—she often did not spare the book. The author, however, interests her much less than the reader for whom the book is destined. In a 1939 monograph titled *Reviewing*, Virginia Woolf explained a distinction very much like the one that Welty practiced: "The reviewer, unlike the critic, . . . has nothing to say to the author; he is talking to the reader" (29).[12] Or, as Welty herself put it:

At the other end of the writing is the reader. There is sure to be somewhere the reader, who is a user himself of imagination and thought, who knows, perhaps, as much about the need of communication as the writer.

Reader and writer, we wish each other well. Don't we want and don't we understand the same thing? A story of beauty and passion, some fresh approximation of human truth? (*Eye* 106)

This is the standard Welty set for herself, and when she reviewed, it was what she sought for the users of writing whom she dignified by supposing that the best of them would bring to reading a potential for passion and imagination similar to her own.

Welty's book reviews are arranged chronologically in this volume. Beneath the title and author of the book reviewed, the title and publication information of the published review are listed. Welty did not compose or suggest these titles; at the *Times*, they were written, often from a phrase within the review, by a staff person to fit the layout of the page, and in other publications a similar process prevailed. Typesetting errors, dropped lines, and misspellings have been corrected and recorded in the endnotes. The endnotes also indicate, whenever possible, editorial changes made to Welty's typescripts or Welty's recorded revisions. For convenient reference, the appendixes contain a separate list of the books Welty reviewed, alphabetized by author, and a list of the sixteen reviews Welty collected in *The Eye of the Story*.

NOTES

1. Eudora Welty's comments in the Introduction are from an interview granted in preparation for this volume unless otherwise cited. Nash K. Burger provided the editor with invaluable information about book reviewing and the *New York Times Book Review*. Hunter McKelva Cole was the first to research Welty's book reviews; he listed them in "Book Reviews by Eudora Welty: A Check-List," *Bulletin of Bibliography* 23.1 (1963): 240. Cole also assisted me with information regarding Welty's *New York Post* reviews and her internship with the *New York Times Book Review*. Noel Polk added to and updated the list in "A Eudora Welty Checklist," *Mississippi Quarterly* 26.4 (Fall 1973): 663–93, rpt. as "A Eudora Welty Checklist, 1936–1972" in *Welty: A Life in Literature*, ed. Albert J. Devlin (Jackson: U P Mississippi, 1987), 238–65. Further book reviews were listed by W. U. McDonald, Jr. in his continuing "Works by Welty" in the *Eudora Welty Newsletter* and were collected by Pearl Amelia McHaney in "A Eudora Welty Checklist, 1973–1986," *Mississippi Quarterly* 39.4

(Fall 1986), 651–97, rpt. in Devlin, 266–302. In *The Welty Collection: A Guide to the Eudora Welty Manuscripts and Documents at the Mississippi Department of Archives and History* (Jackson: U P Mississippi, 1989), Suzanne Marrs catalogues Welty's type-scripts, published reviews, and *The Eye of the Story* papers. Noel Polk's *Eudora Welty: A Bibliography of Her Work* (Jackson: U P Mississippi, 1993) includes complete descriptions of Welty's non-fiction prose and a "Publishing Log for the Career of Eudora Welty."

2. *The Eye of the Story: Selected Essays and Reviews* (New York: Random House, 1978); hereafter cited as *Eye*.

3. Albert J. Griffith, "The Poetics of Prose: Eudora Welty's Literary Theory," in *A Still Moment: Essays on the Art of Eudora Welty*, ed. John F. Desmond, Metuchen: Scarecrow Press, 1978, 51–62; Michael Kreyling, "Words into Criticism: Eudora Welty's Essays and Reviews," in *Eudora Welty: Critical Essays*, ed. Peggy Whitman Prenshaw, Jackson: U P of Mississippi, 1979, 411–22; Harriet Pollack, "Words Between Strangers: On Welty, Her Style, and Her Audience," in *Welty: A Life in Literature*, ed. Albert J. Devlin, Jackson: U P of Mississippi, 1987, 54–81.

4. Michael Kreyling, *Author and Agent: Eudora Welty and Diarmuid Russell* (New York: Farrar Straus Giroux, 1991) 97.

5. "Looking Back at the First Story," *The Georgia Review* 33 (1979): 751–55.

6. Reprinted in *Conversations with Eudora Welty*, ed. Peggy Whitman Prenshaw (Jackson: U P Mississippi, 1984); hereafter cited as Prenshaw.

7. Nona Balakian, who was hired by Van Gelder just as she graduated from Columbia Graduate School of Journalism in 1943, taught Welty her job at the copy desk. In an introduction to a volume of her reviews and essays, Balakian character-izes Van Gelder as a "maverick with ideas of his own. . . . Himself literature ori-ented, Van Gelder saw the *Book Review* as an educative medium. Since the supple-ment is indirectly dependent on advertising, he couldn't ignore popular books of the day, but the reviews he printed of these books invariably exposed what was irrelevant or false or blatantly commercial about them. He had a knack for finding young writers with literary backgrounds . . . (*Critical Encounters* Indianapolis: Bobbs-Merrill, 1978, 15).

8. See Burger's "Eudora Welty's Jackson," *Shenandoah* 20.3 (1969): 8–15.

9. "Pageant of Birds," *New Republic* 109 (25 October 1943): 565–67; "Some Notes on River Country," *Harper's Bazaar* February 1944: 86–87, 150–56.

10. Burger, who stayed with the *Book Review* through all the changes, recommends a *roman à clef*, *The Belles Lettres Papers*, by fellow editor Charles Simmons (New York: William Morrow, 1987), for a humorous version of the situation during this period. Robert Van Gelder also wrote a novel based loosely on *Times*'s personalities, *Important People* (New York: Doubleday, 1948).

11. Welty said it was at Van Gelder's suggestion that she gave a lecture at the Pacific Northwest Writers' Conference at the University of Washington, 4–8 Au-

gust 1947. Van Gelder was also one of the speakers. Welty is quoted in the local newspaper as saying, "Your story . . . should stir the reader's imagination—make him think, feel and act. . . . Plausibility doesn't matter. Many times we are most enchanted by the story that is fairylike and highly implausible" (Joe Miller, "Short Story Writer Speaks," Seattle *Post-Intelligencer* 7 August 1947: S14). "The Reading and Writing of Short Stories," first published in *Atlantic* 183 (February 1949: 54–58 and March 1949: 46–49), is collected in revised form as "Looking at Short Stories" in *Eye* 85–106.

   12. London: Hogarth, 1939, 1969.

A Writer's Eye

But You'll Be Back

By Marguerite Steedman

THE LIFE OF A SOUTHERN TOWN

Saturday Review of Literature 19 September 1942: 22–23

This novel is about a little Georgia town cut off from life by the new highway's leaving it away to one side; and how Miss Cora, the maiden lady in the big house, contrives in one mounting flight of inspiration and ingenuity to get its life back by the homely way of putting every talent in the place to work. It is the account of a great burst of energy out of one character.[1] Out of Miss Cora's energy, everybody cans, preserves, weaves, carves, serves dinners, and hands out flowers to tourists. Miss Cora loves the town, but she does the good deeds also because the hero, in love with her niece, has left Thessaly in time-honored disgust saying it is no town for ambition to flower in, that place being New York. It is to bring Peter back by refuting this (in some kind of maiden-aunt logic) and bestowing him on the languishing niece that Miss Cora schemes over the town and that the town is infected by her ambition and works busily under the spell and accomplishes a great list of things.

This is mostly a novel about things—wanting things, getting things, losing things, stealing and selling things, and getting better things. It does not go very inquisitively into human emotions, touching only the feelings of enterprise that things and their getting can inspire. It is to the detriment of this novel that enterprise is not revealing behavior, in fact it is often the farthest thing from it. At its most ambitious and at its best, the book sets out to be the panoramic story of a town, its threatened life, its death by ruin and fire, and its dramatic renascence. The human story, the emotional story in this panorama, is touched in a vague hovering way, while the success story of getting houses, food, and a man for the girl, is told meticulously and with zest.

The author knows her little towns and is quite sure in her casual observations and in the lighter anecdotes of that life. She knows the South, obviously, and she has a nice habit of good humor. But when the time comes, as it should, to look through the outside of this life to the inside, she backs away.

Several deficiencies might come from its being a first novel. The plot is an account of manipulations instead of a study of human motives. There is no interplay of character, only a one-way effect of an omnipotent Aunt Cora on the others. For this reason there is little human interest in what Aunt Cora accomplishes and no suspense or doubt about the accomplishment. The other characters are just so many stops for Aunt Cora to pull out in her solo performance. She is able to cast such a strong spell over the population that even the town siren begins to cry and borrows á car in order to ride clear away from the hero. It is too bad that the story has to take its root out of a problem of young and unnourished love. This love affair, between Peter the young architect and the niece, cannot be much support when the heroine is asleep (alone) for most of the first eighty pages and the hero takes the train (offstage) to New York on page ninety-six without even telling her goodbye or appearing for one scene with her, and stays till the end of the book. He doesn't even write. One is told that they are in love, but one likes to make up his own mind. Since Marion herself is an unprotesting if pretty young being and makes few remarks, one decides that all this weaving and preserving should be done for the town, but not for Marion.

The jacket advertises the book's characters as "Normal Southern" people, which is a jolting phrase, and one hopes does not indicate that hereafter southern people are to be sub-divided after having already been divided from the rest of the country. This is not to say that Miss Steedman has not touched a relatively fresh field for she takes a whole little town indiscriminately into her story and includes everybody, many "nice people." Her trouble is not stock horror-characters, but stock sentimental characters, for whom "normal" may be the publisher's euphemism. There are the standby creatures, of North and South alike—the little crippled boy who is a genius, the mean old miser, the gamey Civil War general, the long-haired poet, and the treasure of a cook, etc. Miss Steedman is direct in her homely observations, but she does not look with such careful eyes at the things that better require the clear penetration; she notes exactly and well "the sweetish odor of mud on which the sun shines," but when she describes pity or love she contents herself with an old cliché. The description of the fire and the ruined town is good and is the most realistic thing in the book. But about emotion and character one can also be noticing and explicit. The charity and duty described are not emotions, ingenuity is not a force like passion, and though this book deals with charity, duty, and ingenuity, and faith too of a kind, these things cannot come really alive without a more vital breath breathed through them. The author herself has not been emotionally affected by her ethical ideas, one feels. She is sure of them, often enthusiastic, sometimes sentimental, but not possessed. She is actuated by something less and something lighter than emotion, the development of a bright idea. The writing is energetic if not very distinguished, and is done with ease. Ease has permitted carelessness at times, and there are smudgy traces of journalism in an occasional absurdity of phrase and now and then a veil of sheerest hokum falls over the page. Her thesis that no little town need die is laudable and full of interest, but the mind and heart and spirit of the town that would prove this thesis and rise above it are not examined. A glimpse at the town's real core of feeling and a timid hint of imagination are in the last chapter or so, but much more could have been made of the town's story and its overtones of medieval pride and joy in its work.

Sweet Beulah Land

By Bernice Kelly Harris

PLANTATION COUNTRY

New York Times Book Review 7 March 1943: 9

This novel is the story of Beulah Land, a section of river plantation country in North Carolina, over the eight years of time bounded by the arrival and departure of a stranger. The inhabitants include river gentry, sharecroppers and Negroes, and their in-betweens; and their lives when we meet them are intimately known and intimately related, one with all the others, according to the ways of the country. The panorama is given a treatment by Mrs. Harris at once exhaustive in detail and tender in its exactness.

Every last person in this place is shown to us, grouping by grouping, in a series of pantomimes at mid-distance that reveals each situation in its wholeness and in clear light and perspective. There could hardly be hope that all these characters and each of these pantomimes could emerge with equal vitality and strength, and they do not do so; but the average is good, and the procession is engrossing.

The story's development is the effect of the stranger Lan on the people of Beulah; he causes love in aristocratic Alicia's cool breast, he drives parvenue Archibald Hart and his henchman Trent to their worst exploits and villainies, and drives common little Sophie to her flagrancies and self-tortures. He is curse or blessing to every one he meets. Yet to this reader he never comes to life himself.

Perhaps none of the principals, or none of the close-ups, can compete successfully with such a rich background in constant life and stir behind them. Miss Partheny, the old lady sharecropper, is the exception, but she was not one to hold back on any occasion, any more than a righteous wildcat. Hart seems at times a stage villain, sneering and grabbing women's waists and waving mortgages. Alicia is a rigid creature.

Lan wanders in, staggers in, collapses in the road at Alicia's feet; and with him talking wild and strange the while, she nurses him to life and finds herself attempting to mold and order him toward becoming her husband and sharing "Elmhurst" with her. And sure enough, a great change overcomes him when she makes him owner of some land. But the marriage does not happen, and Lan becomes manager of a little store on his land and remains and lovingly tends it for eight years, at the end of which he wanders away again, into the obscurity out of which he came.

The scenes where people, white or black, sit and talk leisurely, tirelessly, and anonymously, on disasters, on "ha'nts," have some quality of the ballad and a solid base in Southern ways. The conversation of every subordinate character is wonderful, real, and a joy to read, though that of some of the principals is stiff and at times destroys a scene's illusion. It might be that the breath of life which [is] in the minor characters has its origin in real people the author has known and listened to, but she cannot put equal authenticity into imagined persons.

But the picture of Beulah—Ridge Road, and Neck—is given extremely well, it has authenticity, balance, rich and well-proportioned detail. Mature understanding has directed it, in addition to a clear and lively eye. Mrs. Harris is knowing of her country. She is completely at ease in every mansion, cottage, or shack—except Lan's, and I don't really think she should have gone in there.

The book has collective life, and never preaches in any social-study manner to rob it of that life. Each little glimpse has concrete narrative, an intimate landscape with its times of planting and harvest, characters filling it by the score with precisely expressive faces, spontaneous pantomimes, colored costumes and possessions and toys in hand, all somewhat like a painting of Peter Breughel's.[2] In the midst of any and all of this, Lan is unreal; perhaps he is symbolic, and so lost among the rich every-dayness which is the life and charm of *Sweet Beulah Land*.[3]

Between the Dark and the Daylight
By Nancy Hale

WOMEN AND CHILDREN
New York Times Book Review 2 May 1943: 8

This is a book of twenty-one short stories. In such a number the quality as well as the kind is sure to vary.[4] Some of these are nostalgic stories of childhood, some trim vehicles for remarks on the war, education, the states of society and other current topics, some full-bodied stories of more inherent weight. Some are concerned in intense, intimate fashion with mood, such as the excellent "Six-Fifteen." This is also among the stories of childhood, which, one feels, are the real stories in the book, the fountains of the others.

All these are female stories. Only a woman could have written any one of them, or have wanted to write them. At moments the reader feels that Nancy Hale is writing wholly as a woman, but is not exercising further womanly functions of looking at and feeling profoundly and instinctively some truth beneath what she so cleverly and easily has seen first off.

The spirit of the stories is tense and antagonistic—against one sex or the other, some section or other of the country, some social class or race, or even, in several of the light sketches, against some mannerism. Antagonism usually makes for heat and fine energy, but dispels another kind of energy, a play of the understanding.

Love is in all the stories. It is a stifling matter of sex in the powerful and exhaustive study of "Summer, 1913," dealing with the oppression and lack of dignity in love which appears also in the sharp tale of "That Woman." In "Summer, 1913" sex is as much a solid, measurable, heavy and opaque a thing as the object on which the young suffering wife fastens her gaze at the story's end, a maple highboy, lacking only the highboy's dignity. In "Who Lived and Died Believing," sex stretches and dissolves into long wavering vistas of nightmare and madness, but it is equally impenetrable. In "Those Are as Brothers," Miss Hale momentarily identifies its importunities with fascism and the persecutions of Hitler; this latter kind of thing is too easy a way to explain unhappiness or even describe it.

Perhaps all this has a connection with the charm of the stories of childhood. Innocence is treated nostalgically and the life of ignorance is tangible bliss, seen, smelt and handled tenderly. It is only in these childhood stories that she ever describes the beauty of the world and the seasons and she does it in a way to make us miss this beauty in the stories of adult life. Indeed, the softness and the beauty of the Southern scenery which comes into "That Woman" is described bitterly and becomes a part of the narrator's anger. Of the child in the title story, Miss Hale writes, "She did not want to grow up and be with people." This seems definitive of the attitude toward people which permeates the entire twenty-one stories here. The childhood stories are evocative of many more things and of many more feelings than the other stories. It is enchantment vs. disillusion that is given us here and perhaps we cannot be blamed if we choose the former and then turn away from the latter to find refreshment again.

Miss Hale says easily and well what she wants to say, as usual, and for this reason any group of her stories has that special interest which attends good writing.[5] Cruelty, which is in some of the stories, has interest as well as tenderness, but one feels that it does not tell as much in the end. The stories of childhood go through a door which the other stories halt before and find locked.

Our Daily Bread

By Enrique Gil Gilbert
Translated by Dudley Poore

EXOTIC, FROM ECUADOR

New York Times Book Review 18 July 1943: 6

It is seldom that we get hands on a book written out of Ecuador. Farrar & Rinehart have published several as a result of their Latin-American Prize Novel Contest. This one, by Enrique Gil Gilbert, received honorable mention. It is a novel that plunges us into a green world where all is excitement, and all is vivid, strange and believable, because we always believe anything that seems so much alive.

The novel is in three parts. The first tells how a rice plantation was cut out of the jungle on the Guyas, a great tidal river in the coastal regions of Ecuador. The second shows the immediate past—how Captain Sandoval, the formidable landlord, got his land, how he was only a guerrilla captain who had made the most of his luck. The last part foreshadows the future— the problems of new labor and of machinery, the disaster that threatens owner and worker alike.

From the start, the jungle absorbs the characters, breeding all deeds and presiding over them. This book grows out of it—like a fern, like a canoe plying its river torrent. Señor Gilbert has written his novel with eyes turned full upon the land—written it with eyes, ears, nose and mouth. When you finish his book you will have smelled and tasted Ecuador, stroked the soft pile of the Ecuadorian night and felt its tropic texture.

The method the author has used is to focus minutely upon a series of episodes. These accumulate significance, of course, but their value remains in their fine, individual clarity. He makes moments stand still while he fills them in with color, sound and fragrance. There is a minimum of dialogue, usually from anonymous speakers—a talk that flows as if from every one, functional to the scene.

This is not to say that Señor Gilbert does not pay attention to character. He shows his people in action and in siesta, in lonely song and in the sweat of intense labor; but by describing them physically, and equally well their physical reaction upon one another, he has no need for long dialogues. His people are mostly engaged in actions that brush words aside: love, and death, and the conquering of a jungle. The quivering drive of life is in all their looks and actions. A vitality that they are almost unable to bear haunts what they do. At high moments, love (by some principle of dynamics) becomes rage, hunger becomes lust. "Daily Bread" includes, in this book, the daily bread of the emotions as well as of the body.

Enrique Gil Gilbert is a Professor of Literature at the *Istituto Nacional Vicente Rocafuerte*. His style is clear, vigorous and dramatic; it is exuberant, yet not wasteful. Above everything, it is imaginative. Colors and scents, the abstractions, too, are described in the terms of their own world—eyelids are wrinkled like alligator skin, frogs at night play their marimbas; "time folds up like an accordion"; green skin is always malaria; the women are like fruits, flowers, jaguars. The vigor of this book is fundamental.[6] The special enchantment of its background gives it a startling beauty and a spiritual meaning all its own.

The Horse and His Shadow

By Enrique Amorim

Translated by Richard L. O'Connell and James Graham Luján

A POWERFUL NOVEL OF THE PAMPAS

New York Times Book Review 15 August 1943: 4

There is no love in this book. Something austere and ruthless animates the action, and a satisfaction that is not a communicable emotion is its result in the characters. Passion and strength in plenty spring forth, but not from love and not from its hope. In place of this emotion is something very special—a code, a law of the land, which commands all the power and dignity we associate with the deepest feelings.[7]

The Horse and His Shadow is the story of a great *estancia* in Uruguay. There live Nico, the owner, his aristocratic wife Adelita, waiting for her child, and his old mother. On his wide plains live the gauchos. Moving back and forth between house and plain is the beautiful servant girl, La Gaucha, really Adelita's half-sister, half aristocrat, half gaucho. Beyond, at the boundaries, are slowly arriving the Polish refugees, attempting to start a new life in South America, people smuggled in, their life in hazard, questioning and hopeful, but beyond the pale.

Instrumental in bringing this element into his brother's life—which is to destroy him—is Marcel, city man, political and historical student, who comes to visit Nico as the story opens.

The gift he brings to the *estancia* is a wonderful stallion for breeding to Nico's mares—Don Juan. As the title suggests, Don Juan towers over the story.

In his shadow events develop and culminate in tragedy and resolution.

Nico is killed by a Polish refugee. Adelita's son is born and dies, the Polish refugee's son dies, and only the illegitimate son of Marcel and La Gaucha and the little colt of Don Juan by a common little mare, secretly bred to him by clowning peons, are to live. So life takes its secret way, the book tells us, and its beauty and profligate vigor are never lost.[8]

Love is as formal as sex, as simple as the stallion led to pasture. Never is a word passed between La Gaucha and Marcel. He looks at her "with vehement eyes," which he narrows "as if taking aim." They meet wordlessly, she becomes pregnant, and he departs. No one in the book expects anything more of another than this.

The more subtle relationship between the two brothers is beautifully told: the ever-doubting appraisal, the challenge always between them; but "the law of the plains" demands that they never quarrel openly in the confines of the house, but always offstage, on the open pampas. The final and critical meeting of the two dominant and opposing forces—Nico and the Pole—is resolved by purely formal combat, as questions in the Middle Ages were settled by a joust. The cause is not even stated by one man to the other; the landowner is slain by the outraged refugee—and the incident, though magnificently dramatic, is as formal as a ceremony.

Yet this is an unfair report if it makes the novel seem superficial. It is only the form of the book which is strange to us—a barrier form, in which life is violent yet ice cold. The story itself is carefully built and presented. The characters emerge splendidly. Nico is a striking person, with the inherited traits of the owner of vast land, settling everything from the back of his horse, "in the open country, without protection, without witnesses, imbued with the animal vigor of the beast on which he was mounted." The old mother is a symbol of time-worn womanhood to whom nothing is explained. She wanders in the maze of her own household, which to her holds all the unexplained secrets of the world, careful, and brooding over every crumb and scrap.

The stallion, with his legendary name, is the startling and beautiful figure he is meant to be, making himself a parapet from which his master may command and shoot. And among the scenes burned into the mind is the blind gaucho's story of the night he spent in the tree, while the flooding river ran and humped like a bucking horse below him, while the tree itself was a Noah's ark of refugees, wildcats and snakes and himself all clinging there together.

The Land of the Great Image
By Maurice Collis

THE GREAT BUDDHA
New York Times Book Review 29 August 1943: 5, 16

This book gives a picture of the society of the little known Portuguese Asia and the land it touched, in the seventeenth century. The author, a scholar writing with deep originality and charm, has used diaries of the day and various other studies for one source, and for another twenty-one years of residence in the East, where he was a civil servant for Britain. As implicit as all his knowledge is his understanding of the Eastern mind and heart. This understanding is never forced. It fills the book like a fresh spring of spontaneity and wisdom and gives it the best authority.

Portuguese Asia, a string of fortresses skirting India's side, was the outcome of a crusading venture which sought to bring the Roman Catholic Church to the East, and which resulted in colonizations, riches, slave raids, the penetrations of missionaries, and many exploits, both crusading and commercial, on the part of the Portuguese. Among these was Friar Manrique, an Augustinian friar, who made a journey from Goa, its capital, to Mrauk-u, the kingdom-city of Arakan, in the course of his busy life. It is his diary that Mr. Collis has at hand among others.[9]

Arakan was a Mongolian state whose people spoke a kind of Burmese but were of part Indian blood, with a dim race-memory of northwest China. The reign of the King, Thiri-thu-dhamma, toward whom Manrique walked, was the most progressive in long centuries of development. The friar's first sight in the land, high up on a mountain pass, was the Great Image, a religious carving of the Buddha of incalculable antiquity, revered in

Arakan as no object can be revered outside the East; it was considered a contemporary likeness of the Master. But Manrique looked at it simply with distaste, and in his long sojourn in this land he never changed or looked with any more effort into Buddhism. On the other hand, it was—aside from the high dangers of travel itself—easy for Manrique to go to Arakan and to live there, for in that day Oriental kings held a keen intellectual interest in all religious subjects, respected all priests, and enjoyed religious discussion.

The curious meeting and linking of king and priest is the theme of the book. In spite of genuine liking they remain separate and go their own extreme ways, alike only in the violence of their end. It is a meeting which passes unrealized, which sees no analogy of the spirit because the ways of the spirit are different. The juxtaposition of the blunt, reasonable Augustinian friar and the radiant, subtle Arakan king is made a telling symbol of the double strand—Christian and Buddhistic—of the seventeenth century vision of conquering and uniting the world in peace and brotherhood. Both these men lived, thought, believed and moved in intense accordance with their place and time. Both were good human beings, only in some degree blind and deluded. Both truly longed that this world be led and ruled by divine love. But Friar Manrique in his specious arguing was in the end a bigot, and King Thiri-thu-dhamma died because his heart was bewitched and terrified by sorcery.

"That he should have died drugged, frantic, hallucinated, ensorcelled was fitting," says the friar. "A Buddhist king who, forgetting the compassion and sanity of the Eightfold Path, opened his mind to the evil suggestions of a wizard and murdered his subjects to obtain occult powers, had lain down with monsters, and because he looked into the abyss the abyss looked into him."

It was unenlightening to Manrique that he was captured and mistaken for a slaver by people who had suffered from slavers and was punished by them. Back home the Portuguese kidnapped annually and brought to Dianga, according to Manrique's statistics, an average of 3,400 Hindus. Of the 3,400 he succeeded in baptizing some 2,000 a year. This represented a religious triumph which blinded him to the horror in the slave trade. That was the universal attitude of the Portuguese in Asia. Manrique's heart had never told him that slavery was a crime against the human being. Now, when at his extreme moment he was rescued, he wept tears of gratitude toward his rescuer and fell on his knees before him, although he was a Buddhist. "But," says Mr. Collis, "his emotion was only momentary, and the revelation it brought went with it. . . . He was not a changed man. . . . His mind remained closed as it had ever been. He did not grow an inch in spiritual stature. Under the violent promptings of his heart, he had seen for a moment. Then bigotry shrouded his vision again."[10]

It would be impossible to outline the actual narrative of this book and indicate its smaller wonders. It is as strategically put together and as fantastically simple as a fairy tale; and it affects us, quite aside from the scholarship of Mr. Collis, with that true belief we gave fairy tales when children.[11]

He gives us this belief out of his artistry, for these fantastic things do not become familiar to us under his hand; they become filled with life, which is better and which is the illusion an artist creates. The things in this book include all the ornament of Asiatic intrigue, all the ceremonies and wonders of the truly far places. They deal with magic and with ordeals, for the belief of that day was in magic on the Buddhist side and in devils on the Christian side (as it is in psychoanalytical terms today, Mr. Collis points out).

Incidents of the friar's journeys are often highly comic: the story of the bribing on the river, the story of the Kandy Tooth, are delightful. There are also scenes of moving tragedy and glory. The land itself is a fantasy and a dream of strangeness. The physical pictures the author gives us are more than beautiful; they are wonderfully neat and often ironic, for his precision can come from both knowledge and ironic intent.

There is charm in all he tells us. It is nice to know the material of canopies, the shape of the fabulous Ruby Ear-Rings (bantam's egg), the exact toys little children liked, what the colors and fragrances were, how people danced, how ladies carried out schemes, and the plans of rooms and designs of cities, and the way the White Elephant was given his bath. The gong and flute sound for us, and we can almost hear the strange sound of the Yattera bell which was rung to bring about ruin in occult ways, by setting the enemy astrologically ajar.

The Land of the Great Image is a vivid, illuminating study written with the care and penetration that an artist as well as a historian must exercise to make the exotic past live and breathe for us.

The Galantrys
By Margery Allingham Carter

VICTORIAN HALF-BREED
New York Times Book Review 31 October 1943: 6, 12

This is the first non-mystery novel by the creator of that favorite of investigators, Mr. Albert Campion.[12] As an admirer of Mr. Campion from away back, this reviewer approached *The Galantrys* with proper respect. But here Mr. Campion's creator has explored a mystery that requires far more than his suave ingenuity for its solution—a mystery that goes as deep as anything we know. This time the puzzle is the why and wherefore of a man, in his time, in his spot on earth—in application, the mystery of a whole culture.

Mrs. Carter uses James Galantry as the focus of her idea. Into her scrutiny of his character she pours her vision of past and future, of England, of society and, I think, a philosophic vision of what could be. Of course, this adds up to an attempt to write the ideal novel; it is hardly surprising that Mrs. Carter does not realize the attempt completely. But the fact that she had the courage to tackle such a theme gives her book breadth and interest.

James Galantry is the product of the century-old variety of English gentry—and the ageless, untamed gypsy. This blend of wildly incompatible racial strains, carrying the stigma of "half-breed" in early Victorian England, produces the fundamental conflict. Its effect on James' character is studied through his growing up, his courtship, loves lost and gained, his progeny, his ideals—all he cherishes and hates. The rococo background, of course, is excellent for this inner—and outer—struggle. The settings—countryside and London—are handsomely done. So are the costumes of the day, the vogues, manners and social credos.

17

The narrative style is, for the most part, as remote as an amused god's view of our cosmos. Occasionally it bends down gently to examine at close range some small incident which may be more enlightening than the rest. Unfortunately this method breeds a certain remoteness in the reader's feelings as well. It is evident that the author knows her people thoroughly—too thoroughly, perhaps. Too often she asks us to take her word for them and not to demand proof in the writing.[13]

James is worked out carefully, and appealingly drawn. Sometimes he is a mirror reflecting his times and his country. Sometimes he is many-faceted. Always he is clear as a transparent jewel that shows its inner texture. . . . But the novel races too fast for its protagonist: events must be summarized, just as we would enjoy lingering over the small details and the conversation. The author, by looking both backward and forward—by reminiscing and seeing into the future at the same point—destroys our present pleasure in her scenes by striving to give them their other dimension.

Not that *The Galantrys* is metaphysical. Mrs. Carter puts down any such budding ideas in her readers—consistently and with wit. Her style is comfortable, with no strange angles at all. Perhaps, if she had been a little more daring, both in thought and writing, her novel might have more compelling interest, more original value.[14]

A Garland of Straw
By Sylvia Townsend Warner

A GARLAND OF STRAW
Tomorrow November 1943: 52–53

These are stories and sketches collected from writings over a period of several years.[15] They range from character sketches and reminiscences to long and serious studies, from dips into the purely absurd to dissections of various war temperaments, in England and out of England. Miss Warner writes well, and nobody needs reminding of that. She should be highly valued if only because a true delight in the absurd is rare, considering how much of the absurd there is in the world. In this book we may sample, and share in, this delight.

Some of these stories are no more than incidents that might come casually to the mind, funny things you might think to put in a letter. Some others go clear out of the eccentricity they exist to praise or condemn, almost to enter tragedy, and more might dare to do this. "The Level Crossing," which is the last story, is satisfying because it, more than the others, attempts a wholeness; others delight in being bits, however brilliant. But I think in general Miss Warner is careful never to lose herself beyond a point where wit will not bring her back.

Nearly all the stories are about eccentrics. It is a safe bet that in real life many of these odd little creatures are puttering about the lanes of England. But Miss Warner's characters are sometimes eccentric in that they are not quite alive, quite in a manner dear to the English heart. This reader could wish at times that her people had a little more life in them, at the sacrifice of eccentricity, however whimsical. There are more ways Miss Warner knows to define a character than by the character's delicious little oddities. A revolutionist who likes Jane Austen does not devastate us; because while he stands before us, aptly talking and holding his book, still, nothing happens to him at all, or, consequently, to us; the story is just the sight of him. The point at stake often seems very light to cause a whole story, points such as a breach of taste in decoration, or a wife's escape from home because of a time-bomb which she welcomes as a chance to slip off and hear Debussy records, which her husband does not fancy, as he, a little better than she, prefers sightseeing in St. Paul's. There is irony here; but need there have been anything?

Humor is in all the stories, and in many is a war-bitterness, but the stories might be a little stronger in constitution, to bear both these qualities well and still seem of vital substance in themselves. Miss Warner is damning several kinds of people in this book, but rather as if she could not bear to write about them; these stories are all she will say. Her indignation cannot be doubted, and certainly her heart is true that she ultimately speaks from; but the feeling in the reader is that if Miss Warner is too nice to say anything further, we must be too nice to notice anything further; which is of course ridiculous; but there is a feeling of good behavior intact in the writing of these stories which can be catching.

And then, proving us wrong in generalizations, Miss Warner produces a propaganda piece like "Apprentice" which is super-violent in effect. And if such a story lacks by nature the virility and power of a Goya *Disaster*, it has nevertheless a kindred briefness, and a brand of humor that shocks like the burn from that same acid.[16] "A Functionary," one of these, is besides all else a fine story. This group is not without a relationship to the other stories; each is a little nightmare, the quaint story turned horror story. "The Red Carnation," however, is very beautiful and quiet.

"Plutarco Roo," "My Shirt Is in Mexico," and "To Cool the Air," easy little pleasantries, are warm and funny, if slight. "Lay a Garland on My Hearse" is a superior travesty on Family and its jollifications and assumptions. And there are several stories of "common people" and these tend to be more human, as indeed common people can be and no blame attached. Action enters the shabby parlors of these stories and conversation takes place which, if less articulate on account of the ignorance involved, is nevertheless more real and moving for being less blossomy in wit, and less futile in direction.

Above all, Miss Warner is an English writer, and if the English fire seems to burn a little bleakly for us sometimes, because it is so well tended, perhaps it is our loss because in our comparative exuberance we expect too much; but I do not think so. Yet, if the absurd is not the medium for indicating the highest truths of character, and if wit, even to the highest degree, is not the exact literary weapon one would choose against such tremendous things as fascism and the lies of the world, let us admit the bounds these stories lie in, and then praise them for their special and rewarding excellence. And we should always rejoice in the very grammar of a neat, sound, exact sentence, like every single one of Miss Warner's.

Waters Over the Dam

By Harry Harrison Kroll

ALABAMA FARM BOY

New York Times Book Review 26 March 1944: 4

This is a disarming book, and a pleasure to read. The first-person story of a young hired man on a farm in Alabama twenty-some years ago, its authenticity is worth something and the pleasure it takes in life is worth more.[17]

Unassuming Mr. Danny, 18, from down on Bashi, is working on Paw Jack Dixon's farm and grist mill—living with the family, and now and then going to school with the children. The farmhouse stands on once rich, now worn out land; the day is that of the T-model Ford, peg-topped trousers, the Youth's Companion, the Rose Killian circus, set-around parties. But more than any of these things it is the day of youth. Life is as alluring and as teasing as a nymph running ahead in the bright woods—and Danny is busy running after her.

The book is frankly recollection, sometimes nostalgic, but not sentimental. It is an honest attempt to recapture the effortless, cavorting, dreaming days of first knowledge and first love. It is a simple narrative, certainly autobiographical, unaffected and beguiling. Though nothing much happens out of the ordinary, there is not a boring word in it.[18] Because a human understanding—and not some kind of "social consciousness"—has directed this work, we have amusement and irony and a summer-like abundance and clarity in Mr. Kroll's story. There is no chastising of character or reader—though the people in *Waters Over the Dam* are poor, have little and get disappointed sometimes.

Mr. Danny, a long-legged, amiable boy, does his work with good spirits, likes and admires the Dixon family and abides by Miss Lucretia, the mother. With an eye out for everything around him, he plays with the children and in polite awe of learning (because he hasn't had much) he doesn't mind sitting at a little desk in the schoolhouse if Miss Parnell Dees can teach him anything. We see Danny plowing the cotton rows, aware of every weather promise, smelling the mint under the plowpoint; eating at the family table, going to the Christmas tree, groaning with malaria, swimming blissfully with little Rennie in the creek, sitting the hours away in the mill with Paw Jack. We see him hugging Miss Parnell Dees on invitation, and sitting cramped at his child's desk in a schoolhouse when his man's muscles cry out for work and being outdoors in the earth's season.

In love, he has wordlessly expected to find courtesy, tenderness of play and forthrightness of passion. He is not too demoralized to learn that, wrenched to its other side, love can become violence itself in its violation. The growth of this double love in a boy's soul—for the flesh and for the spirit—is uppermost in this book. But it is as a part of Danny's whole nature of growing—and he is so close to the earth that it has something seasonal about it too, a genuine primitive.

As Danny grows into two loves and has long vague dreams in the heat of afternoon and in the beauty of night, the loves fight over him. Miss Parnell Dees, the school teacher (plump, tailored, pouting, iron-willed disciplinarian and seducer), is the age-old female dominator imposing her passions with a peach-tree switch. The virginal Rennie Dixon, growing-up tomboy, eager and tender, high-spirited and mocking, with her flying corn-silk hair, her face oval as a bay leaf, is as appealing a picture of innocence as comes to mind. There is true innocence, of deed and character, in this book, by the way, as there is true vulgarity and lust, uncluttered by anything false or gloomy.

This is distinctly a Southern book, in that every word springs straight up from Southern earth.[19] But it is the happen-so of location, not any battleground of problems. There are races, black and white, but living simply side by side from one amiable day to the next. There is poverty—but it is not put down as that by Mr. Danny because a money poverty does not touch him. There is the declining earth, beside the lush and fruitful, of that abandoned Southern country, which gives Danny a feeling of mourning for the rape of the land. But no arbitrary pressure is put on narrative or character to force an unnatural crisis or to prove any contentions. The story flows on like the mill-stream of the book, grinding its mill, passing like time. The dignity and patience of labor, the kindness and cruelty among people, the feel of earth worked in and cared for and of abandoned earth—the dreams that come on a dim road through the woods or beside the river—these more enduring things are this book's concern.

A Haunted House
and Other Short Stories
By Virginia Woolf

MIRRORS FOR REALITY

New York Times Book Review 16 April 1944: 3

This is a posthumous volume to which Leonard Woolf attaches a note saying many of the stories are incomplete or unperfected. It includes six out of the eight stories in *Monday or Tuesday*, published in 1921, seven stories subsequently published in magazines, and five unpublished stories, which Mr. Woolf lets go with some hesitation since they were never revised and are only in the stage "beyond that of her first sketch."[20]

The unperfected work of a perfectionist is interesting not only technically, but in a human way which is not necessarily morbid. All this fastidious pursuit, this delicacy of the inner organism, will perhaps be seen now in its slower workings. We might hope to see in these stories not only the problems Virginia Woolf set herself but the obstacle. The sympathy is ready to flow only the quicker perhaps through channels not so exquisitely cut for it. And yet of course she has left nothing in the smallest way untidy, unstraightened, esthetically out of place in these stories—this was not in her; they are, sentence by sentence, quite perfect as always, and give that same tantalizing illumination, which moves always ahead. Who else in the writing world could have left unfinished work so fine? It is not in feeling that we might notice incompletion; we are not aware of a suspension of belief, a pause, a gap not closed, or any promise meant to be extended and now withheld. Yet it would be only fair to Mrs. Woolf to accept as a fact that regardless of how fine these stories seem to us, she considered many of them not for our eyes, and only temporarily set in their forms.

As they exist, new stories and old, these seem as perfect, and as functional for all their beauty, as spider webs. Indeed they were made for a like purpose: to trap and dissect living morsels in the form of palpitating moments of time, instantaneous perceptions, those brief visions of others, which give us when captured—breathing, even struggling and so betraying themselves—an illusion of life.

The extreme beauty of her writing is due greatly to one fact, that the imprisonment of life in the word was as much a matter of the senses with Virginia Woolf as it was a concern of the intellect. The scent, the gesture, the breath on the lips, the sound of the hour striking in the clock, the rippling texture of the surface in the moving air—all these things she sought with all her being to apprehend, throughout a lifetime—for they were the palpable shadows and colored reflections of the abstract world of the spirit, the matter that mirrored the reality.

Many people then have found it a curious, almost haughty, decision in Virginia Woolf to seize this palpitating life, at the last moment, indirectly. Her stories nearly all come to us once removed—seen in a mirror, actionless, happening in an excruciatingly prolonged moment of dilated perception during the entirety of which a character may be stooping to pick up a pin. She imposes a deliberate, initial artificiality on her stories. But perhaps this treatment is given to a view of life which may well be too intense for us not to watch it through a remove of some kind. Obliquity gives its own dimension to objects in view, and elongation, foreshortening, superimposing are all instruments of the complicated vision which wants to look at truth.[21]

The approach of many of the sketches is that of a probing—a deep probing or a light pricking, these are the moods. A character is filled with some moment's life, becomes iridescent with it and like a bubble is blown free of the pipe for some astonishing moment, then let burst before our eyes. Or some character, seen flat-toned and dull to the eye, full-front, opaque with self-regard, is then subjected to a probing by the imagination which seems surgical, so precise and swift it is, and without the character's knowledge often, as if he were asleep under an anesthetic: this probing—really a silent imagining—usually happens under the more human cover of guesswork or actual fantasy which in the end proves the error or the futility of the examination. Nevertheless, by the science of Mrs. Woolf the opaque character is revealed opalescent in its cocoon, with its past and future wrapping it like butterfly wings. Its flicker of life ticks like a heart under our eyes, and as it emerges from its dull contemplation we almost see it fly in the sun—but not quite. For this would be the miracle beyond science, an illusion.

Instead of science, I should have named painting and music as being most closely allied to the writing of Virginia Woolf, which seem far more obvious counterparts. Yet it is in the science of these arts that the counterpart lies, and in that she is also meticulous as an astronomer and bold as an engineer. The Arabesques of Debussy and of Matisse can be simultaneously kin to the arrested motion of her stories. Whether visual or auditory in their sensory images, her compositions are made by the technique of impressionism. In the broader organization and development of her themes she makes one always think of musical composition, indeed she gives musical terms as titles to some pieces. And in the delineation of character and in detail she makes one think of painting. We are likely to see profile and full face and reflection and dream-image simultaneously. Again, some of the stories are almost devoid of people, which would seem a prerogative of still-life in painting; sometimes in a room momentarily deserted by characters, objects emerge vibrant and meaningful as an apple of Cézanne. And yet it should be pointed out that regardless of the feat thus accomplished, the purpose of her "still-life" technique is to say something always about the human being, the human world; the objects *belong* to someone, and are telling you, though without narrative, something of human thought and passion, as if even objects must speak of this.

The impressionist dictum that light is the most important actor in the picture can also apply to the work of Virginia Woolf—here light does move often as a character and for its own sake from scene to scene and only itself remain unaffected by passion. In "The Searchlight," in this book, light is a character, the main character. But also it must be observed that in her stories the beam of light is manipulated; it is like a wand, it touches from here to there with the undeviating purpose of illuminating the particular in the abstract world. It moves as the stream of consciousness in *Mrs. Dalloway* moves, from person to person, it is time passing in *To the Lighthouse*, a philosophical conception as well as a sensory image.

So near can the sensory come to the philosophic in these stories that the words "breathing," "breath," and the other words which mean this, when they are used so often and with such preoccupation, give us the feeling of a

27

creator breathing life into the creation, so passionate is her belief and desire. Virginia Woolf wrote always, I think, with a sense of mystery and tragedy, and yet so controllably, so strictly, so tightly did she write thus that though her stories are perfect, perhaps the miracle did not always happen. Perfection, even perfection, is sometimes not enough. The miracle after all might come as accident, and might be a crude thing.

Some of the stories in *A Haunted House* are only a page and a half long; they are essences, however, not scraps or fragments, which throws the clearest possible light on the way Mrs. Woolf worked. "An Unwritten Novel," a story from the early *Monday or Tuesday*, seems to this reader in title, intent, form, idea—almost in prophecy—to embody much of this last volume. In this first-person sketch of fourteen pages, a woman writer, riding on a train, tries to read or to reach the inner life of a woman sitting opposite her, a stranger. This virgin relationship between two people is thus posed, and is fully examined, directly and indirectly, and the examination, with the story, ends ironically and passionately. In the experience of observing, the observer is herself observed, her deft plunges into another's obscure background become reachings into her own hidden future, error makes and cancels error, until identification between the character examined and the writer examining seems fluid, electric, passing back and forth. The writer even in a moment of penetration of the other character helplessly imitates a physical spasm, some squirming and twitching in this other person, a complete identification at once hateful and intimate, revolted and compassionate. "She saw me. A smile of infinite irony, infinite sorrow, flitted and faded from her face. But she had communicated, shared her secret, passed her poison; she would speak no more. Leaning back in my corner, shielding my eyes from her eyes, seeing only the slopes and hollows, grays and purples, of the winter's landscape, I read her message, deciphered her secret, reading it beneath her gaze."

Here, like a technique of a technique, is the writer writing before her own eyes. Here are her word-pictures and word-sketches, mounting as if of themselves, in lists, parentheses, impatient naming of brief participants, all spaces filling in with trees, colors, streets, furniture, seasons, objects on a table; choices of deed and character made, as they arise, before the eye; the helpless and magical building up and developing of a moment or scene along the way and its dissolving and ironical elimination which progress with the journey. A world complete with all its people and objects the writer draws up about the twitching Minnie, as if compelled, desiring to see in this way a glimpse of her soul—only to watch that world all go to pieces as Minnie herself gets off the train and is, surprisingly, met. This relationship, made on a journey of unspecified purposes, in a moving vehicle with panoramas flying and fading without, the changing and merging features of persons, landscapes, character, color, motion in place and time, hope and despair, seems to seek at the very source the attraction and the repulsion in each moment of being.

Mrs. Woolf ends her story: "And yet the last look of them . . . brims me with wonder—floods me anew. Mysterious figures! Mother and son . . . it's you, unknown figures, you I adore; if I open my arms, it's you I embrace, you I draw to me—adorable world!"

Crazy Like a Fox

By S. J. Perelman

STRICTLY PERELMAN

New York Times Book Review 2 July 1944: 6

This looks like the unholy work of only one man. Reader, S. J. Perelman has struck again.[22]

"Great, fatuous booby that I was"—these are the words of Perelman himself—"I imagined advertising would be destroyed from the outside. It won't; it's going to bubble and heave and finally expire in the arms of two nuns, like Oscar Wilde." Not if S. J. Perelman can help it, it won't. In fact, here lies the body before us now, with a sign left pinned to its jacket saying *Crazy Like a Fox.*

Advertising is not the only victim of this man. With his Dyak-like tread he has crept up on the movies, on Corn, on Jitterbugging, Bee-keeping, Fashion, then Chichi, and with a maniacal glitter in his eye has done his deadly work.[23]

Read these random notes, torn secretly from the mordant evidence at hand. "I don't know much about medicine but I know what I like." . . . "A Schrafft hostess, well over nine feet tall, with ice mantling her summit, waved me toward the door marked 'Credentials.'" . . . "He caught my arm in a vise-like grip but with a blow I sent him groveling. In ten minutes he was back with a basket of appetizing, fresh-picked grovels. We squeezed them and drank the piquant juice thirstily." . . . "I had gone into the Corn Exchange Bank to exchange some corn." The clues are unmistakable. These are the notations of the Fox.

Even innocent Clifford Odets has not been allowed to escape.[24] He has been dealt with callously. The Fox has down here notes for a play called "Waiting for Santy" and bitingly leaves word that "the parts of Rankin, Panken, Rivken, Riskin, Ruskin, Briskin and Praskin are interchangeable, and may be secured directly from your dealer or the factory." Has anyone seen Clifford Odets lately?

There are other victims, even more innocent than Odets. "Take a small boy smeared with honey," we find here, "and lower him between the walls. The bees will fasten themselves to him by the hundreds and can be scraped off after he is pulled up, after which the boy can be thrown away. If no small boy smeared with honey can be found, it may be necessary to take an ordinary small boy and smear him, which should be a pleasure."

The strange part is, Perelman refers to his deeds as "prose." But Perelman's "prose" was never a simple thing, like mother love, or even like other prose. It is highly complex, deviously organized—the work of some master brain being undoubtedly behind it—and is more like jiu-jitsu than any prose most of us have ever seen.

There is, for instance, that sudden materializing of figures of speech, calculated to throw the bystander, or reader, over the head of the sentence and press a little nerve at the back of his ear. "Mr. Mifflin, in a porous-knit union suit from Franklin Simon's street floor, is stretched out by the fire like a great, tawny cat. Inasmuch as there is a great, tawny cat stretched out alongside him, also wearing a porous-knit union suit, it is not immediately apparent which is Mifflin." (Mrs. Mifflin's presence on the scene does not help any—she "is seated at the console of her Wurlitzer, softly wurlitzing to herself.")

By Perelman's evil plot every too-familiar name of this world is going to get caught in an insidious tangle from which it is doubtful, now, that any will ever become extricated. "In one corner [of Schrafft's] Nick Kenny, Jack Benny, James Rennie, Sonja Henie and E. R. Penney, the chain store magnate, were gaily comparing pocketbooks to see who had the most money." All about, trade and advertising clichés are shooting through the air like bullets. "It's a heller—Altman's, of course?" asks a lady of her daughter Giselle who is in her wedding dress, and Giselle sputters, "Yes, and available in nineteen different shades—among them wine, russet, beige, peach, grackle, stone, liver, lover, blubber, blabber and clabber."

Every reader is entitled to his own moment for collapse, but this reviewer

31

takes hers during a very short play of the advertising underworld when a lady enters on the line, "Don't mind us, Verna, we just dropped in to sneer at your towels."

There are those who think that Perelman no longer slays with the old abandon. They declare that some of that fine early madness is missing, and that one day the Fox may be caught. These are optimists. There is both old and new evidence in the forty-eight pieces here collected—and though Perelman may not scatter the red herrings to which we have become accustomed, something mighty like a herring, and mighty frisky, goes scampering across all 269 pages with every $2.50 purchase of the book, according to the steadier witnesses. Or perhaps it is not a red herring but that which, or whom, Perelman calls "Pandemonium, the upstairs girl."

Artist at War

By George Biddle

TATTERS AND FRAGMENTS OF WAR

[Reviewed under the pseudonym Michael Ravenna]

New York Times Book Review 16 July 1944: 3, 24

"To obtain a pictorial record of the war in all its phases" was the general assignment given forty-two artists by the War Department.[25] One of these was George Biddle, the brother of Attorney General Francis Biddle, who was to organize and act as chairman of the Art Advisory Committee and to go himself to the Mediterranean and draw. This book—fifty-five drawings and maps and an expository text in diary form—came out of Tunis and the Sicilian and early Italian fronts.

Mr. Biddle, after endless red tape in Algiers to "get permission to accomplish my assignment," finally flung himself in a jeep with a driver from Alexandria, La., and was soon where he wanted to be—where he could see. "At the front no one asks for passes." Before he returned to America, he had found himself in desert bivouacs and on maneuvers in Africa; in the first jeep entering Messina and receiving the grapes, morning-glories and hot bearded kisses of the Sicilians; on the captain's bridge of the Boise on D-day at Taranto, giving orders in Italian to Italian craft. He was in the first wave of our men crossing the Volturno. Although he went as an "eye," simply to see and draw what went on, he was by necessity an arm too, with a gun in hand, and on occasion took over a prisoner or dressed a wound or interpreted a conversation. All this time, a veteran of the first World War, he was a man the young boys shook their heads over, as being one of "you old men," that ought to stay home.

George Biddle is, of course, right when he declares in his book that an artist's eye is needed in war in order to tell the truth about it. Art is both more passionate and more dispassionate than reporting, and hence more true.[26] By being selective it can record the essentials better than a photograph which, however official, is indiscriminate, and also carefully censored for horror.

In the midst of this turmoil of battle, Mr. Biddle has made drawings of a strange abjection. It is the incongruities of life that tell the story, he says— the almost surrealist mixture of human bodies, animal bodies, broken columns, scattered fruits, dismembered trees, walls that have shed their plaster "like icing off a cake," the tatters and fragments of war.

All this is true enough; yet the lack of organization in the sketches themselves succeed in giving an impression of feebleness. Of course the drawings were made hurriedly, on the scene. For this they have a value they could not have worked up in another state, but it is to be regretted that they somehow fail in immediate impact, simply through the style thereby achieved. It should be said that this artist has pity, but I think this abjectness is not pity but an artistic conception. Otherwise, of course, it would be bad art, which is different from sad art.

Oddly enough, more of what Mr. Biddle saw comes through in his text— which is interesting in itself.

Biddle himself, quite naturally, mentions the name of Goya more than once in speaking of his task—their intentions are kin; and so it would not be unfair to make one comparison.[27] Where Goya drew disaster in the act— falling bodies, the thrust of violence in its present moment—George Biddle draws the aftermath of disaster, the sprawling pattern in its wake.[28] His bodies in fatigue, in sleep, in resigned pain and in death are quiet, as if they had become simply a reflection of the horror that has just passed over them.

Perhaps that inertness is valid too, as a part of this war, with its speed of destruction, its wholesale dealing out of ruin and passing on, before the victim has had time to assimilate it, or even quite to believe in it. Goya often showed human beings at the moment they met death, but at that moment they were supremely alive, aware—the very passion of his feeling for war's horror seemed to dictate this moment to him for its translation into art.

Mr. Biddle pursues his point of view:

When I picture a battle scene it is not violence, dynamics, or heroism. I see weighted feet, slouching shoulders, and the vacant, expressionless stare of automata. . . . Let us be honest. Our soldiers want to win the war so they can get home, home, home; and never leave it. . . . One reason why our Army does not know [exactly why they are fighting] is because the people at home do not know what is happening to our soldiers.

The artist makes his book a case against censorship and the deleting of the evils and horrors of war. He asks how, as long as the people are ignorant of what our men really do and endure, they can contribute that essential support which is so needed both at home and at the front.

In spite of Mr. Biddle's purpose in showing us waste and ruin lying inert before us, his drawings give a curious feeling of indirectness and lack of eloquence—which does not emanate at all from the artist's verbal descriptions of the scene. Here he has been a competent artist but a good writer, and when he writes in Africa that "the evening star is the size of a walnut," or that Giraud's eyebrows are like a young girl's, and notes that "When soldiers rest they fall back on their packs and lie looking up at you as if from an armchair," we see through his eyes better at such times than we do when we examine his drawings. And he gives a picture of the people simply by telling of that cry for candy, "'*Caramelli! Caramelli!*' For hundreds of years we shall be known in Sicily as the *Caramelli* soldiers."

In drawing and text Mr. Biddle has honestly tried to omit nothing for us. His equable humor and usually sanguine spirit contribute to the validity of what he tells, as does his use of the diary form, for all this gives a matter-of-fact, believable character to his notations. He has an eye out for the absurdities that make life even on the front bearable from one minute to the next. The time when he sketched some Italian prisoners only to find that they, from their corner, were sketching *him*, remarking, "He laughs best who laughs last," is the telling kind of entertainment he finds and passes on to us.

No matter where he goes Mr. Biddle sees the human being. It is the individual Arab that he despises for his cringing and his trickery and filth, and the individual Sicilian that he loves for his bounty of spirits and his adoration of the beautiful, even in pain or despair. He tells of drawing the wounded civilians in a hospital in Nicosia—as a task of morale of some kind—and how they would lift from their cot or litter to exclaim, "What beautiful drawing!"

Mr. Biddle says from time to time that the man in action feels a certain satisfaction or dignity in having his drawing made—in being "immortalized," so to speak, out of his daily anonymity of fighting. This is interesting, and one wonders if the fighting man would agree, or if he does not feel his inner dignity intact in spite of everything—loneliness included—and if he does not hold so still for Mr. Biddle mostly because he is tired. As he draws, Mr. Biddle—quite rightly—thinks of the future and of preserving a record. But even while he poses, the fighting man who lives in the present every moment could scarcely be expected, just now, to appreciate this long-range view, however honest and kind.

As simply a story of an artist at the front this book has a special interest. When before in any of the wars of the world did a government send artists in with their fighting men to tell the people at home what the wars were like? Our Congress, it is true, rather abruptly withdrew this sanction along with the allotted funds, and the work had to continue under a magazine's backing. Nevertheless that the idea occurred at all is rather an interesting and hopeful example of a new, a human and subjective attitude of a country toward war, that may be a sign in itself that we can never tolerate another one.

It would be interesting to see the work of the other artists who have gone overseas on this assignment.[29] The assembled work should present a picture which attains in the whole what it might lack through any individual. Mr. Biddle's work will certainly rank high in the assemblage. His sincerity of work and his undoubted courage in carrying his project through make him an example for the other artists at war.

The Great Fog
and Other Weird Tales

By H. F. Heard

ANIMAL, VEGETABLE, MINERAL GHOSTS

New York Times Book Review 3 September 1944: 5

These are good supernatural stories of science and idea. The ghosts are mold cultures and polar hysteria and the like of that. They raise only the intellectual hair, not the pulling kind, and since it is difficult for us to be really frightened intellectually, they do not have the homely charms of the ghost stories of M. R. James, for instance, which also have their professorial air with little black devils all covered with hair, besides. Neither have they the buoyant enthusiasm of the early Wells stories.[30] But they have their special fascinations.

Mr. Heard's stock of odd knowledge is extraordinary, an exotic cupboard where you can make real finds in puzzling facts about vertigo and balance in the semi-circular canals, about fungi, hypnosis, Gregorian chants, and the tracks on the flagstones of English churches, of the fertility dances from pagan springs. Chemistry, weather, the primeval energies, and the mutations of animal life are not really ghosts; yet their reality, or potentiality, is effectively used by Mr. Heard to make us as uneasy as possible.

Generally, as in "Wingless Victory"—a very long story of penguins in a superior Penguin Eden at the South Pole—startling ideas are developed with the serenity and exacting fullness of an essay, but not quite with the spark we like in a story, no matter how satisfied we are by its strange facts. Perhaps the imagination of Mr. Heard seems too orderly, too ascetically scientific. He always takes his time, a thing we don't like about story writers, and when his Penguins talk they round off their paragraphs as deliberately as scholars.

But there is pleasure in reading these. That faint twinkle that often shines through pedantry lights up a story like "The Swap," when two irritable old professors, of the kind generally known as "codgers," place themselves heart against heart and stare eye into eye, after reading of a Sufi practice, thereby suddenly exchanging souls, only to find themselves thoroughly outraged by each other's bridgework.

Some of the tales, like "The Cat, I Am," are given a rational ending and by losing their supernatural standing are not as effective to this reader as the out-and-out weird tales. "The Great Fog," while notable and interesting, is a moral, and Mr. Heard seems always rumbling a little, morally, underneath. Why is it that the moral and the supernatural don't mix? Perhaps we never can shiver while we are being cautioned about our shortcomings.

The two extremes in the book are "The Crayfish," almost a straight detective story, which turns up a devilish means of murder, by the way, and "Dromenon." "Dromenon" is a narrative astonishing in originality and in pure power of mood. Along with its erudition it has a content of feeling, strange, ardent feeling, which transcends the cold science of the other stories and makes their telling seem by contrast almost old-maidish. "Dromenon," which is actually the story of a gentlemanly antiquarian's investigation of an out-of-the-way church, is a wild excursion into supersensory music, pagan dance, Gothic architecture, and the rhythms of the blood, and in a strange, compelling fashion it is made into a tale of mounting suspense.

It is interesting to note that H. F. Heard is really Gerald Heard, an English author and lecturer who worked with Horace Plunkett during the Irish rebellion and is living now in Laguna Beach, Calif., where he came in 1937 with his friend Aldous Huxley. He is the author of *The Third Morality, Pain, Sex and Time, A Dialogue in the Desert* and other books, as well as two mystery novels, *A Taste for Honey* and *Reply Paid*, also written under these initials.

Sleep No More
Edited by August Derleth
Jumbee and Other Uncanny Tales
By Henry S. Whitehead

GHOULIES, GHOSTIES AND JUMBEES

New York Times Book Review 24 September 1944: 5, 21

Readers to whom the name M. P. Shiel is a password to a delirious and astounding world will only need to be told that *Sleep No More* contains a fine Shiel of good vintage. "The House of Sounds," which Mr. Derleth has winnowed out of England, where it has lain for fifty years, is as wild and gorgeous a tale as "Purple Cloud" devotees could hanker for. Shiel is probably a kind of genius. None of the other writers represented in this collection are, or nearly so, but to have even one genius up an anthology's sleeve is very fine. August Derleth, who tirelessly gathers horrors for readers who have by this time certainly become connoisseurs, has done a careful job with *Sleep No More*, and if you read the book straight through and end with "The Rats in the Wall," by old master H. P. Lovecraft, the potion may work and you may sure enough never sleep again.

Good, dependable horror conjurers here include Prof. M. R. James, the Rev. Henry S. Whitehead, Messrs. John Collier, Algernon Blackwood, H. R. Wakefield and others. What makes this collection different from a great many representing more or less the same authors is that the stories here chosen are not the familiar ones. As the editor points out in a foreword, only three of them are in print elsewhere, and only one of the three in

America. When Mr. Derleth asks to be commended for *not* including once more "The Upper Berth," "Seaton's Aunt," "The Beckoning Fair One," "The Wendigo," etc., we can commend him some, for the stories here, while unfamiliar, are also good. In all of them some strange, intriguing idea has come to the author, but somewhere in the course of his mapping out a story to accommodate it the idea has got thinned out or wasted, or has degenerated into cliché. There are too many things called "The Thing." The idea is not developed, and here is where the old favorites are inevitably superior. Nevertheless, these stories are fun. This reviewer liked the one where the man puts on the wrong overcoat in the New York Public Library and turns into a slobbering Black Druid while riding home in the subway, and this changes the expressions on the faces of the other passengers.

The Rev. Henry S. Whitehead belongs to what Mr. Barlow in his preface calls "the serious Weird Tales group."[31] The stories in *Jumbee* all take place in the Virgin Islands, except for the last one, which suddenly switches to Jackson, Miss.[32] If there is such a thing as the comfort horror tale, this is the kind the Rev. Whitehead writes. It is hard to classify otherwise such gentle, matter-of-fact, rather fatherly stories which produce some of the most point-blank ghosts that have jumped at us anywhere.

The variety of ghosts is fresh and interesting. There is Armand Dubois, who immediately after death pays a visit to a lady he owed $300 to, arriving in the form of a little goat who trots around her night table, first to the left, then to the right, looking at her out of green eyes. And the head of a voodoo bull victim materializes over the mantelpiece in a lady's drawing room, with a bullet hole in his forehead, down which blood slowly runs at tea-time every afternoon.

Mr. Whitehead is careful to give exact facts in his stories. A Martinique fish-Zombi is ten feet tall, with a pumpkin-shaped head, has purple scales and a beak like a scythe, and comes up from behind to take you—as a wasp might take a fly. A Jumbee, on the other hand, stands but a few inches off the ground—perhaps because he hasn't any feet. He comes by families and hangs in a cluster in a tree by the roadside at dawn.[33]

The Rev. Mr. Whitehead, who was born in Elizabeth, N. J., and was ordained an Episcopal minister, had a pastorate in the Virgin Islands. It is a fact that these little stories have charm—perhaps it is the gentleness of the author's personality pervading their horrifying content that makes them piquant.

Enjoy Your House Plants

By Dorothy H. Jenkins and Helen Van Pelt Wilson

FOR THE WINDOW-BOX FARMER

[Reviewed above the initials E. W.]

New York Times Book Review 1 October 1944: 24

This book will prove sturdy, it is hoped, for it's the kind that will be consulted every day by those who cultivate their gardens in a window. It is written to fill exactly this use, providing practical information as well as that encouragement that's needed to take a little plant and raise it in the soot of the city. The authors, opening with a description of their own window as dazzling as a flower show, to lure the timid apartment dweller into the boldness of gardening, then proceed to show how easy it is—providing their common-sense directions are heeded.[34]

The book is well arranged, brisk and clear with its information. At the start there is a classification of plants as to their needs of light and sun, so that gardeners will know exactly what they can attempt in their windows. Only the healthy plant is decorative, say the authors. Their doctoring advice ranges from botanical facts down to hints, sometimes dark, out of their own lively experience.

Plants and bulbs are taken up by variety and fully discussed in terms of the window shelf. For instance, if you crave an African violet you can learn within a few pages where to buy a healthy plant, how to cultivate, divide, repot, water and rest it over, and how to grow it afresh from a cutting.

Both common and exotic plants are discussed. You'll have your cyclamens for Christmas, but you'll be tempted to grow a camellia too, if you're not careful, and before you know it you'll plant your next avocado seed and have a little glossy-leaved tree in your kitchen in two months' time.

In addition to helpful advice on keeping the ordinary plants healthy, warnings or challenges are given you about plants difficult to grow. There is a calendar of monthly duties, a ready-reference glossary, an index, and a useful list of dependable growers for ordering purposes. Excellent illustrations include diagrams to follow in your digging and potting procedures, and photographs of the authors' own very attractive and successful window gardens.

Of Men and Battle
Pictures by David Fredenthal, Text by Richard Wilcox

ONE-MAN SHOW
[Reviewed above the initials E. W.]

New York Times Book Review 15 October 1944: 24

This one-man show by David Fredenthal bears the catch-title *Of Men and Battle*. David Fredenthal, an artist familiar to gallery-goers, who has worked under Guggenheim and Museum of Modern Art fellowships and later as an Army war artist and for *Life*, made these sketches for the picture magazine during the attack on Arawa, New Britain, December, 1943.

The pictures quite capably tell the story they set out to tell, and admirers of Fredenthal's work will find its characteristics as fully evident in these battle-done sketches as in his studio paintings. Here to the number of about sixty they give the slap of massed impact, but the general effect is of a rather messy and incoherent form, out of which a certain admirable brute force and occasional delicacy of line show up to relieve the monotony of their disorganization.[35]

G. I. Sketch Book

Edited by Aimee Crane

DRAWN AT FIRST-HAND

New York Times Book Review 29 October 1944: 20

Penguin has here published, in a neat little book opening the long way, 138 pages—eight in color—of sketches made by American service men in this country and overseas.[36] They have been studiously and well chosen by Aimee Crane, who writes a foreword, and are reproduced to good effect in spite of their modest dimensions.

The sketches, which the jacket describes as "informal," were done in water-color, pencil, or sometimes oil paint applied to ship's canvas. "Informal" is a loose and euphemistic word for a sketch made in a foxhole, on the deck of a burning ship, inside a transport plane, on the cot of a field hospital, in the shadow of a tree in a sniper-filled jungle, or in a traveling LST. It is from such vantage points that these artists' eyes have seen their present world. Though behind part of the work is a background of more or less professional painting experience, the technique is still a technique of convenience, speed and whatever compulsion made some of these artists draw for the first time in their lives.

The GI's painting here are men born in Cleveland, Denmark, Armenia, Council Bluffs, Brooklyn, Knoxville, Mexico, Irvington-on-Hudson, N. Y., and Stoke-on-Trent, England. They range in age from the 54 of Lieutenant Commander Coale, USNR, to the 19 of Pvt. Harry Andrew Jackson, USMC. Their backgrounds in art vary, too. Captain Vidar of the Ski Troops studied at Beaux-Arts, Top Sergeant Wexler invented and produced the comic strip "Vic Jordan," Sergeant Rounds illustrated children's books.

44

Chief Specialist Thomas won the 1938 Pulitzer Art Prize, but Lieutenant Donahue is an ex-drummer with a swing orchestra.

Some of the pictures were done with a definite aim: T/Sgt. Olin Dows, USA, is one of twelve men chosen to make a pictorial record of the war theatres. On the other hand, Private First Class Smith, USMC, forgot all about a little drawing he made until he saw it in *Life* one day and, when questioned, said: "I drew this picture sitting on a foxhole along a river in Guadalcanal after a big drive. It was drawn on the cardboard top of a 37-mm. ammunition case." A remarkable scrap it is, too, setting down the tenacious and straining forms of a stretcher party moving through a tenacious hell of hindering jungle vines.

In fact, the work is almost without exception interesting. The water-colors of Sergeant Loudermilk, USMC, of Comancho, Tex.—who studied under Barse Miller, was a defense worker before the war and took a prize in the South Pacific art contest at New Caledonia [—] are fresh and spirited. The beautiful work of Lieutenant Di Benedetto, USA—who studied at Cooper Union and the Boston Museum of Fine Arts and was overseas with the First Mapping Squadron—is represented by two fine crayon drawings. Lieutenant Colonel Dickson, USMC, who never studied painting anywhere, but while with the first regiment to land and occupy Henderson Field made a series of convincing sketches of these events, produced the now well-known figure of the battle-weary Marine, "Too Many, Too Close, Too Long."

Captain Pleissner, AAF, who has exhibited nationally here, made some stark sketches in the Aleutians he flew over. Lieutenant (j.g.) Jamieson, USNR—of the Abbott School of Fine Arts and the invasion of Sicily—is represented by a greater number of pieces than any other artist in this collection, and it is not too great a portion, for he shows unvaryingly good line, interesting composition and fine dramatic feeling.

It all proves, as an Air Corps man in the India-China-Burma theatre recently wrote home to his wife—the letter quoted by Miss Crane—"The desire for the fine and esthetic is not a shallow, meek appendage to the lives of humans, but a forceful necessity of life."

Six Novels of the Supernatural
Edited by Edward Wagenknecht

HAND-PICKED SPOOKS
New York Times Book Review 10 December 1944: 6

In these 883 pages of supernatural writing there are not enough moments when a soft, careless chill, or even a feeling much apart from the mundane, is likely to steal over the reader. The kind of reader who expects much to happen in ghost stories might even be tired out by the time he gets to the end of the book, from a surfeit of ghostly talk and a scarcity of the real ghost article.

This volume of the handy Viking Portable Library includes: *The Beleaguered City*,[37] by Mrs. Oliphant, published 1880; *The Return*, by Walter de la Mare, published 1910;[38] *The White People*, by Frances Hodgson Burnett, published 1917; *The Terror*, by Arthur Machen, published 1917; *Sweet Rocket*, by Mary Johnston, published 1920, and *Portrait of Jennie*, by Robert Nathan, published 1920.[39]

The dates are given as evidence of an interesting and inescapable idea that what constituted the supernatural in 1880 or even 1920 has undergone not so much a change as a new style. There is style even in the kingdom of ghosts, and the whole world of psychology has opened up since the date of Mr. Wagenknecht's latest inclusion. These novels are old, and old-fashioned, and this is no crime. But they are, several of them, a little shallow, and this is fatal. The old-fashioned documented story, in content and method, has a reputation as a good hotbed for flagrant horrors; but the spirit of this whole collection is mild and faded as a pressed flower. Some of the novels were, under their supernatural cast, sentimental to start with, as might reasonably be looked for from the authors of *Little Lord Fauntleroy* and *To Have and to Hold*, and they seem suspiciously included here for sentiment's sake—so as not to be forgotten.

Mr. Machen's fine story, *The Terror*, seems the purest example of the truly supernatural story, and of all in the book its method of narration seems equal to its idea. It is certainly the most satisfactory novel of the six, for this reader, from the simple point of view of a good story. It is good on any account. But while *The Beleaguered City* and *Sweet Rocket* may be good as supernatural stories, they fail except by the definition of being supernatural. Dullness is the complaint I would make of this book.

All anthologists write little notes in the front of their books in which they beat you to the charge that they have left out your favorite stories. Mr. Wagenknecht says he knows you will expect *The Turn of the Screw* and *The Strange Case of Dr. Jekyll and Mr. Hyde*, but that with only six choices possible he has "been compelled" to leave these out. This sounds dark, and what compelled him to put in *The Beleaguered City* and *Sweet Rocket* is not very clear. The collection would have been better with them out and James and Stevenson in, it must go without saying. And notice: their dates don't matter at all. It's true, Mrs. Oliphant's tale may be less familiar than Henry James'; but there could be reasons for that. Besides the quality of the writing itself, there is another way these stories fall below their peers in vitality. A supernatural story must have that too, even though its characters might all be ghosts. These stories languish too often, they droop and faint. There is a feeling of resuscitation, not rediscovery, in reading old stories which cannot touch us emotionally, even with fright.

There is wide variation in content here. *The Beleaguered City* is predominantly religious—it deals with ritual practice, the miracle, with formal belief, and the setting is French Catholic. *Sweet Rocket*, laid in Virginia, is an almost unrelieved transcendental tract, a round table of resonantly earnest talk which the characters utter in turn and all in agreement. Nothing happens, for crisis would naturally be discommoded in this setting of sweet accord.

The Return is in actual fact psychological, but also vague and whimsical— two curses at birth to set on a psychological story, and it proceeds in constant peril of utter confusion, like the White Knight with ditches on both sides. Surely Mr. de la Mare wrote this in yearning youth, and it seems hardly fair to print it now, for it is not a good sample of his imaginative and fastidious work. Its idea is played with overlong (270 pp.) and plays out.

47

The White People is a modest tale of second sight on the Scottish moors, and its serenity is nice and rather disarms you of your discomfort at its morbid quality which comes probably from its being sentimental.

Mr. Nathan's novel is the one in the collection which will be recently familiar to most readers. Its tinkering with time, lightly and expertly done, is valid supernatural material, and is done with the kind of imagination with which we are more akin. Yet it is first of all a love story—in intention too, one feels.

Some of these stories lay themselves wide open to the home psychologist—which seems a cheap and unfair fate for them. Somehow, for all their naiveté, they should have been spared something worse than being forgotten—the indignity of being seized by that certain kind of glib modern reader who can connect the plugs to mother-complexes and this phobia or that as rapidly and probably as carelessly as a telephone girl. "Man has not learned all the laws of nature yet," says a character in *The White People*, and that is a legitimate theme which should be honored whenever it appears, and be sympathetically received. It is only a pity that the present stories do not scare us more into the notion.

The Western Journals of Washington Irving

Edited by John Francis McDermott

SKIES WITHOUT A CLOUD

New York Times Book Review 24 December 1944: 3

Delightful mode of life—exercise on horseback all the fore part of the day—diversified by hunting incidents—then about 3 oclock encamping in some beautiful place with full appetite for repose, lying on the grass under green trees—in genial weather with a blue, cloudless sky—then so sweet sleeping at night in the open air, & when awake seeing the moon and stars through the tree tops such zest for the hardy, simple, but savory meats, the product of the chase—venison roasted on spits or broiled on the coals—turkeys just from the thicket—honey from the tree—coffee—or delightful prairie tea. The weather is in its perfection—golden sunshine—not oppressive but animating—skies without a cloud—or if there be clouds, of feathery texture and lovely tints—air pure, bland, exhilarating—an atmosphere of perfect transparency—and the whole country having the mellow tint of autumn. How exciting to think that we are breaking thro a country hitherto untrodden by white man, except perchance the solitary trapper—a glorious world spread around us without an inhabitant.

Thus Washington Irving in the Wild West of America in 1832, and though it is dubious if he himself had made the camp, ridden the chase, rounded up the turkeys or stirred the brew, assuredly he was under a green tree, and writing it down momently in a journal.

That the original New Yorker ever had the experience of washing his own clothes and eating stewed polecat for breakfast was more or less a happy chance. It was just after his return from seventeen years abroad; at the time he was probably weary of the lavish welcoming fetes accorded him in New York, and certainly highly curious about the new world opening up at home. An opportunity came for him to join Bean's Rangers on a minor military expedition—one gathers, as a kind of combination guest artist and responsibility.[40] He rode horseback and sat on rafts, met the Indians and lived the life for three months—covering land and river from St. Louis across to Independence, down through the present States of Missouri and Kansas to Fort Gibson, then a big loop over the Oklahoma prairies and back.

The five extant Journals kept by Irving were copied by Mr. McDermott, who provides also an interesting introduction. The book is charmingly put together; Mr. McDermott makes excellent correlation of this and contemporary material into some amusing counterplay. There are maps and reproductions of Irving's casual and fluent pencil sketches, and a sample chapter from the *Tour of the Prairies* resulting from the notes, for comparison's sake, rounding out the book in a satisfying and scholarly manner.[41]

That Irving spent his days in delight is evident everywhere. He seemed to meet new things, new people, the excitements and pleasures of a strange life with an emotion somewhere justly between intoxication and amusement, between curiosity and pleasant objectivity. The notes are set down with an un-selfconsciousness that is still elegant. Their directness and spontaneity have the charm which Irving himself would probably shrink to consider achieved until his writing was "finished"—and prevaricated on and romanticized, says Mr. McDermott—as in the *Tour.*

Chances are, such delicacy seldom went West. The writing that was to spring out of the West would never be like this; and Irving's work is unique in Western annals because it is not robust nor rambunctious nor raw; there is not any smartness or swaggering in any word of Irving's writing any more than there was in any bone of his body.

Perhaps the most appealing thing about Irving here is his marvelous eye for detail—that dateless quality. He takes time to note: "Intense curiosity with which an Indian watches Dr. ODwyer while he shaves," and "Little dog looking on at shoeing horse as if studying the art or waiting for his turn." The notes are generally pictorial, often beautiful—he remarks ahead the "blue lines of untrodden country." He is swift to compose a whole little landscape; then fill it with action:

A ground near natives house—show boat on the Illinois shore with flag—groups assembled there—rifle shooting—horse race along shore—negro laugh—sunset—party breaks up—some in boat across glassy river singing ballad—others on horseback through the woods—some on foot—some loiter on shore—beautiful, clear evening sky—moon nearly full—rising over the Kentucky shore above tufted forest—night hawks.

Camp-fire-meat roasted on sticks—savory—our salon of trees lighted up by fire—sky and stars in center—bat flitting across—faces of men & black boy roasting meat—greyhound with spectral face—we sit on bear skins & the meat put on spits before us—cut it off with knife & eat—coffee.

These word-pictures, set down in their immediacy, make valuable records of their time. They prove that Irving was a good reporter.[42] Especially, he was fascinated by Indians, as he always was by the romantic and legendary in American life which related it to the Old World. He seems never to have caught sight of a new Indian without noting it.

Pass several Creeks—one with scarlet turban and plume of black feathers like a cock's tail—one with white turban with red feathers—Oriental look—like Sultans on the stage—some have raquet with which they have been playing ball—some with jacket and shirts but legs and thighs bare—middle sized, well made and vigorous. Yesterday one had brilliant bunch of sumach. They look like fine birds on the Prarie.[43]

He was equally meticulous to enter little bits of Indian legends when he ran across them: "An old squaw left alone when her party had gone hunting prayed the Great Spirit to make something to amuse her—he made the mosquito." But there is marked absence of any of our own Western tall tales in this book, samples of our wild humor or ways of talking. One single bit of laconic speech is set down, "Old Genl Nix used to say God made him two drinks scant."

It is apparent that Irving never identified himself with all this. He remained ever the detached gentleman and observer, seeing the pageant through urban eyes. When the Western scene threatened vulgarity, he suddenly saw it romantically, instead. Thugs heightened to Gypsies, and Mason and his gang, Irving understood, gave back money to poor people, like Robin Hood.

Before daybreak howling of wolves—at daybreak imitations of cocks crowing, hens cackling, among youngsters of the camp—horses driven in—

breakfast—Whistling—singing—dancing—hallooing after horses—joking, laughing, scampering after horses—Bugle sounds. . . . Cries of "Who has seen my horse? & c"

These are like stage directions for a spectacle. They are not a participator's words. Irving does not consciously condescend—and is a great defender, of course, of the Indians—but he does refer to the guides and such in the party as "servants" and the Frenchman Antoine as "the half-breed," and there is a quiet impression that everybody else waited on Mr. Irving. There is appraisal without rapport.

The West was a curiosity; Irving was the visiting New Yorker. He rather expected to find things romantic, and he did: "Fires lit in dell—looks like a robbers' retreat." He enjoyed himself. He never did learn to spell "prairie," though.

Three Who Loved

By Edita Morris

FINE-SPUN FANTASIES

New York Times Book Review 18 February 1945: 4–5

In "Kuhlan," a bouncing servant girl from the North Country of Sweden hires out to a depressed family in town, where she transforms the house to gaiety and the sad daughter to an ambitious one, and after taking three lovers several rounds for May Day goes back to the North Country.

In "The Melody," a little boy is born and grows up in a gloomy, gossipy village and transforms it to a village of painted houses and flower gardens and sweet spirits, melts the heart of the mean rich man, and inspires the silent fiddler to compose a song.

In "A Blade of Grass," a Catholic sister who literally follows her feet, goes from an island to a large dirty town, where she goes up a stair and takes charge of a poor children's *crèche*. She transforms the dirty, evil children to clean, good ones, and the particular love she has for one child she crushes, after which she is content as before.

It is disconcerting for a reviewer when a book has been read and put down to find no vivid after-impression haunting the memory, no image of a character to cherish. This is an unusual book, by a talented writer. Yet it is as if these *Three Who Loved* ended when the book ended, and never had life of their own. Why is this? Mrs. Morris, the author, does not normally lack the power of charming story telling, and her two little girls of *My Darling From the Lions* are surely remembered as freshly as ever for their distinct, lively quality.[44]

We wish through the whole book for the flesh-and-blood gaiety that was in *My Darling*, the rambunctious energy and candid play, the imagination and the humor. Here the glowing Scandinavian setting of Mrs. Morris' other stories is muted, stylized, or symbolic. The action is just so, for the stories are really fables, set and molded from the start. All is still—fresh winds do not blow except when allowed by the author for a specific, hushed purpose.

How abundant the similes are in these stories! Kuhlan is "an apple, a red, red apple." The child of "The Melody" is "like a white candle with a bright, bright flame." Moreover Kuhlan, besides being an apple, is, in her various bodily parts, "like" an orange, a radish, a cat, a clapper in a churchbell, and more. She is like so many things we never get a long enough or straight enough look at her to understand for ourselves anything deeper than her surface and her symbol; she is as "made" in this respect as a rag doll. Indeed, with constant references to her "two legs," "two eyes" and "ten fingers," she seems peculiarly doll-like, for people, we take it for granted, have the usual number of legs and eyes.

In all three stories the emphasis is on the difference between the main characters and the others around them. The "Three Who Love" are extraordinary human beings, not actually very human at all. They "seemed to live according to different laws from others—laws of animals and plants, maybe—whose movements were guided by powers outside [themselves]," and they "made one wonder if [they] understood the ordinary happenings that went to make up other people's lives." The girl of "A Blade of Grass" is "incapable of unhappiness," "a stranger to emotions."

For the rest, the characters are all lumped together, and consist of our old friends from the folk tale and *opera bouffe*—the Gossip, the Drunk, the Mean Rich Man, the Little Hunchback Seamstress, the Poor Servant Girl, the Poor Fiddler; Mrs. Morris seems through with these once they are typed, or invoked.

Perhaps this amounts to an unfair complaint against the very object or design of these stories—a design *not* to present people in the round, but more decoratively in the flat; *not* to tell a warm story warmly, but an elusive and flitting one in a lyrical way. But the longest story is seventy-six pages, perilously long to spin out the lyric form, until the elusive story or pretty fable is likely to seem somehow childish after all.

The author seems to be writing so delicately, in order to keep her distance from such extraordinary characters, that we seem specially to notice her tiptoeing. This is true around the little boy of "The Melody" most of all. What is he? He is some symbol of universal love. He has no root in nature—no such one would run about holding his skirt over the crocuses blowing in the wind to "protect" them—yet he can revive dead dahlias.

Somewhere in these fables there is nobility and tenderness, but not enough vitality to support their thesis. For it must be paradoxically true that "selfless" love becomes empty of meaning in a story that does not make that self real to us. The characters live no lives of their own away from the stories because they are not equipped to do so. Afterward, so tenuous they were, so dependent on a phrase of the author's, they seem to have existed only as a part of her decorative style.

Roger Conant, A Founder of Massachusetts

By Clifford K. Shipton

SALEM AND ITS FOUNDING FATHER

New York Times Book Review 25 February 1945: 4

Salem, Mass., was settled so long ago that by the time Jefferson was President some six feet of earth had filtered over its first foundations. The man who in the main made Salem's foundations possible is the subject of Mr. Shipton's careful and affectionate study.

Roger Conant, like most of the Massachusetts founders, was a West Country man, son of a well-to-do yeoman of Devon. Like them, his motive for taking ship to the New World in 1622 was not a hot-headed one, though it was warm and burning; it sprang from neither adventurousness nor aggressive religious differences. Mr. Shipton thinks Roger had simply come to a considered judgment that in a growing and changing world he would do well to become a useful part of the side which favored human rights and individual enterprise as against the side which didn't. It was this strength of character itself that was of such value to the Massachusetts colony, and the reason why Roger Conant—whose doings are conflictingly recorded in the history books, whose appearance must be imagined from composite Conant features, whose letters and journals all have been lost, and whose very grave lies somewhere unmarked—remains for us a figure of force among the founders of New England. It is to Mr. Shipton's credit (and our pleasure) that he has succeeded in making Roger Conant a real person in this first biography of him.

From the four winds of contemporary letters, documents, court and church records, notes on the weather and crops, the straws of the developing state of mind among the settlers concerning themselves, the Indians, and the mother country across the sea, and a warming assortment of domestic detail, the author has gathered the bits and put back together again an image of Roger Conant lively and circumstantial enough to give a good illusion of the "solid, useful, gentle, honorable man," he considered him.

Roger, young out of armada-touched Devon, in his London apprenticeship as a salter was on hand not only to see Shakespeare fresh but to witness his countryman Raleigh's head roll from the block, and to listen to Capt. John Smith spin his New World tales in Salter's Hall. When he and his wife Sarah and his little son embarked in midwinter, 1622, he knew as well and as poorly as any man of his day what he was leaving and what he was going out to. The list of necessities he would take with him, ranging from medieval trappings to "nayles of all sorts," is both formidable and touching. Besides this he had the tales he heard to go by—of the unicorns and rampaging bears of New England, "a deer whose horns extended backward to the rump and then forward again 'a handful beyond their Nose,'" and "Pond Frogs as big as a Child of a year old." On land the geographical knowledge was skimpy enough for many settlers to expect a glimpse of the South Sea with Spanish galleons on it over any next rise of ground. Till Conant's death it was generally believed that New England was an island. This continued ignorance was due not so much to lack of enterprise in exploring as to the press of time and the simple problems of survival. "One speaks . . . of the 'lost colony' of Roanoke as if that had vanished into thin air, whereas actually Englishmen knew where Croatan was, but in spite of their eagerness to rescue the colonists, could not get around to it for three generations."

In showing us Roger Conant as settler, manager for the Dorchester Company, organizer of the Salem church, planter, selectman, juryman, judge and surveyor, Mr. Shipton gives a picture of the Massachusetts colony that is singularly whole and altogether lively. The career of Conant followed the pattern of the great number of Old Planters; he moved from Plymouth to Cape Ann and finally, and most significantly, to Salem, which he established with a little group of twenty souls. His special importance is that, aware of the larger and deeper forces at work on both sides of the sea, he was ever concerned with making ready a refuge against the day when the civil war threatening despotic England broke out and a whole new society would move pellmell into the little colony. It was in clinging to and strengthening this refuge, the town of Salem, in spite of all hardship, that his greatest service was done and the greatest proof of his character was required and given.

The book is a scholarly piece of reconstruction, painstakingly fitting together not only the lockpieces of important history but minutiae of family and neighborly life. Mr. Shipton's examination of the Puritan way of thought and feeling, revealing it in modern perspective as the radical and tolerant offshoot springing away from Old World absolutism, and carrying the seed of all we hold precious, shows how near to our own democracy their hope in its essence lay.

There are interesting comparisons in the book of Roger's Old Planters with the grim Plymouth Pilgrims and with the gentlemen-settlers of Jamestown. Luminous figures of the day gather in every chapter, and through the narrative run the names of Miles Standish, Roger Williams, John Smith, Endecott, Winthrop and many an enduring Massachusetts name along with Conant—Balch, Dodge, Lathrop, Higginson, Bradford.

It is the rich domestic background that makes us see the Old Planters best as human beings, of course. In Mr. Shipton's warm descriptions we see the man of the house stepping to his door of an evening and emptying his bell-shaped gun at random, to bring down a dozen ducks—the wife with "her children foure or five" busy by the fire, the chickens protectedly feeding under the dining table, where also a stray Indian, after peeping through the window, may slip in and sleep the night and at dawn leave a gift, like the fairies—at any alarm the neighbors stalking the thickets in their heavy black armor in which they look "like black lobsters"—the little pigs feeding on clams when the walnuts and acorns give out. And in the bitter winter we see Roger scraping the bottom of the meal barrel to feed the Indians, while the little Conants sternly bite their fists not to cry.

The houses of New England were no log cabins in which the settlers could have kept warmer, for the English were not axemen but sawyers. Before the saw pits could be built, families burrowed into the sides of hills and lived behind the thick earth walls. When the new little plank houses were built, there was no resemblance to a Western frontier settlement, such as Hawthorne represented. In fact, Salem looked like nothing so much as East Budleigh in Devon, the birthplace of Roger Conant.

From the first, when there was not cold and famine, there was exhilaration. In the New World all the Puritans *felt* better. "In this invigorating climate, English hens promptly learned to crow and grew spurs with which they broke their eggs." There were also, to be sure, "Little Flyes called Musketoes," and pineapples growing on trees which looked familiar from Dutch engravings, but which when picked turned out to be wasps' nests. And the first beast encountered at Salem was "a squuncke." They wrote back to England a frequent message, "Here is good living for those that love good Fires."

Apartment in Athens
By Glenway Wescott

TOLD WITH SEVERITY AND IRONY
New York Times Book Review 4 March 1945: 1, 16, 18

After the war—the Helianos family in Athens thought—they would try to tell their friends who had got away from Greece what they had been through in the occupation, "but it occurred to them that they might not be able to. It is not easy to tell this kind of domestic ordeal and do it justice without either exaggerating it or making a mockery of it. . . . It should be told with severity, irony . . . " Glenway Wescott here states his own task and the conditions it imposes. It is not surprising, for the writer he is, that he has fashioned it well, with severity and irony—and that he has added also compassion.[45] His story of an Athenian family during German occupation is a fine study of humiliation and nobility, and their culmination in tragedy and desperate resolve.

The Helianos family, occupying a small apartment in the center of Athens during the war, is conventional upper middle class. Mr. Helianos is a liberal, an ex-publisher, intelligent, gentle, priding himself on his dialectic and his ironic observations. Mrs. Helianos, passive, womanly, ailing—her heart is weak—depends on his wisdom and her intuition. When the Germans come they are descended upon by an officer who seems the milder sort of tyrant—a middle-aged, quiet man of no bad habits. It would seem that this situation is not nearly so bad or horrifying as it might be, that the Helianos family might have reason to congratulate themselves on their comparative good fortune. It is the evil of this very luck, latent in this very mildness of situation, that Mr. Wescott has searched out and shown. The power of the story lies in the dignity and middle-course position of the Helianos family and in the mildness of the invader.

The account of the German's stay with the Greek family is without violent incident: there is instead the threat or the parody of violence—the slight, almost accidental cuffings; the quailing fear of arousing anger; the sleepless, huddled nights; the dangerous fatigue of ceaseless anxiety to please; the infliction and endurance of hunger. Constitutionally inept at servitude, inefficient in ministering to the invader, the family find the keeping of their house a make-believe by day, and by night a withdrawing into an animal-like intimacy among themselves to shut his nearness out.

The war has already softened the Helianos family for destruction. Cimon, the elder and promising son, has been killed in battle. Their surviving children are inferior—Alex, 13, uncontrollable, who has "a sense of evil rather than a dread of injury," is a perverse little creature; Leda, always silent, "a shameful child" but "an innocent," is "like a bird in a cage. She is both bird and cage, and forever shut." A cousin Petros, the family hero—always offstage—is a cause for alarm to the Helianos in his desperate, extreme deeds. A brother on the other side of the family is a cause of disgrace for his suspected collaboration with the enemy.

To the little family of victims the German is a mysterious character. Helianos is led from intellectual curiosity to fatal conversation, prodding into the way this conqueror is made. The children embarrass their parents by feeling the mystery as attraction—Leda is charmed into fawning on the captain, Alex into tempting him mischievously to show his cruelty and spite. Mrs. Helianos finds him a domestic enigma—he does not relish food or any creature comfort, and for this she blankly distrusts him and hates him by instinct.

When Kalter arrives—a man whose asymmetrical German features were to the Greeks like sculpture where the hand of the sculptor had slipped—the Helianoses are oppressed, but it is when he comes the second time, after a leave in Germany, that they feel worse disquiet. Kalter comes back from his leave changed, a "freakish . . . kindness" in the place of his bullying. "It was not natural for him not to get his own way, it was not natural for him to control his temper, it would end badly," Mrs. Helianos thinks. For the humiliation the German inflicts has its own development. The family are to endure servitude—then inexplicable softening and toying condescension—then an abject begging for pity—and finally treachery that extends and acts even after death.

Kalter carries the seed of death in him, and his secret is that personal misfortune has come to him and he cannot bear it. He himself has been bereaved by the war while on leave—his sons both killed in battle, his wife dead in an air raid. He dramatizes the story shamelessly as he finally tells it to Helianos. And though Helianos finds his threat of suicide "too sudden and incoherent for a Greek mind," he realizes and acknowledges the sincerity of Kalter's grief with a sincerity of sorrow, and in a moment of human recognition and pity cries out against the Fuehrer who has brought such a thing about. The human outcry is his doom.

Kalter has him arrested. From then on, evil opens upon evil, until the tragedy is resolved. In the end, the tragic mother will send her remaining son and daughter forth to avenge the death of their father.

The villain of the book destroys himself a little more than half way through the tragic story. This is significant of Mr. Wescott's purpose. "Forever and forever history will give us another chance," says Kalter of the Germans. Speaking of them as a people but also speaking for all intents of himself, he says:

> Although he dies, no matter; he lives in his fellow-German, his compatriot, his kind. For us Germans, I tell you, this is our immortality. What if one man is imperfect, still there is the type; and sooner or later the type will come to perfection. If you believe that, there is vindication and a remedy for everything. If the one man is defeated—one and then another, no matter how many—the triumph will come, nevertheless, in the end.

The Greek mind sees that

> The clever thing all Germans did was to get everyone talking in terms of the future, as if the present did not exist or did not matter; and for Helianos, with his Greek sense of the value of a lifetime and the absoluteness of death, there was something wrong in that.

This is illuminating as perhaps the reason for Mr. Wescott's choice of Greece as the scene for his story and its lesson.

Mr. Wescott's thesis is that all Germans are evil—that the world is doomed by this Hydra who can time after time be mutilated only to rear another live, ugly head, unless he is put down for good and all. The character of every German in the story develops alike—an evil flower opening only to show deeper layers of evil petals, then its inward evil heart bearing prolific seed. "Good" Germans are the worst of all. Mr. Wescott puts this in

the actual form of a message—the letter Helianos writes from prison which
he wishes delivered to America.

> . . . I would not listen, I forgave him, especially one midnight. I was sorry
> for him, especially that last afternoon. Therefore now here I sit in the evil old
> prison writing you a long, illegible, impotent letter. This is my story. I think
> there are millions of men as foolish as I, in every nation; and I want them to
> know what I know now.
>
> It is something for us to beware of: the good moods of Germans, their
> suddenly reforming and seeking to please, the natural changes of their hearts.
> That is the moral of my story.
>
> In fact the likable and virtuous ones are far worse than the others as it works
> out, because they mislead us. They bait the trap for the others.

Helianos predicts the return of health and virility to Greece:

> There will be a great passion in Greece when the Germans depart, there
> will be wondrous children, oh my darling, like the Cimon of our youth,
> faultless and promising! There will be a little new generation begotten in a
> night, the progeny of our very pain and hunger.

But he warns:

> Germans mean to come back, to bludgeon our new generation into a psy-
> chopathic stupor, to set up their slaughterhouses all anew. . . . Greeks dying in
> battle to the last man cannot stop it; it will take the nations altogether to
> prevent it. . . . They will let us come up again for a season; then when the time
> is ripe for them, mow all our lives down again in a disgusting, useless harvest
> like this.

It is in delivering this impassioned message that the story ceases to follow
a classical form. Helianos is allowed to address us from offstage, from
beyond his doom, and give us a moral message. It can break from the mold,
for it bears the very essence of the book.

Except for this, the form of the novel invokes a traditional Greece. The
use of myths, of place and character names (Leda, Eurydice, Mount Olym-
pus), the classic physical postures and attributes (Mrs. Helianos' serpentine
locks tossing on her forehead in her disaster), all have their part in creating
by suggestion and synthesis a background, emotional, decorative—which is
as much mood as actuality. The conversation is dialectic, oratorical or
lyrical—there is consistent formality of speech, in telling contrast with the
almost unbearable intimacy of the action. The novel is slow of movement,
with the retarded progress of the inexorable story, the plot bare and un-

adorned. The violence is all offstage; news of it is brought by messenger or (as in Kalter's death, which must take place in the apartment) by sound from another room.

Mr. Wescott thus keeps his story pure to the point almost of abstraction, he identifies his characters with the spirit of Greece. Here is Mrs. Helianos standing at the kitchen window, looking at the Acropolis, in her grief following her husband's arrest:

> Then as she stood and looked she assumed an attitude which in physical sensation corresponded to her thought, her spirit. It was an attitude prompted perhaps by unconscious memory of ancient sculpture that she had seen all her life (although without caring for it especially), or perhaps merely exemplifying a racial habit of body from which that style of sculpture derived in the first place—a classical attitude: her fatigued thickened torso drawn up straight from her heels and from her pelvis; her head settled back on her fat but still straight neck, her soiled, spoiled hands lifted to her loose bosom. . . .

The author has also taken unostentatious but subtle advantage of the prerogative of the chorus to lament, to prophesy or to warn, now and then.

But we are constantly reminded that the drama here is not spectacle; it is confined, domestic—we are withdrawn from the general scene to the hearth of tragedy. The scene is intimate, the figures of the drama cannot be colossal, for they are low, aging, or they are children, bearing the little paunch of starvation.

Of these characters, that of Mr. Helianos is remarkably realized, subtle, appealing, and the core of the novel. He was "a civilized Greek." "Even fighting for his life, even (as it was in his case) having lost the fight, hoping against hope, a Greek ought to keep that moderation and strict sense of reality which, he reminded himself, Greeks had invented in the first place." He is doomed because "he was too sedentary and philosophical for the time of war."

For this reader it is in the character of Mrs. Helianos—in many ways the most touching in the book—that the faults that exist in the story come out. She is wholly believable as a "poor bereaved creature" who feels "uncompromising unhappiness," when "instinctively she stood on guard against the mystery of the German. It was her nature to be mistrustful." She sees clearly that while for her husband "the past was his hobby, and his weakness," for herself there is "no help for it, no refuge from it: her Hellas was contemporary Athens, and what did that amount to, what had it been reduced to? Dust, stench, fatigue, disgust, fright, constant fright, and beggars and cadavers."

But believable as she is in her personality, when she acts especially in crisis, she seems unbelievable. Granted she is hopeless. But she lies down to keep from fainting, instead of going to her husband's side, when Kalter orders his arrest. When Helianos is thrown in prison, eight days pass before she feels she must do something about it; until then she does "her weeping, palpitating, fainting," and spends her time in "recollection of what a fine man he was and what great obscure, profound things he said." Instead of going herself to see what has happened to Kalter when the shot is fired, she sends little Alex—because she has been "spoiled all her life." When at last a letter comes from Helianos written in prison on little bits of paper, she postpones reading it and then "once in a while she grew discouraged and was tempted to put it all away in a box or in a drawer as a mere keepsake, unreadable."

Perhaps it is wishing for a ruinous thing or a paradox to wish that all these characters—so subtly imagined and developed, embodying so much—should be more human. They embody human virtues and faults and strivings and weaknesses, in delicately mixed proportions, but they are not human in themselves—they seem not to have been conceived as live characters but put together first, then brought alive. Almost as if he would make up for this, Mr. Wescott has insisted overmuch, in his constant use of the words "dear," "little," "poor," "soft," "womanly" and "manly" and other compassionate adjectives, that his characters are thereby authorized to be human. But somehow they do not let us see it for ourselves.

The children, deficient in life as they are actually, from starvation, reach reality in the end. "[Leda] is not really psychopathic, I have decided," Helianos writes. "She is only horror-stricken and paralyzed by fright." As for Alex, we see that in this classical story perhaps it was not for nothing that he was a pre-Hellenistic figure, his archaic "crescent smile" and mysterious liveliness held abated, with something prophetically as well as historically fierce, barbaric—his future lies in the Underground.

Apartment in Athens is a shapely story, a work of art in the true sense. If it is synthetic, it is so through intense awareness and consciousness of purpose. It is careful work, by which a noble and original piece has emerged from its material. Its moderateness, lack of exaggeration, serenity are admirable as the Greek ideal they reflect and honor. Everywhere is the dignity of a style in which there is nothing wasteful and nothing wanting in saying an explicit thing.

Fireman Flower and Other Stories
By William Sansom

FIREMAN FLOWER
Tomorrow May 1945: 69–70

William Sansom is a young British writer already published in England by the Hogarth Press.[46] *Fireman Flower* contains twelve short stories, all distinguished by good writing and by their curious subject matter and intensity of treatment; but the title story is the master story of the volume. "Fireman Flower," the longest as well as the most concentrated piece of work here, has in plenty the qualifications of an imaginative writer of deep talent.

It will be seen at once that these are stories of the spirit. Although they often employ familiar symbols and are often moral, their symbolism is in turn penetrated by, or overridden by, an imaginative search toward abstractions lying beyond morality. To our greater pleasure, there is more of poetry than of allegory in Mr. Sansom's ideas.

Along with their fantastic or dreamlike quality, the stories are extraordinarily vital—perhaps, for one thing, because they are visually concrete and startling. It is the essentially wonderful or terrifying thing, which is at the same time commonplace, that Mr. Sansom uses for his material. Many man-created things—lighthouses, mazes, buildings on fire from air raids—have become familiar and commonplace, and Mr. Sansom seems to be attempting, on one level, to restore their essential mystery or terror.

In "Fireman Flower," the author has written a fable of complexity and power out of a Brigade Regulation for the Home Guard: "First proceed straight to the seat of the fire." The story, taking place within a burning building, is the story of search. The burning building continuously changes its aspect like the edifice of a nightmare; indeed, the whole story is night-marish and in the end the fireman comes out of it as one throws off a dream. Castle, cathedral, goods warehouse, a simple burning house ("the tradition-al fire of hearsay"), a chaos ("with fearful vertigos of infinity"), an arena, a familiar home with an old friend ensconced, a pleasure bath, "a titivation of the senses," are some of the changes the burning edifice undergoes in the eyes of the searcher for the fire's core. "How many matters composed the fire," Flower is brooding, experiencing as he goes its havens, seductions, deceptions, exhilarations, its pure beauty, its menace. He finds himself in a mirror at one point, as he finds the story of his life in the fire and its spell of past and future in the rooms, the long corridors with vistas like streets in Chirico's paintings.[47]

Finally escaping the nightmare itself by running up the long stair through the burning building and surveying the extending world from the rooftop, Fireman Flower is consumed inwardly by a vision of love—a quiet love for all he sees and knows through the greater vision of the world, "so that he loved a single rusted nail as he loved the Gioconda smile, the factory's timeclock as he loved the mould of autumn leaves, a mausoleum as he loved the crèche, a cat's head in the gutter as he loved the breasts of Joan."

These adventures are set down with the questioning and slow motion with which the passionate energies of a dream are regenerated and recalled. The use of startling and beautiful images is unforced and effective—the giant golden cockerel which a great machine on fire seems to turn into, which Fireman Flower climbs and on whose head he sits, is a fine example. Observations such as, "Compared with the bite of fire, the eyeless munch-ing of a dinosaur seems thoughtful and tender," taken outside the story, show how startling is Sansom's power to surprise; yet they seem almost inconspicuous in the context.

An energy reaching degrees of urgency seems to propel this book, and produces an abundance of surrealist effects, wonderful and explicit and authentically "sur-real." But it would be incorrect and misleading to call the stories surrealist. It must be remembered that these effects come from an energy at work not for its own sake, in free-association or in any form of irresponsibility, but altogether purposeful and highly in control. The tales are moral and spiritual. Their power and intensity make them notable, and Mr. Sansom's talent is an exciting matter for the new American readers of his stories.

Names on the Land: A Historical Account of Place-Names in the United States

By George R. Stewart

PLACE-NAMES AND OUR HISTORY

New York Times Book Review 6 May 1945: 1, 14–15

Outlaws X-Roads, Shiloh, Schenectady, Santa Fe—how did we get these names? And when?

The record of our place-names is of course the skeleton story of our nation; in that array the intrinsic and underlying structure shows. Exploration and claiming—Cape Fear, Louisiana; colonization—Jamestown; immigration—New Rochelle; Revolution—Lafayette; expansion—Deadman's Gulch. Our names tell us everything if we can read them. But every name has a name behind that—a one more story, a sea-change. The ambition of this book is staggering—like a demonstration of our national character in itself. Mr. Stewart uses the X-ray method on his material, but he has the zest of a Forty-niner, and what he makes is not a case, but a strike, and his book is a beauty. Only a passionate lover of facts, of facts rooted in the country and the people and the history of the land, could have written it. Mr. Stewart of course has written a meteorological novel (*Storm*), and a factual account of the Donner party.[48] But what facts are closer to people, more revealing of people's hearts, than the names they bestow?[49]

The scope here is so large, and the details so minute—taking in the whole country from the beginning on (with a nod at the Ice Age) and from one end to the other—that the story would collapse under its own weight in the hands of a man less deft at organizing it—a problem which was only one to tempt Mr. Stewart, one imagines, and lead him on. The lay reader such as the present reviewer has no way of knowing what degree of accuracy the work reaches, but will bet that it is good and high. Mr. Stewart has a reputation for getting data. In dealing with this material there must be guesswork and deduction in addition to the mountainous research; indeed, part of the fascination of the book lies in its ingenuity. A knowledge of languages including the Algonquin, a familiarity with American history from the earliest times on, a clear geographical grasp of the country from all four corners, a knowledge of law and land-grants, miner's slang, Indian beliefs, agricultural developments, Mormon saints and weather—a sizable background appears behind this book.

In the United States (Mr. Stewart does deplore that makeshift name for our country) are places named for battles, for a lost comrade, for the day of a saint, for a homesick moment, for a lure to bring neighbors, for kings and queens; places named for the namer, for a dead pony, for Lafayette, for a tavern sign, for a future wife, for a murder, for a deer in the creek, for a night of bad cards, for a rock that looked like the bosom of a lady, for a cockfight, for a poem in Scotland. Tradition, hope, love, pride, delight in the romantic, the bawdy, the beautiful, hope of gain, a keen and seeing eye, and likely a strutting fancy—these went into the naming of places in America. All Europe and Asia gave us names—and Puritans, Huguenots, Mormons and Quakers, miners, missionaries, outlaws, fishermen, scholars, traders, trappers, surveyors, priests and planters' wives.

The astonishing variety of our names is to be expected, Mr. Stewart holds—after all, four centuries of changing peoples and changing aspirations went into the naming. Variety comes too, because in giving names to places we cherished their strong link with actual persons and events, gave names "which seem to have stories of life and death behind them." "Variety also sprang from democracy—that stubborn local pride in the local name, and the feeling that I have just as much right to give and keep a name as you have." Chicken Bristle, or die. So we have Lexington and Union and also Sweetwater, Marked Tree, Gunsight Hills, Cape Disappointment, Broken Bow, Roaring Run, Massacre Lake. And we have always loved a revolutionary, Mr. Stewart points out, and honored him, no further questions asked, with a town name—Kossuth, Kosciusko, even Ypsilanti did not stop us.

In the beginning the French were hunting a passage to the South Sea; the

Spanish were looking for treasure in a fabulous kingdom and the elixir of life; the British were nosing for present holdings; the Dutch seeking trade. In all these pursuits, naming a place was an important point, a gain on the rivals. The differences in naming were clear-cut from the start. The Spanish always named places after the saint's day on which they found them, so that their maps are really calendars on which voyages can be read like diaries. The Dutch gave a practical name to each little kill and hook of the river they settled on, but they never did name the Hudson—it was simply "the river"—the English reproached them. The English of course drew upon courts and houses in England, gained favors or obeyed the king.

Ranging over four centuries, with pages packed with names and events, the book remains clear in trend, felicitous in pictures of the times which build along the way. We see the whole complexity and confusion of that early time when Joliet and Père Marquette with their boatmen, in two birchbark canoes, set off down the Mississippi:

> At last, near the middle of June in 1673 they came to the great river, which was already known by name. They wrote the word as Mississippi. But Marquette, it would seem, called it also Conception, and Joliet called it Buade, after the family name of Count Frontenac, the Governor. Thus all at once the river had three names—an Indian name for the boatmen, a religious name for the priest, and a political name for the officer.

In all the conglomeration of detail, the major design is not lost sight of, and we are shown panoramas of the nation as a whole at a given time, as

> . . . in the reign of Charles II, new great names arose, until twelve colonies and the Province of Maine were well established. In addition some cities and all the great rivers and capes and bays and islands of that coast had their names. Inland, the French had scattered names as far as Lake Superior and Kansas and Arkansas, and the Spaniards even further to the southwest. Since 1607 almost every year had seen the establishment of some new great name. In 1681 La Salle first used Louisiane; within a year Pennsylvania and Philadelphia were established; about the same time the Spaniards were beginning to use Texas. But the next two generations of men were to give few great names; instead they would fill in with thousands of little names, and establish new habits.

As he proceeds, the author shows how habit of life determined the kind of name. In the Virginia colonies, towns took the names of plantations, of little private chapels and churches, which were often named with Elizabethan fancy (Orphan's Gift, Chapel Hill, Chaplin's Choice, Jordan's Journey, Flower dieu Hundred). In the middle colonies, especially in Pennsylvania, towns took the names of the tavern signs, whose pictures survived as village names (Bird-in-Hand, Broad Axe, King of Prussia, Red Lion). When the Mormons went west they had a whole private holy book to draw names from and their own population of saints, and needed no dim-memoried dragon-killer to name a town St. George after. When the Forty-niners went West they were in such a hurry that big things like mountains and rivers got names that were simple pinning-down affairs, the explicit "West Fork of the South Fork of the North Fork of the San Joaquin," so they could be found again. It was in the naming of the mining camps that they gave vent to their real enthusiasm and high spirits, for "No censorship restrained them; society was of men only. Most of them looked upon their sojourn in California . . . as temporary and riotous adventure . . . Doubtless the more sophisticated often invented the most outlandish names; two Harvard men named Shirt-tail Canyon."

Mr. Stewart pays close attention to the change of temper and mood of the country as reflected in its styles of names. In the eighteenth century the Yankee name ascended over the Puritan. A town in Vermont was named by honest combat, fought out on the hemlock plank floor of a new barn, the winner rising full of splinters to shout, "There, the name is Barre, by God!" Canton, Mass., was named "at the instance of a prominent citizen, who maintained that his Massachusetts town was antipodal to the Chinese city," and all around, other prominent Yankee citizens came to the conclusion that they were antipodal to Canton, too, and Cantons sprang up thickly. "Actually, such an opinion was startlingly wrong . . . The very perversity of the story is almost an argument for it. It seems just what a crotchety Yankee of 1798 would be likely to maintain." He points out how "Illogically, as the religious fervor of the Puritans declined, biblical names grew more numerous. Perhaps they began to seem less holy." A town in Connecticut could be named Borzah in spite of Jeremiah 49:13. ("I have sworn to myself, saith the Lord, that Borzah shall become a desolation, a reproach, a waste, and a curse.") And he points out also, in defending, for example, an Alabama schoolmaster who named a muddy little river in his neck of the woods the Styx:

> The classical interests of the later eighteenth century are as much part of
> the history of the United States as the existence of the Indian tribes or the

Revolution. To maintain, as many have done, that Rome and Troy are mere excrescences on our map is to commit the fallacy of denying one part of history in favor of another part—or else to be ignorant of history. The ideals and aspirations of the Americans of that period deserve their perpetuation.

There are accounts given of all the great expeditions, full of flavor and detail, always contributing to the general picture of growth, of changing habits of thought, of the great surge westward. The Lewis and Clark expedition flowed with the indulgence of proud and extravagant fancy, heralding the great day of the West ahead, as when Captain Lewis commemorated his lady love:

> I determined to give it the name, and in honour of Miss Maria W———d, called it Maria's River. It is true that the hue of the waters of this turbulent and troubled stream but illy comport with the pure celestial virtue and amiable qualifications of that lovely fair one; but on the other hand it is a noble river.

while Captain Clark was writing down: "This rock which I shall call Popy's Tower is 200 feet high and 400 paces in secumpherance." This grandiose spirit led straight to the times when a camping party, sitting around a fire at night, would get up a hilarious game to name some mountain range. And they named mountains differently from the mountains of the east: instead of Sugar Loaf and Haystack were Saddle Mountain, Two Top, Rabbit's Ears, Nipple Butte and Coffin.

The book deals constantly with the Indians, of course, and manages to correct many an error about Indian names. Transference, translation and false etymology are the three ways in which a place name can be passed from language to language, Mr. Stewart points out. So the Indian names enduring as such are of course not the actual, original Indian names—they are what the French priests wrote down, what the Spanish thought they sounded like, what the English thought they undoubtedly meant, what the Dutch made sound as nearly Dutch as they could. Schenectady, for instance, is an anglicized form of the Dutch conception of a New York State Indian word. Mr. Stewart points out the important difference in the ways an Indian and a white man named a river. The European conception of a river was of a stream with a source, to which it and all its branches could and should be traced, and it had a single name. "What is the name of this river?" excited explorers would ask the Indians. "Big Rock," the Indians would answer, pointing to a big rock in front of them. "Big Rock" was the name of the river *there*. At the bend it would be named "Little Bend." Mississippi, a French version of an Algonquin word, probably means "big river," but could never mean "Father of Waters" as the geography books told us—an abstract term no clearheaded Indian would ever give a river for name. In the same way, the Indians running out to greet the white man in the southwest yelled "Techas! Techas!" This meant simply "Friends!" The Spaniards immediately thought the Indians were referring to some wonderful kingdom lying just back of them—Texas. But the Indians were hardly ever referring to anything except what was up at the moment.

The book abounds in the modest tale along with the mighty, telling how places were named:

> Once a surveyor named Strange became separated from his comrades and hopelessly lost in the forest. Years later, forty miles from where he last was seen, men found his bones beneath a great beech tree. Against it leaned his rifle, the shotgun pouch still dangling. In the smooth bark could still be read the carved words in plaintive doggerel:
> Strange is my name, and I'm on strange ground,
> And strange it is I can't be found.

So the stream once known as Turkey Run became Strange Creek.

Mr. Stewart deals with the great namers, John Smith, Penn—perhaps the greatest, Col. William Byrd (who decried the first Lover's Leap, naming the Blue Ridge) and many more. He enumerates the towns named after Washington, Lafayette, Lincoln, Jackson. He writes also:

> Of all Americans to have their names preserved in large cities, John Young is the most obscure. He came as an early settler in 1798. Untroubled by modesty, he named the place Youngstown; then, according to tradition, he traded a deerskin for a quart of whisky, and celebrated his immortality.
>
> He was a man of no importance. But why should not John Young stand as a symbol? If he was a man of little note, so also were nearly all his fellow frontiersmen. They died; their wooden grave-markers (if they had any) rotted into dust, and they were forgotten. But if we believe in democracy, why should not John Young, whisky and all, stand as their symbol, with the blast-furnaces of Youngstown flaming to their memory?

This book is a labor of love, such as few people would have had the energies, much less the abilities, or the pure courage, to undertake—and finish. The whole is written with a grace and engaging humor belying the work behind it. The nation from Seldom Seen to Possum Glory, Hog Eye to Bug Tustle, does owe Mr. Stewart a debt of gratitude for getting the tremendous material here between the covers of a book. "As the train announcer calls out the stations for a Philadelphia local, half the past of the nation unfolds." "It is a rich and poetic heritage," indeed.

True and Untrue, and Other Norse Tales

Edited by Sigrid Undset

Russian Fairy Tales

Translated by Norbert Guterman

French Fairy Tales

By Charles Perrault

FALL HARVEST FOR THE YOUNG READER

New York Times Book Review 11 November 1945: 7

Here are three beautiful fairy tale books. Sigrid Undset has made a collection of Norse tales which she presents with a warm, informal introduction showing her own pleasure in the tales.[50] They are delightful. The old Norse magic of trolls, of feats East of the Sun and West of the Moon is here, a native magic. As Sigrid Undset points out, it makes the fairyland of these people not so different from the world they live and move in every day. There is an interesting male counterpart of Cinderella in the Ashlad and other creations American children will be charmed to meet.[51] The illustrations, black and white, are on the conventional side, but very pleasing, and distinguished in one unusual respect, at least,[52] in that all the magic swords, fairy horses and the rest were drawn by the artist in interludes from fire while in combat overseas.

In the preface to the *Russian Fairy Tales* it is explained that the tales endured for centuries by word of mouth, in a country and time when only sacred, orthodox matters were put down on paper. Their vigor was undiminished, for the tales were everlastingly popular among the poor, and there was a custom for rich and noble persons to keep in constant touch with story-tellers (usually old blind men, and often in threes) to put them to sleep at night with tales.

Afanasiev, the man who finally made a collection of the stories about the time the brothers Grimm worked in Germany, happened to be a lawyer. The hundreds of stories in this book come from his exhaustive collection and are translated, many for the first time, by Norbert Guterman.

These Russian tales are rambunctious, full-blooded and temperamental. They are tense with action, magical and human, and move in a kind of cyclone of speed. They are full of priests, firebirds, little uncles and old women, Ivan the Fools and Baba Yaga the Golden-legged—the world and the fairy world are simultaneously rich here.

Mr. Alexeieff's illustrations are witty and individual; they might confound a child because all the people and animals look to be made of tin with cut-out designs in them—like cookie cutters.[53] They are amusing in themselves and royally plentiful, with hundreds of small black and white pieces and thirty-two full color page illustrations. Ought a fairy tale book be expensive? Or weigh too much for a little girl to hold up? These questions occur to any reader who insists on loving both children and fairy tales. Perhaps this is quibbling, as is a faint feeling that the "folkloristic commentary" is a little too mighty, too learned and long, coming in front of these gorgeous tales themselves.[54]

The present edition of Perrault is glorified with the marvelous Doré illustrations.[55] One's instinct says that these are what the child longs to see in fairy tale pictures—the stuff of serious enchantment, the woods deep and multifoliate, the giants and beasts literal, the fairies beautiful and fairy-like. Puss in Boots—in rampant pose, with his sure-enough boots on and a murdered mouse tied to his belt, towering there and imperiously stopping the King on his ride for the pursuance of a little scheme of his own—really looks the magnificent, magical cat, fierce beyond resistance and wholly believable as a fairy character. The stories are the real Perrault, the Wolf actually gobbles up both the Grandmother and Little Red Riding Hood and never gives up either one. Here is one reader who grieves for the omission of Bluebeard, but otherwise has no feeling but joy in the book.

Gumbo Ya-Ya, A Collection of Louisiana Folk Tales

Edited by Lyle Saxon, Edward Dreyer, and Robert Tallent

CREOLE GET-TOGETHER

New York Times Book Review 30 January 1946: 5, 14

"Gumbo Ya-Ya" is a dish made of left-overs, pretends to be no more, and like many left-over dishes has the luck to be seasoned highly enough to get by. Evidently, the WPA Writers' Project of Louisiana, after finishing the admirable *Louisiana Guide*, had many an unused bit it would be a shame to throw away—stories, legends, gossip, interviews, write-ups of special stuff.[56]

So why not? Here's a book called *Gumbo Ya-Ya*. The expression refers typically to a gathering of Creole ladies for an afternoon and means "Everybody talks at once." The subtitle, *A Collection of Louisiana Folk Tales*, is not troublesomely accurate, the book being a casual collection of almost everything else WPA writers gather.

The Creoles and Cajuns, the Voodoo priestesses, the slaves, the ghosts, the madames, the racetrack boys, the pirates and hoodlums and sports and saints—here they all are. The way the Catholic saints' days are celebrated, what the street criers called, how to play the numbers, how to get a three-day burial in St. Louis Cemetery No. 1, for looks—your coffin in on Friday and out on Monday—all varieties of information are here. Much of the text is direct quotation—interviews with some of the original people on this earth, surely.

The book opens with a rather potent account of Mardi Gras time, entitled "Kings, Baby Dolls, Zulus, and Queens." The sections following are also out of the common range as to content but make less invigorating reading; they are not edited sharply enough, perhaps, to escape being ordinary and long-winded at times, and toward the end the material seems still somewhat unclassified. The book peters out like some wonderful evenings of conversation about some delightfully curious subject—so much rushes to be said that it ends talked out, with babbles, sighs and yawns.

Gumbo Ya-Ya is fresh, colloquial and easy-going in approach—is no "study" at all. Now and then a kind of master-of-ceremonies attitude toward the things they are telling dulls what some of the narrators say—so that the curious, even the ungodly, turns self-conscious or facetious.

There is an abundance of original material, in Louisiana, and it was a good idea to gather it, but there is a feeling that if one man had really pondered on the whole and then written a book which did more than stir everything up together and dish it out, there would have been more value to the work. But then it wouldn't be *Gumbo Ya-Ya*, and it is beside the point to wish of any book that it had been another. At any rate, the material here is uneven in its powers of fascination. The reader finds himself wondering if the editors discriminated often enough between what was indigenous to Louisiana and what was simply interesting in human nature and its vagaries. Much of the ghost-story section, for example, could find its obvious parallel everywhere in the world, the stale old Headless Horseman has been much farther afield than the Bayou Country. Many of the ghost-seers, cult leaders, etc., presented with the master-of-ceremonies style mentioned above, still appear what they would be anywhere, rather pathetic neurotics of well-known types, adding glamour to nobody's geography.

The book is like an old desk belonging to no-telling-who, so outlandish, occasionally, are the stuffings of the pigeonholes; the accumulation is curious and interesting, but only some of it worth keeping. Still, there is a romantic, or a hilarious, or a wild note here and there that justifies your looking through the book. And there is one idea the book gives, perhaps beside its purpose—that Louisiana, different from everywhere else in many ways, is still part of the rest of the world, the same old ghosts are stalking it, human beings when investigated come up with curious but not wholly unprecedented answers.

Westward Ha! Around the World in 80 Clichés

By S. J. Perelman, illustrated by Al Hirschfeld

HIGH JINKS TRAVELOGUE

New York Times Book Review 8 August 1948: 5

It was years ago that a certain writer filled the pages of *Judge* with simulated woodcuts of agile characters ("'Back to the mines, men, there'll be no strike today,' hissed Boss Dismukes") and under them some very reproachable jokes about ladies, cads, and *la vie Parisienne*.[57] He was cherished then by this reviewer who (like thousands of others, no doubt) used to carry his work around in high school hidden in the back of *Silas Marner*. Today, S. J. Perelman—for it was indeed he—has rewarded that faith and followed *Dawn Ginsbergh's Revenge* with *Strictly From Hunger, Dream Department, Crazy Like a Fox, Acres and Pains* and the rest.[58] It's our same Perelman who writes the prose of *Westward Ha!*

Westward Ha! began when the editor of Holiday magazine commissioned writer Perelman and artist Al Hirschfeld to go around the world and send back funny copy for the subscribers.[59] They visited and traveled and tracked down persons from Suez to Malibu, but they didn't have a very good time. That the book is amusing despite all that was, of course, inevitable, considering the talent involved. Just as inevitably, it must be classed with Messrs. Perelman and Hirschfeld's minor efforts.

In the course of travel the collaborators look up personages of various kinds and converse with them in Berlitz-imbibed languages. "To put him at his ease," Perelman tell us as he meets Bao Dai, "I inquired sociably whether the pen of his uncle was in the garden."[60] He turns his deadly gaze on every travel-book convention on earth. "It must have been an off-night in Macao, for when I reached my room and undressed, there was not a single haft of a knife protruding from the small of my back."[61] The eighty clichés referred to in the subtitle is the page count.

Every now and again Mr. Perelman pulls back a moment from his high jinks—and, with a candid gaze that alarms us by being the real thing, delivers an aside that is barefaced fact. Coming out of his seizure, he addresses us as a citizen—tells us that Bangkok is "indescribably pleasing." It's ungracious to react with a "Who? What?" Yet we only feel at home again when we meet the Tungku Makhota, for example, and he stands there "preening himself with a small jade preening knife."[62]

Perelman prose at its pure best, as everybody knows, is highly concentrated stuff. Every line and word count; it is as deadly accurate, as carefully organized and as impressionistic as high comedy or poetry. When this special stuff is given us in its natural form—the set piece—it is wonderful. But when it's made to cover a world journey, it loses its charms with its shape. When writing that's really a high comic performance has to serve for a long sustained account of a trip, taking us over actual hill and dale and following true-life narratives and the known maps, not to mention keeping two strange characters—Perelman and Hirschfeld—alive and in recognizable human guise before us, then the demand on the prose is not a fair one.

Mr. Hirschfeld's drawings are apt, plentiful, amusing, and telling, and go well with the text. The book is attractive and gay to the eye. We ought not to look for anything unmitigated in this day and time, they tell us—especially joy. But it would have been nice to have our Perelman straight, not constricted by a job to fulfill.

Our Gifted Son
By Dorothy Baker

SOMNOLENCE AND SUNLIGHT, SOUND OF BELLS, THE PACIFIC SURF

New York Times Book Review 15 August 1948: 5

Mrs. Baker's third novel, like her first, is about a musician, this time a gifted young Mexican composer.[63] The novel is laid in a coast town in Mexico, a scene Mrs. Baker has done beautifully. Somnolence and stir, moonlight and sunlight, the streets, the Pacific surf, the cool large interiors, the sounds of bells and of fountains—these things provide the pleasure of the book. Otherwise, it seems unreal, contrived, and mannered.

The plot is the gradual exposure of a rotten situation. It's like peeling away layer by layer an apple which looks browner and browner toward the core. If the story is one of those which are possible only owing to people's not telling one another the right answers to questions before it's too late—and it is—then the characters have to be people who won't talk, either through perversity or being slowed down through love. I don't think it's fair, though, for all the characters to be holding their tongues or lying until the plot signals green, or rather red. They are following the demands of a romantic and arbitrary thing—a plot, but not life.

The gifted son is Jose Richter, a Harvard student who comes back to his home town, Las Palmas, to spend his vacation finding out about the several mysteries which have twined about his boyhood and, as coincidence would have it, intertwined about each other. All is entwined yet again with the solemnity of his attaining his full manhood. So the plot is not too lenient a one; the conspiracy is cut to order.

The compound mystery of his mother's death and his father's stubborn silence (but he is a German) and of the American lady's strangely besmirched reputation bedevils Jose's mind and blocks his clear, shining road into the future. The mystery does not seem so deep to the reader, but Mrs. Baker has held back its solution to provide a fair amount of suspense. However, in giving the solution she stamps the story with final superficiality; for she doesn't "solve" Jose's life at all. If it is implied that now he can create his music in an unfettered way, this overlooks the fresh fact that his unfettering has cost the persons closest to him their lives. It's not surprising that the story ends in violence, death, goodbyes, and a single note struck very softly on the piano by the hero's finger.

Just as in real life, it seems too bad in fiction for a whole handful of people to have to give up everything as a matter of course for one person who happens to feel he is chosen and picked out—talented—and who is able to take the sacrifice for granted, if not to hurry it up. Jose hurries it up, and his pity at the tragic turn of events seems a little late, like everything else.

The fact of the matter is that Mrs. Baker has created some promising characters, full of interest, and then not let them do anything on account of the plot. Jose seems likely as an artist and as an attractive young Mexican; but he must busy himself on attaining manhood, as if it were a certificate. The father speaks in sentences of translation-German and seems (perhaps on account of his immovable cruelty) the one person least likely to get up from his seat and go riding in a car, which he has to do in order to get killed.

The heroine is gallant in almost the old Michael Arlen tradition, and flings herself away with pensive abandon, bearing her anguish with independence and a nice set of sport clothes. She has appeal and interest too, partly for being 40 years old, but she is made to perform so foolishly that only the climate seems any reason for her behavior. The American school friends of Jose's and Jose's sister are both pleasant and intelligent, doing what minor characters are always doing, showing up the other characters. But it doesn't matter to the plot what happens to them, they have inferior futures.

Mrs. Baker's style has a deliberately offhand, tomboy quality, which under its surface swagger, is soft, blurred, and rather sloppy. Her indistinct, often careless, sometimes ungrammatical sentences show a disregard for accuracy and clarity in the interest of manner and mannerism. She seems to give a kind of imitation of simplicity. Instead of being disarmed, the reader is likely to arm at once. It strikes one as too bad the author didn't let the characters in this novel take it over more. It wouldn't matter so much, even, if Jose couldn't begin a symphony precisely on the last page, if he'd just begun to be and to feel outside the strictures of the pages preceding.

City Limit
By Hollis Summers

INNOCENTS IN THE WOOD
New York Times Book Review 19 September 1948: 18

Here is a touching and original novel. It is the story of the Babes in the Wood, except that the innocents do overcome the enemy in the end of *City Limit*, and convincingly, though almost miraculously. The author has set the story in a small Kentucky town, in the high school, one or two interiors and a country spot just outside the city limit.

The story is of two high school students who play hookey one fine day to go to the country, of their discovery that they are in love, and the consequent and immediate bearing down upon them of all the ugly suspicion and authority of their elders. This drives them to running away in earnest and living in a little house, hiding. They are inevitably routed out again. Meantime, they preserve their innocence, in an intuitive struggle—not without confusion, terror, some dreadful enlightenment and blind reckonings, and their love is pushed into a strange, triumphant and touching maturity in a little matter of days.

Would young lovers love and be really innocent? It never occurs to any of the powers of the town that automatic suspicion might not be as correct as it is self-righteous. All the frustrated anger, revenge and general busybodiness of the world of grown people, and the holding over influence of the dead, too, must turn upon the children to rout them out, charge and punish them.

The children are treated in the round, are real persons. They are admirably done and eminently believable. Ignorant and intuitive, sensitive and absurd, stubborn and inconsistent, the high school mind is presented as the material of precious innocence in the world, which can somehow endure. Widely different from each other, the two young people between them raise up a sturdy tenderness under our eyes, like a little plant, and it is known to all that this is their protection. But it's a matter of suspense until the end.

The complete account of this little adventure goes unemphasized. There is not a hysterical word in this story of youthful love. The unit of Mr. Summers' style is the simple declarative sentence. Perhaps it is over simple at times, but thereby is its eloquence too. The quality of the writing is certainly one of monotone simplicity, which at proper moments is able to transmute thoughts anything but simple.

A play-by-play account of behavior, the story is told and the scene described in the very opposite of poetic images. Instead, we have here, described meticulously, a factual world, which at moments of expanded imagination on the author's part, and without abandoning the factual account, suddenly becomes a metaphysical one. There are almost no adjectives or adverbs. The explicit verb tells the story. But the fear of death can hover over the heroine in the being of a bird with a wing spread of a certain number of feet, and the girl and the field, and the bird and the world are still real, but death itself is flying over.

To state it another way, this factual account has intensity, which distinguishes it, and the intensity comes from a quality of meditation. It is a story of knowing and learning. "Everybody was tied to himself and everybody had to die." Harriet, the girl, knows this: the boy learns it, and learns thereby to comfort her. The people in *City Limit* are as unpoetic as they are unimportant; the world about them is not a lyrical one, but Mr. Summers shows that it's the commonplace that best bears the strange moments of illumination.

Everybody in the book experiences moments outside himself, even Trudy Bates, the Dean of Girls at the high school and the true villain of the book. Her moment comes, appropriately and realistically enough, when she is surrounded by "the girls" on her day to have the two tables of bridge; it comes as a transforming anguish for the harm she has tried to do the young lovers. Thus the achievement of moments when the everyday event, the monotonous word, and the familiar landscape suddenly fuse with the passionate idea. Fate, identity, love, passion, God, take outward shape with the mundane, even obnoxious surroundings.

It is correct to say this is a psychological novel, but it is the reviewer's glad impression that the story was written not following after Freud no matter where,[64] but out of observation and intuition and study of behavior down to its smallest manifestations, and a conception of it on the general scale. It succeeds because of the author's honesty and care for his work. It could be improved upon—for instance, the beginning of the book is not as well done as the rest, and has an overlong prelude in italics which endeavors to "place" it, a service it does not need. But it stands as it is a very respectable piece of work. The author has compassion, a good eye not conditioned by anything, a good ear conditioned by some worthwhile anger, and a view of youth and innocence that is fresh, dignified, and rewarding.

Intruder in the Dust
By William Faulkner

IN YOKNAPATAWPHA
Hudson Review Winter 1949: 596–598

What goes on here? Grave digging. "Digging and undigging." What's in the grave? One body or maybe another, maybe nothing at all—except human shame, something we've done to ourselves. Who digs? Who but the innocent, the young—and the old and female, their burning-up energy generating a radiance over Yoknapatawpha County and its concerns? Not forgetting the Gowrie twins—like the vaudeville team that follows behind the beautiful stars with its hilarious, mechanical parody, the Gowries from the hills dig too.[65]

Intruder in the Dust is a story of the proving of innocence, this proof a maddening physical labor and a horrendous, well-nigh impossible undertaking, full of riddles and always starting over. The real innocents are the provers, the technical innocent is old, black Lucas Beauchamp in danger of lynching for murder of a white man—and Lucas is a lightless character, high-and-mighty and gorgeously irritating, who would be so temptingly guilty if he weren't so irrevocably innocent, just the kind of man to get in just this kind of fix, who has been building up to it all his life, and now, by hints, condescends to be saved, offering cash fees, and requiring a receipt. The provers, exhumers that they have to be, are Miss Eunice Habersham, "a practical woman" in her seventies, who "hadn't taken long . . . to decide that the way to get a dead body up out of a grave was to go out to the grave and dig it up," and the sixteen-year-olds, Charles Mallison, white, Aleck Sander, colored, who end up dog-tired and a step along in man's wisdom.

Gavin Stevens, the articulate uncle who by his character partly forecasts and foretells for Charles, and the sighing mother—wonderfully done—are near at hand, summoned or pushed back, and beyond and dipping down is the menacing fringe of the Gowries from the ridges of wild Beat Four. Out of the digging comes a solution and an indictment, defining a hope, prayer, that we should one day reach that point where it will be *Thou shalt not kill at all*, where Lucas Beauchamp's life will be secure not despite the fact that he is Lucas Beauchamp but because he is.

The action of *Intruder* is frantic—and meditative, not missing a minute. The more-than-possible failure of the task overhangs it like a big cliff. The suspense is of the chase—sometimes slow-motion, sometimes double-time; leg-work, horses, mules ("unspookable" for this business), pickup trucks, on up to a fast Sheriff's auto, bear the characters toward their grave-robbing with greater and greater urgency. The setting is the open country at night lighted by "a thin distillation of starlight," and a few dusky interiors, smelly. (How Faulkner can show us that making things out in the dark is a quality of perception as well as a quantity!) In counterpoint is the Square, back in Jefferson, with the Face of its crowd, the immobile, inflexible crowd around which sentience strives and threads and skirts, until the crowd's final whizzing away like a battery of witches on brooms. Even when old man Gowrie gets his Vinson back, brushes the quicksand off and takes him home to bury again tomorrow, is this story going to stop? "This time Hampton and his uncle could go out there tomorrow night and dig him up" is the boy's sleepy valediction that night.

Intruder is marvelously funny. Faulkner's veracity and accuracy about the world around keeps the comic thread from ever being lost or fouled, but that's a simple part of the matter. The complicated and intricate thing is that his stories aren't decked out in humor, but the humor is born in them, as much their blood and bones as the passion and poetry. Put one of his stories into a single factual statement and it's pure outrage—so would life be—too terrifying, too probable and too symbolic too, too funny to bear. There has to be the story, to bear it—wherein that statement, conjured up and implied and demonstrated, not said or the sky would fall on our heads, is yet the living source of his comedy—and a good part of that comedy's adjoining terror, of course.

It doesn't follow that *Intruder*, short, funny, of simple outline, with its detective-story casing, is one of the less difficult of Faulkner's novels. Offering side-by-side variations of numerous words, daringly long, building ever-working sentences (longer than *The Bear*'s, maybe, if anybody is counting), moods and moments arrested, pulled up to peaks, wilfully crowned with beauty and terror and surprise and comedy, Faulkner has at once re-explored his world with his marvelous style that can always search in new ways, and also appeared to use from beginning to end the prerogatives of an impromptu piece of work.[66] It could be that to seem impromptu is an illusion great art can always give as long as profundities of theme, organization, and passionate content can come at a calling, but the art of what other has these cadenzas? Even the witty turns and the perfect neatness of plot look like the marks of a flash inspiration. If *Intruder* did come intruding in a literal way, shaped from the dust into life before the eyes, then we have a special wonder here; but it's none of our business, and the important thing is the wonder, special or not.

Time shifts its particles over a scene now and then, past and future like seasoning from a shaker, and Yoknapatawpha County we know now too, while the new story in its year, month, and ticking hour of day and night, emerges in that illumination and shading which Faulkner supplies to the last inch and the ultimate moment. The political views in *Intruder,* delivered outright as a speech, are made, rightly enough, another such shading to the story.

As in all Faulkner's work, the separate scenes leap up on their own, we progress as if by bonfires lighted on the way, and the essence of each scene takes form before the eyes, a shape in the fire. We see in matchless, "substituteless" (Faulkner's word for swearing) actuality and also by its contained vision: "Miss Habersham's round hat on the exact top of her head such as few people had seen in fifty years and probably no one at any time looking up out of a halfway rifled grave." Every aspect of vision is unique, springs absolute out of the material and the moment, only nominally out of "character" or "point of view," and so we see hats and happenings and every other thing, if not upwards from a half rifled grave, then down the road of the dark shuttered cabins, or up a jail stair, from the lonely ridge where Gowries come; or see in accompaniment with the smell of quicksand (a horse is there to get the smell and rear up), by the light even of impending conflagrations. Old Man Gowrie turning over a body that's the wrong body, not his son's, becomes "only an old man for whom grief was not even a component of his own but merely a temporary phenomenon of his slain son, jerking a strange corpse over onto its back not in appeasement to its one mute indicting cry not for pity not for vengeance not for justice but just to be sure he had the wrong one, crying cheery abashless and loud, 'Yep it's that damned Mont-gomery damned if it ain't!' " The boy's feverish dream of Miss Habersham trying to drive around the mob to get back to her own house, a vision of How the Old Woman Got Home, is this writer's imagination soaring like the lark.

Of course it's a feat, this novel—a double and delightful feat, because the mystery of the detective-story plot is being ravelled out while the mystery of Faulkner's prose is being spun and woven before our eyes. And with his first novel in eight years, the foremost critics are all giving cries as if (to change the image) to tree it. It's likely that Faulkner's prose can't be satisfactorily analyzed and accounted for, until it can be predicted, God save the day. Faulkner's prose, let's suspect, is intolerantly and intolerably unanalyzable and quite pure, something more than a possum in a tree—with its motes bright-pure and dark-pure falling on us, critics and non-critics alike.[67]

The World Next Door

By Fritz Peters

VETS' MENTAL HOSPITAL IS SITE OF MOVING NOVEL

New York Post 18 September 1949: 16M

Most of us have been at some time in our lives touched closely, at least fairly closely, by the presence of mental illness. *The World Next Door* is an account of such an illness as told by one who experienced it; the illness is a world, and it's not very far away. A note in the front of the book says this is "based on actual experience"; with names and characters fictitious, it is presented in the form of a novel told in the first person.[68]

David Mitchell, a young war veteran returned home, is taken by force in Chapter I to the veterans' psychiatric division of a hospital in the East. There, in time—a comparatively short time, one gathers—he is cured. What the book attempts, and I think, succeeds in doing to a startling degree, is to tell the interior story of what happened.

It discloses horrors and cruelties and violence in plenty, but nothing remains as horrible and cruel as the inner life of the patient through whose eyes we see things. Mr. Peters' book does not seek to be sensational—to the contrary; on the other hand, through its very "interior" quality, it is one of the most sensational novels to come out in recent years.

This is one way in which *The World Next Door* differs from other books of its general subject matter. With uncompromising honesty and unsparing revelation, it describes a level of experience deeper, darker, further down than the other books have gone, a level more personal and yet strangely more impersonal—so abstract does suffering render "the world next door." It reaches points of wild and terrifying humor. There are some passages of peace and beauty there, too.

It seems that even while he suffered, this patient was concerned with thought itself, with suffering itself, with delusion itself—their processes, in peace and in violence, during the course of mental illness. And the book is addressed to the intellectual understanding—there are no emotional appeals, no sensational exposes for exposing's sake.

The book has logic, it is written logically, and in its way it is dealing with logic itself. The belligerent, ingenious and heartbreakingly lucid assaults and compromises and trickeries and bargains the mind makes with what has so distressed it—these make present to an excruciating degree the narrow margin that lies between insanity and pure logic—between simply, the sick and the well.

This book is the revealing document it is by its intense focussing on what is personal and firsthand. In dealing with mental illness this book is about the individual's problem first, and society's problem by the way. It does not preach—directly, at any rate. In its anguished and brilliant progress it examines and implicates man himself. It is in part dedicated "to the veterans, of war and society, in all psychiatric institutions."

As a performance of writing, *The World Next Door* is an astonishing example of what must be almost total recall. How could it help being of high value to doctors? It is certainly of absorbing interest to the general reader, to whom the development and cure of the illness of David Mitchell become a matter of highest suspense. There is the excitement of a detective thriller in its powerful, penetrating and unequivocally sincere account of a journey into madness and return.[69]

South

By William Sansom

FIREWORKS IN ITALY

Saturday Review of Literature 23 September 1950: 16–17

South is the Mediterranean world. These are stories of Ajaccio, Nice, Naples, Monte Carlo, Florence, Siena, Milan.[70]

First of all, Mr. Sansom, who takes joy and sustenance from the physical world, can communicate that world and that joy—no mean achievement.[71] Here is the impact of the South on the sun-starved North, personified in Mr. Sansom with a notebook, for all this overwhelming detail—fresh, instant, exact, inhumanly brilliant—must have been put down on the spot, or Mr. Sansom is a wizard twice over.

This author in three books has already proved he can make you see, hear, taste, touch, and smell to his order: ride in a bus, put your head under water, anything he likes.[72] Here you see the street dealers in Ajaccio: "one tall Senegalese walking slowly from restaurant to restaurant like a priest in his red fez, a single blue-black crayfish weaving its worried feelers from his purple-black hand." He leads you down boulevards "straight, leaf-shaded, with shop windows glinting darkly in the night of high noon" into "squares so spacious and beaten flat by years of the changeless, flowery sun." He shows you the trees on the Florentine hills "like darts thrown at random into the brown earth by a fond divinity." He can take you under water—there's "a hermit crab pouring out its soft body to pull the shell a labored inch along the floor." He can give you Monaco and a hangover at the same time: "The yellow extraordinary terraces broke over him with mad impact—this place could not be true! He felt as if small birds were pulling cotton strings from each side of his forehead, his head was expanding dangerously."

Mr. Sansom's descriptive power is a steady fireworks.[73] Like fireworks, part of its necessity is contrivance, an occasional "set-piece." These are stories wholly evoked by places, limited by the evocation, and purposely so: "Aspects and Images" Mr. Sansom calls them on the title page. For the most part the "native" characters are personifications or figures in a landscape— they do not enjoy private lives apart from the purposes at hand and so are not very near us or quite animated. (But some of Mr. Sansom's animals—he has several for characters—could make you stand on a chair.) All but one of the stories take place in a public place—park, museum, casino, the square of a town—with a visitor as protagonist, more accurately as witness, for he seldom acts for other reasons than, ultimately, to sight-see. "Poseidon's Daughter," the exception, is told from within, but develops an analogy between incident and myth, and so once again the story appears at a remove.

In "Afternoon" two old Florentines feud back and forth between the Boboli Gardens and the Pitti Palace. In "Landscape with Figures" an escaped snake wanders into the Galleria Vittoria Emanuele in Milan, where he is charmed by one of those girl bands "in pajamas of viridian satin" playing outside a cafe. "Three Dogs of Siena"—highly amusing—concerns visitors, too, dog-sight-seers, confronted with the statue of the wolf-mother of Romulus and Remus.

The most highly developed story is "My Little Robins," for it is concerned more specifically with human situations and reveals aspects of people while it gives images of Ajaccio. It tells of the little dealers of the streets, specifically of one, tracked down—literally—by our observer; we see him morally, too: an odd sort who shoots robins for selling, one of "the breed of the loving hunter." "Here was the predatory esthete, a fine mind if a dark one"; "he faced up to the cruelty of life and lived his part of it."

But the towns remain the real characters; it is they that enjoy the moods and the motives, are comic or tragic, cut up antics, threaten or bewitch— the square, the crowd, all the abundant and wasteful life of the Mediterranean, with its espresso machines, plane trees, and palms, octopi, mistrals, casinos, fireworks, and that old refrain *"Qu'est-ce que c'est que ça?"* "For private tragedy no city stirs—only perhaps, like some immense impassive beast, listens inwardly for a moment wondering where over all its great hide the tic has bitten."

The "aspects and images" remain the brilliant products of a remarkable vision, of eye and intuition, historical embellishment, a beautiful and formidable amount of on-the-spot detail. They are lacking in the overtones, the ragged edges of Mr. Sansom's prouder stories which deal with human beings in the stress of self-devised problems.

The stories are surely what Mr. Sansom intended them to be and they succeed. The limitations suggested are in a measure another proof of the author's virtuosity; he evidently enjoys a challenge, and he has already shown in other books that he can go deeper and further than *South* when he takes the notion.

The World My Wilderness
By Rose Macaulay

WISE AND WITTY NOVEL
OF EUROPE NOW

New York Post 12 November 1950: 16M

In her first novel in ten years, Miss Rose Macaulay[74] applies the gifts for which she has long been valued toward a work of acute contemporary significance.[75]

We follow Barbary, a young girl whose English mother Helen has brought her up, or let her bring herself up, in France during the Resistance, a child who has learned her mores from the Maquis, to the very proper London household of the mother's divorced barrister husband and his new wife.

But it is rather in the ruins of the old merchants' rows around St. Paul's that Barbary unerringly finds her true dwelling. Her French half-brother, subjected to the same transference, says of the wild-flowered ruins, "'This is more for us. It is chez nous'."

Through this wilderness the driven Barbary carries her own despairs and secret horrors, finds her solace, nourishes her terrible dreams, grows into a consuming life of black marketing and thievery, rushes pell-mell toward downfall—it is all like an acted-out nightmare.

She is the living comparison of one physical wilderness with another in the war-ruined world, of both with the wilderness of the spirit—she is more than its comparison, indeed, she is its identity.

But she is not the heroine. The real heroine is Helen, not Barbary; for it is the mother whose great full figure stands behind that of her daughter, casting it into its more temporary proportions.

She is almost THE Helen—lastingly beautiful, wise and learned, a woman who is forever the lover and the pagan.

It is Helen who would beg the question of Miss Macaulay's book—the moral question of what is one to do, for oneself and for others, what should one have done, with this shattered world on our hands? Standing outside the question and taking a not uncruel advantage thus, as Helen initially does by reason of her personal endowments and convictions, she is not loth to be a cause of turmoil, its center rather than its resolution, as in myth her prototypes have been.

The characters, of great variety and charm, contribute as they can and must to Miss Macaulay's searching theme. At one end of the scale, which could be described as that of human perception, is poor Pamela the second wife, at the other, Helen.

(Who would ever not know Pamela, with those proper answers and those clothes of the kind that are "cheaper in the end!")

A closer pair of opposites are Gulliver, Helen's divorced husband, and Barbary—born enemies, both strongly endowed but limited by the circumstances of their worlds so as to see only the single extremes they tend toward, wrenched, but relentlessly holding on, each with a violently active integrity.

Nearer the center, more nearly alike, are the two Frenchmen: Helen's lover, one more of that whole knowing, charming, tired, but still amused Mediterranean world; and her son Raoul, whose French father has been set in an equivocal place before him and has been murdered as a collaborator, which, actually, he wasn't.

Just outside this dangerous line-up, and pushing and working at it with a most domestic zeal, is the old nurse—the hold-over from other days, other kinds of days, and even other kinds of novels, helping everything along, providing footwork and warning cries for action, the bosom for the refuge from it, and tears for its denouement. She keeps up a chorus of comment, and sees that all respectably takes a turn for something, if not for the better, with a nannie-like love of crisis.

The settings are impeccable choices for their own supporting roles—the French Mediterranean Coast, haunt of Helen; bombed and unbombed

London; wild Scotland with its shooting boxes where still the right clothes are being worn for shooting properly at each wild creature—a place Barbary can't bear for longer than a single day.

The assembling of these contemporary complexities—of personality, place and time, and of the larger poetic shadows which haunt them all—is a brilliant assembling, and not an answer—Miss Macaulay has given us high honesty and unswerving clarity, which are the best a writer can give. There is no facile answer to be found in this novel—knowing, poetic, witty, terribly melancholy as it is, and a joy as it is to read.

The Witch Diggers
By Jessamyn West

A SEARCH, MADDENING AND INFECTIOUS
New York Times Book Review 14 January 1951: 5

This is a good, long, warm, generous and curious novel. Its detail rounded
and rich, an enormous number of vigorous characters abounding, it is a
physical panorama concerned morally with man's infatuation with plans and
calculations, from the noblest of them to the maddest, and most useless and
hopeless, and how this infatuation distorts, ruthlessly opposes, and even
dooms his powers of love.

The scene is a Poor Farm in rural Indiana at the turn of the century, the
characters the Conboy family who run the institution and those who come
into relation with them. The title refers specifically to a brother and sister,
inmates of the Poor Farm, who believe that the truth is something as actual
and literal as a piece of paper, actually and literally buried in the ground
somewhere, to be unearthed by diggers if they dig long enough, then to set
mankind free. A curious splendor is in these witch diggers, maddening and
infectious.

This novel about love, responsibility, fate, is presented in a physical world
of earthly beauty and ugliness, of vigor, fecundity, and general stir, in many
scenes, a number of them expansive—holiday groups and community gath-
erings. *The Witch Diggers* could be Indiana, 1899, Breughel.[76]

The characters are alive and vividly struggling, explained fully and yet
remaining, I thought, opaque to a degree, as real-life people do, but this
gains them a curious wholeness in the context. We see that the characters
are sometimes ignorant, sometimes innocent but never simple; they have

the makings of complexity without the tools for its expression. In another guise the witch diggers might have been poets.

All are charged with the business of living, strongly opinionated, strongly sexed, acting for the most part in good faith toward one another and sometimes (as they are able) toward themselves. Their conflicts are, hence, simply their differences as individuals. Placed in the uncontroversial times, in the simple setting, within the order only of the seasons, the novel is left free for its characters to move under their own stars. Some of these—the Poor Farm inmates—have been relieved even further of worldly impediments; and these are the characters who run to the greatest extreme of all in variety of personality and in action—from the catatonic to the frenzied. Stripped to the utterly physical, the physical of the Poor House pigs at times, the book reaches here its moral bone—which is Miss West's triumph.

How responsible for each disaster to another human being do our separate sins make us, how do they combine? What is the limit of the harm we inflict on other people—all too often "for their own good"? How far is ignorance to blame? Could these people, indeed, have escaped their own doom?

Link Conboy, superintendent of the Poor Farm, a man of scruples and conscience and nobility, is essentially inarticulate—he who had the best chance not to be. And this is the key, I think: so is every other character in the book inarticulate, from whence stems his fate and his disaster. Not that everyone in this countryside does not talk all the time—wise men, fools, fanatics, lovers, and just women—but nobody is able to communicate at all, except when it is possible through sexual behavior or strangely ritual symbolic action, as the witch diggers do.

If *The Witch Diggers* is a novel of the distinction it is because in dealing with the passions, Miss West is dealing also with passion itself. Charades is a favorite game in this Indiana locality. In a sense all the action in the novel is a charade, the characters moving on the scene in sides or teams or alone, to present their allotted syllable the best they can. It is calculation which futilely and frantically turns over the earth in a vanity of witch digging, ignoring, fatally ignorant of, the simple and revelatory power of love.

Short Novels of Colette
By Colette

A COLLECTION OF COLETTE: SIX NOVELS IN ONE VOLUME
New York Post 30 December 1951: 12M

Here are six short novels by a major French writer too long known to most of us only by name and reputation, presented in one fat volume of translations, by various hands, extending over a number of years; one was made by Janet Flanner, in 1921.[77]

The novels are: *The Indulgent Husband*, written in 1902; *Cheri*, 1920; *The Last of Cheri*, 1926; *The Other One*, 1929; *The Cat*, 1933 and *Duo*, 1934.

Colette's life and her writing are presented us here by Mr. Glenway Wescott, who has enjoyed both a long familiarity with all the large output by Colette, and her friendship.[78] It is good to have the information and the special illumination given out by this essay, which is brilliant, loving and long. Mr. Wescott's fervor, always informed, is still uncontained and catching, like that of an audience waiting for the curtain to go up on some surprising and beautiful experience; it is doubly pleasing for being so justified.

Colette, born in 1872 in a village in Burgundy, is today confined to her bed in an apartment in the Palais-Royal—still writing, by night, under a light shaded by blue paper, one of the familiar sights of Paris to strollers in the gardens below. She has enjoyed not only length of life but an enormous variety of it, including a period on the stage.

How strange—or is it?—that she first wrote as a drudge; taken off into the country by her first husband, a journalist and hackwriter known as Willy, she was, a girl in her teens, "locked in her room for four-hour stretches while she inked up a certain number of pages." But it was her joke: she liked writing—mercifully for her, and for us. Eventually—and released—she was writing with a kind of genius.

It is in her writing itself, not in the separate pieces as novels, that I find her greatness. In the best of it, her virtuosity, even seen through the veils of translation, shimmers marvelously. Colette is instantly recognizable as a master. Authority, rightful authority, is apparent with every sentence, every word.

Colette is an impressionist surely more kin to the great [painters than to the] great writers who were and are her contemporaries.[79] She uses light and reflection as purposefully as Monet or Renoir. The senses can read her paragraphs as clearly and uninterruptedly as the mind can, with an even more certain, even more immediate, understanding, disturbance, delight. In exactly seen interiors and exteriors her novel's characters (always few in number), perfectly lighted, are marvelously exhibited in motion and repose alive with illusion.

There is one quality which I find in Colette's writing by power of its absence—heart. She writes indeed of love—of loves, passions, infatuations, cat-loves, strange loves—a perfect rainbow of loves. But she writes not with her love—or so it seems to me, reading her for the first time here. She writes frequently out of a force which is much more explicit, cryptic, arbitrary, witty and undismayed.

Look not for compassion in Colette; yet it is this withholding (I do not say lack) which is in some way a part of her strange power. There is nothing vulnerable about her writing, as there is nothing clumsy. Dazzling it is, but not daring. Its material, its matter, is somewhat banal and shabby; its profundity is in its treatment—by intention so, and by the genius of achievement.

For brevity, for wit that began back in the observation of the eye which produced it; for the loving openness, almost transparency, of all the senses to the moment passing, its time and place; for a recognition of the essence of that tension (of whatever name or quality) existing between and among the human beings and sometimes the cat in a room together; for a recording of feeling as strict as a seismograph's; perhaps best of all for a real gaiety, a real laughing gaiety—for these things we will value, honor, study, and above all delight in Colette.

Don Camillo and His Flock

By Giovanni Guareschi

WHEN GOOD MEETS BAD

New York Times Book Review 17 August 1952: 4

These are thirty-four stories or sketches about Don Camillo the priest and his adversary, Peppone the Communist Mayor, laid in a small village near Milan in the valley of the Po.[80] *The Little World of Don Camillo* is the title of an earlier book by Mr. Guareschi, and in the preface to the stories he bounds the *Little World* and explains that the happenings to follow grew in its atmosphere.[81]

The stories are all brief, around six pages long, and are cheerfully alike in nearly every other way as well. Being moral in their intention, Italian in their nature, and playful in their habit they attempt not much more development than anecdotes, which essentially they remain. Their pleasure for the general reader is likely to lie in the warmth with which they are written. Each takes the form of a battle of wits or fisticuffs between the good (the Roman Catholic Church) and the bad (the Communist party) to see who gets the better of whom, and it doesn't take long to get this settled until next time.

"You have a trick up your sleeve" is the motif, and the level, of the book's conversation. It is the truth, too. One reason the stories must be such cheerful, possibly speedy, work for Mr. Guareschi, who writes with plenty of zest, is that there is a *deus ex machina* in Jesus, who, speaking up in the vernacular of the Po from His crucifix on the wall, carries on helpful conversations with Don Camillo when things get too tough; so an occasional miracle helps out the good side. At other times, mere foxiness does the trick, or mere force of arms.

In the pattern of these tales, a problem arises (there is never a dull moment in the Little World), there is a contest of prowess, with matching feats of wit or strength, an aside if necessary between Don Camillo and Heaven, and the punch ending, with Peppone going off with his tail between his legs. The stories are set out to be as innocent as Peter Rabbit—though in this their taste may not indeed be as faultless, or their charm as great. The cards are a good deal more stacked in the Little World than in Mr. McGregor's garden. But the stories are kindly, and sometimes engaging.

The fillip to the tales is of course meant to lie in the sturdiness of Don Camillo and the innately soft heart of misguided Peppone. Don Camillo is in there using fisticuffs, kicks, guns, disguises, slams with pitchfork handles or brickbats to achieve his ends, and Peppone on his side and with equal exuberance is doing the same. The difference between adversaries so evenly matched—who seem really inclined to like each other in their warm, Italian way—is in their backing. Stalin is too far away to do Peppone any good.

The West Pier
By Patrick Hamilton

THE SEEDS OF EVIL
New York Times Book Review 5 October 1952: 5

In *The West Pier* Patrick Hamilton tells of the formative years and early manhood of Ernest Ralph Gorse, born in 1903 in Hove, England, and introduced to us as, practically from that year, a member of "the criminal class." At the novel's conclusion, the young Gorse has successfully sown his seeds of evil in Brighton and is just setting out for London, with a trophy of youthful and petty crimes all undetected or unpunished, presumably to carry on in the future on a grander scale.[82] His ruthless spoliation of a young love affair is his most serious and significant act. This bears on the rather curious image which dominates the novel and gives it its title.

The West Pier, sticking out in the water at Brighton, is seen as "the battleship of sex." On this pier the four chief characters—two young couples—meet by chance in the opening chapters, picking one another up as happens every day, the author points out, on the West Pier. Young Gorse, almost lacking in such human feelings, being wholeheartedly preoccupied with the inhuman, proceeds to make use as he can of the human feelings of others.

Mr. Patrick has organized his novel with calmness of purpose—that of sober, thorough investigation—and with patience toward what he finds always staring back at him, the character's ultimate inscrutability, and its ubiquity in the world as well. It follows that a certain quality of fatalism pervades the work.

To its credit, *The West Pier* is never sensational. It is unadorned and strict as a lecture, the style plain and in its plainness foreboding. Set down in a laudable attempt at dispassion, it is, however, without passion. It is true that a curious effect of reality does somehow result from sheer accumulation of fact: the drearier the facts, the more accumulation it takes, and sometimes the heavier the going. The novel is warmest, or only warm, in the depiction of the secondary characters. The young lovers are appealing, but helpless as a pair of baby chicks under the shadow of a hawk.

The character of the poisonous young villain is never gone into much below the surface of his behavior—for the reason the author gives that it is opaque. Will this do? Nobody knows, says Mr. Hamilton outright, what makes his Ernest Ralph Gorse the way he is. This is the way he appears. Take a look at him, listen to his dreary words, see how meanly he acts, and know there is a whole "class" like him.

There is little humor, except what lies in mordant reporting of school-room and seaside repartee, and little sensory feeling in the scene, these not being Mr. Hamilton's tools here. But the reader feels that the use of them at moments, in treating of life however sordid, might not come amiss—and might even bring light to bear on this work, which promises to extend beyond the present volume.[83]

Charlotte's Web
By E. B. White

'LIFE IN THE BARN WAS VERY GOOD'
New York Times Book Review 19 October 1952: 49

E. B. White has written his book for children, which is nice for us older ones as it calls for big type.[84] Most of the story takes place in the Zuckerman barn through the passing of the four seasons. "Life in the barn was very good—night and day, winter and summer, spring and fall, dull days and bright days . . . with the garrulous geese, the changing seasons, the heat of the sun, the passage of swallows, the nearness of rats, the sameness of sheep, the love of spiders, the smell of manure, and the glory of everything." The book has liveliness and felicity, tenderness and unexpectedness, grace and humor and praise of life, and the good backbone of succinctness that only the most highly imaginative stories seem to grow.

The characters are varied—good and bad, human and animal, talented and untalented, warm and cold, ignorant and intelligent, vegetarian and blood-drinking—varied but not simple or opposites. They are the real thing.

Wilbur is of a sweet nature—he is a spring pig—affectionate, responsive to moods of the weather and the song of the crickets, has long eyelashes, is hopeful, partially willing to try anything, brave, subject to faints from bashfulness, is loyal to friends, enjoys a good appetite and a soft bed, and is a little likely to be overwhelmed by the sudden chance for complete freedom. He changes the subject when the conversation gets painful, and a buttermilk bath brings out his beauty. When he was a baby he was a runt, but the sun shone pink through his ears, endearing him to a little girl named Fern. She is his protector, and he is the hero.

Charlotte A. Cavitica ("but just call me Charlotte") is the heroine, a large gray spider "about the size of a gumdrop." She has eight legs and can wave them in friendly greeting. When her friends wake up in the morning she says "Salutations!"—in spite of sometimes having been up all night herself, working. She tells Wilbur right away that she drinks blood, and Wilbur on first acquaintance begs her not to say that.

Another good character is Templeton, the rat. "The rat had no morals, no conscience, no scruples, no consideration, no decency, no milk of rodent kindness, no compunctions, no higher feeling, no friendliness, no anything." "Talking with Templeton was not the most interesting occupation in the world," Wilbur finds, "but it was better than nothing." Templeton grudges his help to others, then brags about it, can fold his hands behind his head, and sometimes acts like a spoiled child.

There is the goose, who can't be surprised by barnyard ways. "It's the old pail-trick, Wilbur. . . . He's trying to lure you into captivity-ivity. He's appealing to your stomach." The goose always repeats everything. "It is my idio-idio-idiosyncrasy."

What the book is about is friendship on earth, affection and protection, adventure and miracle, life and death, trust and treachery, pleasure and pain, and the passing of time. As a piece of work it is just about perfect, and just about magical in the way it is done. What it all proves—in the words of the minister in the story which he hands down to his congregation after Charlotte writes "Some Pig" in her web—is "that human beings must always be on the watch for the coming of wonders." Dr. Dorian says in another place, "Oh, no, I don't understand it. But for that matter I don't understand how a spider learned to spin a web in the first place. When the words appeared, everyone said they were a miracle. But nobody pointed out that the web itself is a miracle." The author will only say, "Charlotte was in a class by herself."

"At-at-at, at the risk of repeating myself," as the goose says, *Charlotte's Web* is an adorable book.[85]

Nine Stories
By J. D. Salinger

THREADS OF INNOCENCE
New York Times Book Review 5 April 1953: 4

J. D. Salinger's writing is original, first rate, serious and beautiful. Here are nine of his stories, and one further reason that they are so interesting, and so powerful seen all together, is that they are paradoxes. From the outside, they are often very funny; inside, they are about heartbreak, and convey it; they can do this because they are pure. The whole nine have an enchanting ease about them, a deceptively loose-appearing texture, a freshness and liveliness which might bid fair to disarm the reader, as he begins, say, the remarkable "For Esmé—with Love and Squalor." Nothing could be further from what Mr. Salinger is about to do to him.

The stories concern children a good deal of the time, but they are God's children. Mr. Salinger's work deals with innocence, and starts with innocence; from there it can penetrate a full range of relationships, follow the spirit's private adventure, inquire into grave problems gravely—into life and death and human vulnerability and into the occasional mystical experience where age does not, after a point, any longer apply. Mr. Salinger's world— urban, suburban, family, mostly of the Eastern seaboard is never a clue to the way he will treat it: he seems to write without preconception of shackling things.

He has the equipment of a born writer to begin with—his sensitive eye, his incredibly good ear, and something I can think of no word for but grace. There is not a trace of sentimentality about his work, although it is full of children that are bound to be adored. He pronounces no judgments, he is simply gifted with having them, and with having them passionately.

The material of these stories is quite different, again, from his subject. Death, war, the flaws in human relationships, the crazy inability to make plain to others what is most transparent and plain to ourselves and nearest our hearts, the lack or loss of a way to offer our passionate feeling, belief in their full generosity, the ruthless cruelty of conventional social judgments and behavior: the persistent longing—reaching sometimes to fantasy—to return to some state of purity and grace; these subjects lie somewhere near the core of J. D. Salinger's work.

They all pertain to the lack of something in the world, and it might be said that what Mr. Salinger has written about so far is the absence of love. Owing to that absence comes the spoliation of innocence, or else the triumph in death of innocence over the outrage and corruption that lie in wait for it.

The feeling may arise from these warm, uneven stories (no writer worth his salt is even, or can be) that Mr. Salinger has never, here, *directly* touched upon what he has the most to say about: love. Love averts itself in pity, laughter, or a gesture or vision of finality possibly too easy or simple in stories that are neither easy nor simple in any degree.[86]

Mr. Salinger is a very serious artist, and it is likely that what he has to say will find many forms as time goes by—interesting forms, too. His novel, *The Catcher in the Rye*,[87] was good and extremely moving, although—for this reader—all its virtues can be had in a short story by the same author where they are somehow more at home.[88]

What this reader loves about Mr. Salinger's stories is that they honor what is unique and precious in each person on earth. Their author has the courage—it is more like the earned right and privilege—to experiment at the risk of not being understood. Best of all, he has a loving heart.

Marianne Thornton:
A Domestic Biography

By E. M. Forster

THE THORNTONS SIT FOR A
FAMILY PORTRAIT

New York Times Book Review 27 May 1956: 5

Miss Marianne Thornton of Battersea Rise, 1797–1887, had the good fortune and good sense characteristic of her family in having for a great-nephew Mr. E. M. Forster. Her benevolence, characteristic too, gave him a comfortable start on his way toward becoming a writer. Here is fresh cause for rejoicing: a "domestic biography," the perspicacity, the virtue and the persuasion of which could hardly be overestimated. The subject: Marianne.

The daughter of Henry Thornton, M. P., and Marianne Sykes Thornton, she was born the eldest child of nine into a household characterized by "affections, comfort, piety, integrity, intelligence, public activity, private benevolence; and transcending them all an unshaken belief in a future life where the members of the household would meet again and would recognize each other and be happy eternally." Marianne's Papa, a prosperous banker and a man of outstanding intellect, "was fertile in devices for improving her." He had provided for her happiness before she was born by building Battersea Rise, in Clapham Common; the house is the heart of the book, as it came to be the heart of Marianne.[89]

We see the house with its beautiful oval library that William Pitt designed, with the garden beyond its glass doors, and its thirty-four bedrooms and the nursery upstairs brimming with life and good spirits. Here is the family assembled for prayers; here they are at table. ("Prayers before plenty, yes. But plenty.") The neighbors—William Wilberforce, the famous abolitionist; the Zachary Macaulays (little Tom was a terror in tableaus), or some of the "able and alarming Stephen family"—are likely to be guests for the evening, for we are very much in the thick of the Clapham Sect.

Conversation races around the table—foreign missions, abolition, education, *infant* education, politics, the Apocrypha, Napoleon. And the irrepressible young daughters of the house are going to take the best of it down in diaries before they go to bed. "To distinguish six maidens is never easy, especially when the sound of their laughter is gone," says Mr. Forster, but he knows that any of them can call up Jane Austen today. "On the whole the way of life they discovered worked, and they could pursue it to the glory of their God without self-torture or torturing others."

Marianne grew up with a first-rate mind and an affectionate heart, and inclined to accept the responsibilities of both. She had seriousness, gaiety, exemplary judgment in conduct, faith in reason and God: she was unsuspicious of a world that could do so well with improvement, and unshocked and unscared by its bugbears. She rose to a crisis, she rose higher into detachment; she came down to earth and enjoyed fun and nonsense; she could throw herself into the joys of travel; she gave and received love.

She took her understanding from the domestic orbits, none more instructive or demanding; she could reason out from those into the wider circles of society and human nature which she saw as reaching toward heaven. Really a child of the eighteenth century, she lived almost the length of the nineteenth, and the numerous acts of her good life, indeed each of her letters, she launched like so many little lighted boats on the stream of Continuity, going confident into the night. They would be safely received at the other end.

The Clapham Sect could have hardly failed to be a primary force in her life. "Wherever she walked the child found herself surrounded by assorted saints." "The friend of friends," William Wilberforce, is given a full-length domestic portrait in these pages; no public portrait of any man could be half so remarkable. "It is with the saintly, gay and innocent side of his character that [Marianne's] Recollections deal; they ignore the cleverness and astuteness which are evident in his public life and sometimes remind us of Gandhi."

When Wilberforce went as one of a deputation of three from the House of Commons to persuade Queen Caroline to give up being crowned and the lady "all but kicked them downstairs," it was to the garden of Battersea Rise that he repaired for the sight of a moss rose. "'Oh the beauty of it. Oh the goodness of God in giving us such alleviations in this hard world. . . . And oh how unlike the Queen's countenance.'"

Hannah More, "that bishop in petticoats," when she was not at Battersea Rise, could be descended upon in Somerset, "where the two cats called 'Non-resistance' and 'Passive obedience' were fed by us all day long . . . crowns of flowers were made for ourselves, garlands for the sheep. . . . We were fed with strawberries and cream and told to lie down in the hay whilst Charles the coachman made us a syllabub under the cow." "Unlike Wilberforce," says Mr. Forster, "she never married and so she never altered. Childless herself, she became the family life that does not die with death." And so, we are brought to feel, did Marianne.

We move with Marianne through her successive phases of daughter, sister, aunt, great-aunt. "She passes into spinsterhood without regret." The crises of her long, full life were few in number; its daily animation and its depth had purer, less accessible sources. The fabric of the family (for others married, and often had ten children) remains strong, consistent in quality, the same on both sides, and exactly what it seems, goodness itself. It is given a variation in sheen by the occasional introduction of rainbow threads—for example, the Rev. Charles Forster, who married Marianne's sister Laura and turned out to be E. M. Forster's grandfather.

It is toward the end of Marianne's life that Imagination, with a radiant, inquisitive 5-year-old face, takes its first real look at the family. Edward Morgan Forster, that dragonfly of a little boy, the son of Edward Forster and Alice Clara Whichelo, darted across Marianne's last days and with the evident satisfaction he brought her (he had to wear corkscrew curls for her pleasure) was borne some inkling perhaps of what she was not to see for herself in this life. She left a bequest. This made possible Cambridge, then travel, "which inclined me to write." It was while staying with "Aunt Monie" that the little boy had made at the age of 4 at least one discovery that would have confounded a Thornton: he was already able to read to himself. "From that moment I never looked back . . . . No one taught me to read and no one managed to teach me to write."

The family papers on which this work is based are copious, varied and descended from a number of hands old and young; they date from about 1750 to 1900, and only those of a domestic nature have been drawn upon;

there are others of a different importance. Framed by the rest are Marianne's own—a lifetime's letters and her Recollections, which she began writing out for young Edward Morgan Forster when she was an old lady. Time, kinship and the female human heart—formidable combination—have not now held out against him. Marianne appears, a human being—waving whatever useful domestic implement she happens to have in her hand, possibly her quill. We shall never forget her. So, while he has been about it, have appeared a great many other vigorous, attractive and irreplaceable people out of Marianne's world.

Mr. Forster has created them all out of, or in spite of, what might almost be called an embarrassment of riches. What the choices must have cost him! On every hand he produces the tangible, the direct, the explicit, the spark that catches fire; he shows the letter, high-minded or gossipy, with the spirit still intact like the gentian that was folded in Marianne's letter from Switzerland, still blue.

The reader, who has fallen in love with Marianne on account of the book, can only feel how beautifully she persists in pages so thronging with all that signified life to her: her family around her and extending in both directions, Battersea Rise and the tulip tree that Napoleon never succeeded in invading England to cut down, the beloved friends, the visits and parties and jauntings, the letters and sketches and books and babies, everybody who ever was drawn into the whirl and sweep of the Thornton galaxy, from Nurse Hunter to the Mohawk who was persuaded to dance and sing when he happened in to pay his respects one day—all in a marvelously ordered account of cloudless focus, felicitous and witty and wise.

To the Thornton mind, imagination threatened a danger a good deal less calculable than that of Napoleon; neither did the Thorntons possess the sense of mystery or of poetry. Mr. Forster's best gifts are not mentioned here to belittle theirs—what could be more inappropriate?—but to observe for our own improvement that our foremost writer of fiction is exactly who is needed to comprehend human beings who *have been* real as well as those who are going to be.[90] He is doubly valuable if they have been both real and good; triply valuable if they are receding rapidly in time but are still able to give evidence through their effects and if the effects are miscellaneous.

Mr. Forster has employed powers Marianne might not knowingly have countenanced, but she has not been hurt: she has been celebrated and loved. Continuity has been taken care of; and we are the gainers.

The Green Hills and Other Stories

By Walter Macken

IRELAND WITH FIGURES

New York Times Book Review 5 August 1956: 4, 12

The author of several novels of Irish life published in this country,[91] Walter Macken has written here a group of short stories with a dedication to his home town, "the Citie of the Tribes."[92] With the location in common, they are otherwise mostly independent of one another, but from the whole one gets a picture of a little town of the west of Ireland facing the Atlantic, with a beach of yellow sand between mountains and sea, slopes of heather with mountain lakes and blue bog holes, stony fields, salt-laden winds, mountain streams full of poachable salmon, and the little frail currachs going out to brave the sea for the catch.

Of the people, one sees sides of their independence, vigor, pride and a certain Western recklessness of spirit, but the picture is less clear because, oddly enough, it is more general. Some of the characters come curiously close to types. Perhaps this is the price any author pays for the too-close view; outlines long familiar tend to blur.

Some of the characters, like Gaeglers, and the two old brothers in "The Gauger" for example, seem alive and kicking. Others, like the "atheist" who lived apart on the mountain top and gave his life to save a little boy lost in the storm on his way to see him, didn't strike me as half as real, and I wondered if that was because this kind of character belonged not to the story itself so much as to old and established tales of the family fireside. It gives rise to a question of whether the stories here could be perhaps of two categories—one group experienced (in the artist's sense), the other in some form grown up with, heard told, their sharpness and unconforming edges rubbed away like a stone's in the sea.

Mr. Macken can indeed tell a very good story—witness "Gaeglers and the Wild Geese," "The Currach Race" and "The Gauger," to take the very first three in the book. The vitality of the telling is attractive and has a certain momentum of its own. The style is a close approach to the spoken word. "After last mass on St. Patrick's Day in the village there were hundreds of people gathered on the two necks of land which embraced the sea on either side of the strand." (This is for "The Currach Race.") " . . . The sun was cold looking and there was a good breeze traveling from the direction of America. You would swear that the sea was clapping its hands because somebody had told it there were four fools who might otherwise have remained out of its grip at this time of the year."

A few of these stories are too pat—pat because the anecdote and the symbol lie in wait for them, as of course they always lie. Mr. Macken doesn't estimate them as dangerous. He apparently trusts them as the friends of Ireland that they are, and once or twice has turned his story over to them and they have gobbled it up. This is a pity, for the least of the stories opens full of promise. All any of them need do, one feels—for one responds to the attraction of the place and the exuberance of the author—is be allowed to follow their own inherent direction and bear out their implications.

The lone English lady who comes to live in a shack on the edge of town and takes her national walk in rain or shine on the wild lonely Irish road, sounds full of provocation, but all she does is accept a kitten, and beam at us, beam away her mystery; it is forgotten for sentiment—wasted, and Mr. Macken could have done a real job on her. Perhaps he is an author who hesitates to let his characters grow real without the scope of a novel; as it is, in the stories it's the place of their origin that has the towering reality.

Last Tales

By Isak Dinesen

A TOUCH THAT'S MAGIC

New York Times Book Review 3 November 1957: 5

The Danish-born author (Baroness Karen Blixen)[93] who writes under the pen name of Isak Dinesen has the straightout gift for performing illusion, and the resources of mind and heart of a great lady who has lived for a good many years in many different parts of the world. In her tales, one of the extraordinary things is that the spell—for they lie in the realm of magic and romance—gets done by the speed of wit, takes its turn within the circle of morality, and keeps its hold, through irony, which usually attends on learning and experience, not enchantment. But I haven't found anything out, for the spells work, too, through the pure delight of the senses.

Isak Dinesen has, of course, a long time ago made herself master of the tale and her three previous books, *Seven Gothic Tales*, *Out of Africa* and *Winter's Tales*, are well known in this country.[94] Austerely objective in their execution, true to her credo of the storyteller's story, her tales are also extremely personal in their point of view, in their great style. They have a vigor which persuades us that vigor perfectly solves the secret of delicacy, for her stories are the essence of delicacy.

She has a marvelous gaiety, and what makes it more marvelous still are its transpositions, true gaiety's other key. Her tales are glimpses out of, rather than into, an extraordinary mind. Sometimes one feels that Isak Dinesen's stories come toward one like the flashes and signal-beams from a lighthouse on a strange and infrequently sighted coast—a coast beautiful and precarious, for it may be the last outreach of magic, but resting on bedrock.

Like all her tales, these twelve (her first collection in seventeen years) are like no other tales. They range from country to country, the North to the South—from point to point in time, from here to there in reality. There are tales joined onto other tales, tales inlaid in tales, and one long, disturbingly beautiful, unfinished Gothic tale called "The Caryatids." What is their inner relation and their true domain?

In "Night Walk," a story happening in Italy some centuries ago, a betrayer of his friend, who afterwards cannot sleep is told that if he walks through the streets of the city, proceeding always from the larger street into the smaller and narrower, until he can turn no further, he will find sleep at the end. He reaches the place: "This moment was a return and a beginning. He stretched out his hand, took care to draw his breath lightly twice, and opened the door. By a table in a little, faintly lit room, a red-haired man was counting his money." Who was the red-haired man? That's the story.

Her tales all have a start in other tales—for a tale must have its "start," as good bread must; as good flowers must, proliferate how they may. Her "starts" are the fables, the fairy tales, stories from the Bible and the Arabian Nights and Ancient Greece and Rome. Sometimes they can be felt to be passing, like a procession not more than one street over; sometimes we see their old rich banners and colors, catch their songs and sight their retinues of seraphic or diabolic origin, and sometimes that procession and the procession of her story cross and mingle, they may even dance, and all the queens and lovers then, the magicians and children and beasts and hunters and wives and gypsies and country gods and artists and angels are of a company together.

Are these tales human? Whatever they are *not*, is irrelevant.

"The divine art is the story," a storyteller says in one of these tales. "In the beginning was the story. . . . Where the storyteller is loyal, eternally and unswervingly loyal to the story, there, in the end, silence will speak. . . . We, the faithful, when we have spoken our last word, will hear the voice of silence."

Remembering her *Out of Africa*, surely one of the most sensitive personal accounts written in our time, we are moved to think how it is the same eye that saw the Giant Forest Hog on the path in the Ngong Forest that sees the primeval boar in the Gypsy's spell of the water wheel in her tale "The Caryatids." And we realize so clearly that they are visions both, even perhaps of the same thing, one life gave to her and one a story gave to her. Both visions she has let us see, but kept them two.

It is enough to open this book and start reading:

"It was a lovely spring day, and the almond trees were blossoming. . . . From the terrace at the top there was a wide view over the landscape, and all the shapes and colors within it . . . in the cool of the evening were as beautifully harmonious as if an angel had stood behind the shoulder of the observer and poured it all out from his flute."

"Are you sure," a lady asks a storyteller in this book, "that it is God whom you serve?"

"The Cardinal looked up, met her eyes and smiled very gently. 'That,' he said, 'that, Madame, is a risk which the artists and priests of the world have to run.'"[95]

Granite and Rainbow
By Virginia Woolf

UNCOMMON READER
New York Times Book Review 21 September 1958: 6

Of course, an editor who sent out a new book called *Men Without Women* to Virginia Woolf knew what he was doing.[96] The *New York Herald Tribune* received a very farsighted review. (The title she decided merely "to stare out of countenance.") She thought Hemingway's characters talked too much, but she would, "if life were longer," care to read the stories again. Hemingway "lets his dexterity, like the bullfighter's cloak, get between him and the fact. . . . But the true writer stands close up to the bull and lets the horns—call them life, truth, reality, whatever you like—pass him close each time."

This 1927 review is published in *Granite and Rainbow*.[97] It seems there were still pieces left out by Virginia Woolf herself when she put together both series of *The Common Reader* and that eluded her husband when he published three books of her papers after she was dead.[98] Two lady scholars[99] from America—a country she always thought showed signs of being restless—found them, and are thanked for this collection by Mr. Woolf in a foreword. Seventeen years after her death appear twenty-five essays and book reviews—eleven written before 1920, twelve written during the Twenties, one in 1930, one in 1940. Writing them earned her the time to write her novels, and the least of them is a graceful and imperturbable monument to interruption, though it saddens us to see her "whipping the heads off poppies," as she called it to Lytton Strachey—and Marie Corelli was surely a poppy—with *The Waves* waiting in manuscript on her table.[100]

The essays, of course, are the heart of the book. For one thing, she is back in invited company—Sterne, Defoe, Jane Austen, Peacock, the old cronies. The finest and longest piece, "Phases of Fiction," was written for the old *Bookman*, which published it in three parts in 1929.[101] "There is . . . some design that has been traced upon our minds which reading brings to light," she says, and brings it to light.

That beautiful mind! That was the thing. Lucid, passionate, independent, acute, proudly and incessantly nourished, eccentric for honorable reasons, sensitive for every reason, it has marked us forever. Hers was a sensitivity beside which a Geiger counter is a child's toy made of a couple of tin cans and a rather common piece of string. Allow it its blind spots, for it could detect pure gold. It could detect purity. In the presence of poetic fire it sent out showers of sparks of its own. It was a mind like some marvelous enchanter's instrument that her beloved Elizabethans might have got rumor of and written poems about.

She has told how, after the enormous pressure under which she wrote her fiction, the intensity of feeling she lived through, the exacerbations she suffered, writing criticism was, for her, release. Critics, she once observed, are persons who have "done their work as a good housemaid does hers; they have tidied up after the party was over." The reading and re-reading she set herself to do for *The Common Reader*, for instance—"to go through English literature like a string through cheese"—would, she said, be good for her mind—"rest it anyhow," for "one day, all of a sudden, fiction will burst in."

In the early pieces there are no early sentences. "Far be it from us to hazard any theory as to the nature of art" is, so far as I can see, the only slip she ever made. Her early recognitions range from fine ("No one felt more seriously the importance of writing than she did," of Katherine Mansfield) to finest: once she saw that streak of vulgarity in Henry James, she was incapable of being scared by his ghost stories until she got to *The Turn of the Screw*; a masterpiece made her afraid of the dark.

She scatters treasure everywhere she reads. "The novelist [of all those practicing the arts] . . . is terribly exposed to life. . . . He can no more cease to receive impressions than a fish in mid-ocean can cease to let the water run through his gills."[102] This aside comes in the course of reviewing a second-rate novel, about which she presently observes that "a hundred pages have flashed by like a hedge seen from an express train."

And now what we can do—for no farewell glimpse is ever satisfactory—is what Virginia Woolf herself loved to do in her own reading: let the work as a whole swim up into the mind. "Breaking the mold" she called the task she set herself. The novel, of course, was never to be the same after the day she started work on it.[103] As novel succeeded novel she proceeded to break, in turn, each mold of her own. It is a perilous life. The innovators of fiction, like the Jumblies of Mr. Lear, come from lands that are far and few, and they go to sea in a sieve.[104]

"Every moment is the center and meeting-place of an extraordinary number of perceptions which have not yet been expressed," she wrote in one of these essays. It was 1927. She was forming her prophecy of what the novel of the future would deal with. She was just in time: *To the Lighthouse* was about to burst in.

The Most of S. J. Perelman
By S. J. Perelman

ALL IS GRIST FOR HIS MILL
New York Times Book Review 12 October 1958: 4, 14

Give him a cliché and he takes a mile. "The color drained slowly from my face, entered the auricle, shot up the escalator, and issued from the ladies' and misses' section into the housewares department." And, "I sent him groveling. In ten minutes he was back with a basket of appetizing fresh-picked grovels. We squeezed them and drank the piquant juice thirstily." Spring returns to Washington Square: "It lacked only Nelson Eddy to appear on a penthouse terrace and loose a chorus of deep-throated song, and, as if by magic, Nelson Eddy suddenly appeared on a penthouse terrace and . . . launched into an aria. A moment later, Jeanette MacDonald, in creamy negligee, joined the dashing rascal, making sixty-four teeth, and the lovers began a lilting duet."

Our garden of prose has no more been the same since a certain silky party put in an appearance than the Garden of Eden after the Serpent called. S. J. Perelman—for it was indeed he—has this to say by way of a concluding note to this collection of thirty years' work:

"If I were to apply for a library card in Paris, I would subscribe myself as a *feuilletoniste*, that is to say a writer of little leaves. I may be in error, but the word seems to me to carry a hint of endearment rather than patronage. In whatever case . . . I should like to affirm my loyalty to it as a medium. The handful of chumps who still practice it are as lonely as the survivors of Fort Zinderneuf; a few more assaults by television and picture journalism and we might as well post their bodies on the ramparts, pray for togetherness, and kneel for the final annihilation. Until then, so long and don't take any wooden rhetoric."

"There has never been a year like this for the giant double-flowering fatuity and gorgeous variegated drivel," Mr. Perelman said in "Caution— Soft Prose Ahead" and that was back in the Thirties. If the only trouble is that all he's lampooned has now caught up with its parody, it's anybody's fault but S. J. Perelman's.

The book is put together chronologically, which is as good a way as any to see what was going on, prosewise, from 1930 to 1958 when Louella Parsons, whose syntax Mr. P. recommends for its narcotic value ("You don't even need a prescription") sets him the scene for "Nirvana Small by a Waterfall." Each reader will make a leap for his own favorites. Here's "Strictly From Hunger," the masterpiece on Hollywood (" 'Have a bit of the wing, darling?' queried Diana solicitously, indicating the roast Long Island airplane with applesauce.") Here's "Farewell, My Lovely Appetizer," the one that gets Raymond Chandler right between the private eyes, both of a dusty lapis lazuli; and "Genuflection in the Sun," in which a gourmet journeys to pay his respects to the author of a piece of fountain-menu prose—"the finest thing since Baudelaire's 'The Flowers of Evil'." (" 'Did you ever get any figures from Liggett's? Were there many conversions?' ")

Shall I not simply list some of the old friends you will find again here?[105] The Schrafft hostess, "well over nine feet tall, with ice mantling her summit." Mrs. Lafcadio Mifflin, of "Kitchenware, Notions, Lights, Action, Camera!," "seated at the console of her Wurlitzer, softly wurlitzing to herself." And Mr. Mifflin, "in a porous-knit union suit from Franklin Simon's street floor, stretched out by the fire like a great, tawny cat. Inasmuch as there is a great, tawny cat stretched out alongside him, also wearing a porous knit union suit, it is not immediately apparent which is Mifflin." And, as a matter of fact, Gisele Mifflin, who delivers that indelible speech about the shades her wedding *tailleur* comes in at Altman's—"among them wine, russet, beige, peach, grackle, stone, liver, lover, blubber, blabber and clabber."

There are "my escort, a Miss Chicken-Licken"; "Pandemonium, the upstairs girl" (she entered on a signal); "my hostess, Violet Hush" (of Los Angeles, of course); "my brokers, White-lipped and Trembling"; "kindly old Professor Gompers, whose grizzled chin and chiseled grin had made his name a byword at Tunafish College for Women." "John J. Antennae, spiritual father to millions, . . . fox-nosed, sallow, closely related to God on his mother's side." Manual Dexterides, who knows a lot about Tommy Manville; Hyacinth Beddoes Laffoon, "queenpin of the pulp oligarchy embracing Gory Story, Sanguinary Love, Popular Dissolution, and Spicy Mortician." There is Rosy Fahrleit (she plays over your face), and old man Huysmans, owner of a delicatessen. ("In slicing Huysman's brisket," it comes to be asked, "does one go with or against the grain?")

Here are the well-known biopsies of the fashion magazines—a certain June issue of Vogue "was certainly a serious contender for the ecstasy sweepstakes." "Cloudland Revisited" is here, those vignettes of the Twenties—Dr. Fu Manchu and Victims to the left, Theda Bara and Victims to the right. Here are the plays about (I mean, anent) the advertising world: "You mean that the finger of suspicion points to Loose-Wiles, the Thousand Window Bakeries, whose agents have recently been skulking about in dirty gray caps and gooseneck sweaters?" Here is *Westward, Ha!* and *Acres and Pains.*

Here, in the Hollywood pieces, we find Perelman among colleagues "listening to the purr of their ulcers," or noting how the movie *Stanley and Livingstone,* "by an almost unbelievable coincidence, was released the very same day luminal was first synthesized." Groucho Marx, for whom, of course, Mr. Perelman has done his share of writing, seems imminent here and once appears in person; we get an intimate glimpse of him indulging "his passionate avocation, the collecting and cross-fertilization of various kinds of money."

As always, Mr. Perelman's sources are allowed to play about upon each other. When he, "together with five hundred other bats, hung the rafters at Loew's Strabismus to see Joan Crawford's latest vehicle," we are shot from there into a parody of a Ventura column on a Barbara Hutton story.

In my dictionary is an engraving of most intricate design, labeled "human ear."[106] When I consulted it recently, in connection with this review, I was forced to exclaim, "But this must be the ear of S. J. Perelman!" When I looked up "ear" also in my Nouveau Petit Larousse and found the very same picture of the very same ear, I think I may quietly say it can hardly be laid any longer to mere coincidence. Mr. Perelman misses no mad word we write or say, and its image and essence he translates back to us with an artistry acute, brilliant, devastating, and, Heaven keep preserving him, funny.

Now for the sequel.

Henry Green:
Nine Novels and an Unpacked Bag
By John Russell

LIFE'S IMPACT IS OBLIQUE
New York Times Book Review 2 April 1961: 5

In this country it was 1949 before the first of Henry Green's novels was published, *Loving*, which came midway in the eight so far now written; after which we eventually got all but the first, *Blindness*. We still can't read *Pack My Bag: a Self Portrait* unless we send to England for it, which we do, because it is a good book and unique and because it is, like the novels, the work of a writer of steadily astonishing powers and of a truly original mind. As a novelist of the imagination, he stands almost alone, a pure artist in our times.[107] He enriches us, all by himself, more than do the others put together of those writers, not artists, of whom there are so many.

All of a sudden three books have been written about Henry Green's work at almost the same time. And by young men, if one supposes rightly—which is encouraging for the young men. This of John Russell's is a worthy study. It is plain, and makes good sense to start with, that Mr. Russell (of the English Department at the University of South Carolina) has been seized by the delight that Henry Green's extraordinary prose can give, for delight I think does open the door to this writer whose work then comes to be so moving. And he is also aware that past the door there is a great deal more to meet with.

"The mere exchange between two human beings in conversation is mysterious enough. . . . That we talk to one another in novels, that is between strangers . . . is nothing less than miraculous if you once realize how much common experience can be shared. My plea is that we should not underestimate this." Using this and other remarks of Henry Green on fiction to form a "wedge into Green's world," John Russell begins his book with a general but concentrated discussion of the author's theory, technique and style. Then he takes up the novels separately or in combination, pressing on as far as he can by the light of their singularity and by that of certain relationships he finds between them.

Mr. Russell recounts sanely, interprets with imagination and without insistence the cryptic plots. He imposes no harness on the author along the way, being engaged simply in tracing through the novels a course from optimism to pessimism—a pessimism from which he is able to find in the end that "wholesome and positive attitudes may be constructed." His terms are precise and sensitive to the complexities of his subject. His approach has a zest congenial to the novels and might have caught it from them.

Mr. Russell says that basically, to Henry Green, "existence is an enigma, not a trap: 'We shall never know the truth,' says Mr. Rock at the end of his day" in *Concluding*. "Green resists being placed in a niche alongside other contemporary English novelists. His humor seems to derive from the rational, limited view of man prevalent in the eighteenth century; his near-morbid insistence that man threads an obstacle course to death from the Continental writers I have named." (Kafka, Celine.) "That he should also be a symbolist is the most fascinating and perplexing thing about him, for there is an energy of passion in much of his symbolism."

But—derive? It does seem difficult to think of Henry Green with sources not of the living present world. And as to comparisons, these illuminate, but do they hold? For instance Laurence Sterne is here mentioned, and isn't his humor essentially that which emanates from formlessness, while Henry Green's relies on, comes jumping out of, form?

"Green is remarkably sensitive to human beings' needs," Mr. Russell says with perception, "though aware that it is potentially dangerous to have longings and need fulfilled." And he quotes from *Pack My Bag*: "We seldom learn directly; except in disaster, life is oblique in its impact upon people."

Mr. Russell, to this reader, does well by the characters, especially those in "that great gallery of restive souls from which Green populates the comic novels." Mr. Russell says, and this is important: "Although his tendency to concentrate on exterior behavior of characters is foreign to the methods of Joyce and Mrs. Woolf, Green's criteria remain aesthetic ones. . . . Speaking of his attempts to be selective and non-representational, Green once said: 'The Chinese classical painters used to leave out the middle distance.' He himself leaves out a middle distance—the analyzed minds and motives of his characters—and is enabled to work his figures into tableaux almost mathematically precise, and aesthetically satisfying." He carefully qualifies this: "Form is a medium for Green, not an end."

Relishing the marvelous dialogue, Mr. Russell observes that the characters "talk not with phonographic realism but just far enough from it to freshen the idiom as inflection freshens speech," and suggests a way this might have been done. Good advice, but let another writer try it.

The author speaks sane, if perhaps too sane, words about Mr. Green's dazzling style; for instance: "From first to last he evolved no series of styles, but . . . was equipped early to cope with what challenged him." And: "Because Green's writing is so flexible, I feel that judgments of his style are apt to be unrewarding, unless it is granted right off that his restraint and his ability to pull out stops are ever waiting on his vision."

It is through the forms and structures of the novels that Russell seems to this reader to have caught the most and given the best of his feeling about Henry Green's work. He shows himself sensitive to their proportion, balance, framework, their motion through space. At the same time, he is not afraid to look deep.

It's illuminating how unlike in approach, method, and mood are this book and Edward Stokes' *The Novels of Henry Green*, published last year.[108] Both are serious, scholarly works devoted to the marvels and riddles of the novels.

It does charm the imagination to think that while Mr. Stokes, at the University of Tasmania, was running up a table of comparison how many times the color red was used in *Loving*, Mr. Russell in South Carolina was drawing a little hexagonal diagram of the emotional ties in *Nothing*. But Mr. Stokes was seeing *Nothing* as a stream of conversation flowing into whirlpool and then out again, and *he* was making a quadrilateral involving six triangles out of *Doting*. It just goes to show that a work of art is infinitely accommodating.

The Freudian pattern is next to be imposed, we gather from an interpretation of Pye in *Caught*, quoted by Mr. Russell in a footnote, from a critique yet to appear.[109] The heart may quail, but the mind applauds: if there must be any analyses about this writer (and this is certainly in the air), let there be many, all different.[110]

The World of Isak Dinesen

By Eric O. Johannesson

THE ACCEPTANCE OF LIFE IS A DEFENSE
OF THE STORY

New York Times Book Review 17 December 1961: 6

This painstaking study could not have been easy to write. As we all know, Isak Dinesen's work is very much something of her own: curious, elaborate, beautiful and mercurial, very strange and at the same time very much what it seems.[111] It is lord of its time and place, and reflects such a sense of fun. You cannot put salt on its tail. It might at different times in different stories seem a dedication to passion or a toy and as either, full of delicacy and marvels, grandeur and high jinks, with everywhere more dark to it than light. And for some of us *Out of Africa*, the autobiography, outdistances all the rest she has written for its intensity and beauty of personal feeling.

Eric O. Johannesson is a fellow Scandinavian, an assistant professor of Scandinavian at the University of California; he acknowledges thanks to a number of Scandinavian scholars in this work. We can thus be grateful for an opportunity to learn special information from him, as we do at the start when he pays attention to the Dinesen family and the Danish background.

He has followed what would seem to be an admirable purpose and plan. "In this study I have sought to describe the neat and orderly structure which is the world of Isak Dinesen. . . . I have also sought to define what I believe to be the underlying theme of Dinesen's tales: the defense of the story and the art of storytelling, a theme so pervasive[112] that it has come to form the very basis of the author's world view. I have not felt it in my power to deal with the fascinating personality of Isak Dinesen herself."

He has chapters called "The Art of the Story," "The Gothic Tale," "The Mask," "Marionette and Myth," "The Art of Acceptance," "Aristocracy," and "Africa." He writes about the exotic settings, the element of artifice in the tales, the use of metaphor and simile, the relation of the Dinesen stories to the old stories and myths, about illusion and the stage. This is all well.[113]

Mr. Johannesson tells how Miss Dinesen, writing from Germany during the last war, spoke of her faith in "the strange kind of reliance on the grace of God, which one calls humor"; and when he brings forth this sort of first-hand thing, it is worth all our literary comment. He says of this, and goes to the root of the tales:

"Humor, as understood by Isak Dinesen, is an affirmation and acceptance of life in all its forms, the opposite of rebellion, . . . a kind of yes-saying to life, an acceptance of whatever fate will bring, and the theme of acceptance is a profound one in Dinesen's tales. But, in saying yes to life, the figures in the tales are also acknowledging the authority of the story and the divine storyteller. Thus Dinesen weaves her tales in such a way that the two themes become one: acceptance of life is a defense of the story."

Again, in discussing the theme of the mask, he says—and one feels he has again touched base—"A deep and fundamental skepticism lies at the basis of this view of art and life."

If he could have gone ahead, saying simply what he thinks! But Mr. Johannesson has an unfortunate willingness to prove his observations out of the stories, in a way fatal to any rapport with the stories themselves. "A good example," says Mr. Johannesson, "is seen in the final speech of the fish in 'The Diver': 'Man, in the end, is alarmed by the idea of time, and unbalanced by incessant wanderings between past and future. The inhabitants of the liquid world have brought past and future together in the maxim: *Après nous le déluge.*'" A good example of what? Of "the habit of some of the figures in the tales to pluck quotations out of the air and use them very consciously." What in the literal world has Mr. Johannesson got us to talking about?

He uses Miss Dinesen's tales and stories as if they were so many yard-lengths of solid and consistent material. He states some point in general, then sets forth a list of examples from the stories; he attaches to the quotes the title of the story in parentheses and by its initials (SGT), to keep the scholarship straight. Otherwise he uses her work like a fishpond.

What good is a haul-in of similes? He has found good ones, but out of context their original purpose is gone, and so their meaning, which belongs to fiction, and to a sentence in a page in a certain story.

It would be hard to know how, in a study of a writer like Isak Dinesen, to lift out just the bits that are wanted to bear out some theory or observation. It would be like undoing a mosaic. Something gold and twelve feet high is not to be conveyed by any one pebble between the broken fingernails of the most devoted hand.

Behind this somewhere may lie the requirements of a thesis or dissertation. Which is no sin, except that there is another involved—the author who is the subject of it. Such a book is written to *solve* the work of Isak Dinesen. And one doesn't solve stories as if they were riddles, even when (as hers may do) they resemble riddles. One reads them. An encounter takes place, which is more than, and different from, an exchange of a riddle and a guess at an answer; otherwise, one would really need to read anything only once.

Of this author—and one is sure Mr. Johannesson respects her deeply (even though he never refers to her in any way except as "Dinesen")—he nowhere says or gives any strong evidence to show that he has been stirred, delighted, touched, bored, maddened, even baffled. Indeed, the sad thing about this study is that its author does not seem to have felt any excitement in her work.[114] He is thorough, sincere, and believes that he has finished with her. In one sense he has, for one feels her stories will never trouble him again. But what a fate, for the books we love never to stir us again, never to compel us to read them again and again, as hers can do.

The Stories of William Sansom
By William Sansom

TIME AND PLACE—AND SUSPENSE
New York Times Book Review 30 June 1963: 5, 27

Since the appearance of his first book of stories, *Fireman Flower,* 20 years ago,[115] the enormously talented English writer, William Sansom, has been warmly read and warmly admired for his stories, novels and travel pieces in this country.[116] This is a welcome collection of 33 of his stories, here presented with an excellent appreciation by exactly the right fellow-writer, Elizabeth Bowen.

One sees different things, or sees familiar qualities differently, in re-reading at a stretch a good writer's work. One gets to know better the long thoughts, the cast of mind, the range and play of mood, the feelings that have lain deeper for their weight and reserve than the faster-flowing ones that color the separate stories and impart the first effervescence.

The flesh of William Sansom's stories is their uninterrupted contour of sensory impressions. The bone is reflective contemplation. There is an odd contrast, and its pull is felt in the stories, between the unhurriedness of their actual events and their racing intensity. In fact their speed is most delicately regulated to suspense. The suspense, which is high, has not a positive, but a negative, connection with the pace at which things happen. Things happen slowly, even in slow-motion, but the suspense mounts fast and high because all the while it has been compressed within. And it is the suspense that the stories are really about.

The wall, in "The Wall," takes three pages to fall. The story is three pages long. The wall that falls is the story, and those three pages are the length of excruciation that we can bear. We have been given the measure.

For conveying in the short story how places, hours, objects, animals, human beings in their behavior look and feel, and sound,[117] this writer can hardly be surpassed. One after the other here are the wonderful set pieces of description that characterize his work, the flourish of flags in Siena, the masterpiece of a centerpiece of fresh, dead fish in a Marseilles restaurant—but to start naming them is not to be able to stop.

"How Claeys Died," "Various Temptations," "Episode at Bastein," "Three Dogs of Siena," "Among the Dahlias"—here are his best-known stories, sinister, comic, tragic. Here is "A Saving Grace," a true original among ghost stories. What a marvelous conviction it brings, that there is an affinity quite unassailable between what is dead and gone and what has been altogether foolish and delicious, a connection delicate and wistful (if slow to arrive) between human memory and a certain hilarious vaudeville quality that living life will ask for till death comes.

Here are the fine comic stories. How did Patten meet his wife? "A Game of Billiards" tells us Patten got caught in the deserted billiard room of the upstairs floor of his pub on his way to the "Gentlemen's" by a lunatic who wanted him to keep score for an imaginary game of billiards with an imaginary opponent. Patten had indeed day-dreamed of being closeted with a madman some day and has always imagined that "he would crumble instantly. But now—surprisingly—it was the opposite. He felt capable, alert, strong. After all, the rehearsals had been of some use." But the game goes on, and how is Patten ever going to get out? And then the door of the billiard room is opened by mistake: a girl is looking for the "Ladies'." "She stood like the embodiment of all heroic rescue—the figure of sudden salvation, the sworded angel . . . in her pink dressy blouse and her blue serge skirt." She isn't really the one who sounds the alarm for the rescue, she only takes his signaling for a friendly direction. But back safe in the pub, whom does Patten see first, to tell his story to? "It was his saviour in the satin blouse."

In Mr. Sansom's humor lie both caprice and tolerance; his wit goes along in splendid partnership with fantasy. And his comic stories do not go on for long without the element of threat, or peculiar danger.

The stories of scenes are well represented here. These are highly complex and extremely accomplished works of art. Time and place, in the stories, not only exist to an intense degree—they create the characters out of themselves, and then belabor or nourish or trick or lure or teach or obliterate or exalt them.

In "A Waning Moon," we go into the giant, metallic, malevolent outside of the Western Highlands from the claustrophobic and malevolent inside of a trailer with a husband and wife on holiday. The story is at once terrifying in the true nightmare sense and comic—for a certain length of time—in the domestic sense. How Mr. Sansom can write about place! It is so marvelous, for example, to see the slate hillside in this story marbled in moonlight and the marble chips moving and turning out to be goats.

In "Pastorale," a loving pair traveling in remote wilds on the Corsican coast, who have been completely absorbed in each other, feeling no need to even say "Thank you" or smile, are suddenly confronted by the sight of the Calanches: "precipitous cliffs of fierce, red granite, a steep convulsion of weird rock . . . figures deep in thought about themselves, their stone thoughts cowled and draped with red stone . . . An aeolian music sang round them, but it was too ancient a sound for human ears." The lovers shudder at last and run back to their bedroom. They are, it seems, town-dwellers.

In "Time and Place," a man and woman who are, on the contrary, nothing to each other, self-sufficient fellow guests of a hotel, take a casual walk into the Highlands and are caught in a Scotch mist: "The circular blindness . . . and wherever they looked it was circular and perpetual, round and round, and round overhead. It seemed, too—but gently, slowly—to be thickening still and closing in. But perhaps that was the illusion of their eyes training for some point of definition—any mark for their human eyes." What can they do in the long run but lie down together on his mackintosh and wait for the mist to lift? Back in the hotel, of course, a mere nodding acquaintance is resumed—or rather avoided.

In these scenic stories, as in the war stories, there lies an element of allegory. It is the situation itself, which he sees as already existing as he began the story, that has inspired or directed or driven Mr. Sansom. One feels the surer of this because all of a given story's attributes, aspects and elements, from its title on, are each in their own way parts of one whole; and this whole has been conceived, one needs hardly say, as a work of art.

"A World of Glass" happens in Trondheim—where everybody wears dark glasses; there is the landscape of snow and icicles and ice-bound lakes, the clarity, the frozen beauty, transparency, and cruelty. And we learn that the story is, in fact, the story of an eye, the eye of a young girl, a lifelong resident of this city; the eye is then revealed as being glass; her blindness is revealed to have been caused by glass, a broken bottle in the hand of her husband, a deed of unseeing drunkenness. And there are also elements of reflection, of things in reverse: Trondheim's architecture is false Greek in the snowbound north.

The narrator himself is not a simple tourist. He is an actor who must disguise himself to hide his famous identity. It is with the blind young girl, the victim, he tells us, that eventually he explores and examines this strange city—it has become all but an abstraction—"through her eyes." And before he can leave he is arrested for assault. He attacks a tourist he sees there from his own country, and punishes a perfect stranger. The scene, the characters—*both* the characters, the prevailing figures of speech, the action, the words of dialogue, the title, the whole conception is this, and to make this, a world of glass, the glass eye. And it all reveals very well another vein, perhaps the deepest, of Mr. Sansom's feeling: the need, in every place and every thing, for the human element.

William Sansom has never been anything less than a good writer. I think as time passes his writing becomes more flexible without losing its tightness of control; the flexibility is its own sign of such sureness. And what is perhaps more unusual among writers so good, his work with time seems to have gained, not lost, spontaneity.

The very act and mystery of writing a story is central to his work, this reader believes. And which came first, the work or the mystery that brought it about? One wonders how he might have even escaped the allegory form of *Fireman Flower*, for instance, given the raw experience of firefighting in wartime London out of which it came. He makes us wonder how often, indeed, as life works it out, is the allegory not the literal, the literal not the allegory. In fact, it is pretty much like the two snapshots of her sailor son, who is growing a beard, that the lady bartender in "Eventide" shows her customer. The cleanshaven one she puts on the bar for him to see.

" 'That's how he is really,' said the woman and then showed him the other photograph, of a similar young sailor, but with a beard.

" 'And that's how he really is.' "

The Gayety of Vision: A Study of Isak Dinesen's Art

By Robert Langbaum

COOK, CARE FOR THE MAD, OR WRITE

New York Times Book Review 7 February 1965: 4, 44–45

The story of Karen Blixen's life is almost as well known as the stories she wrote under the name of Isak Dinesen: her birth in Rungstedlund, near Elsinore, where she died in 1962, her long sojourn in Africa during and after her marriage to a cousin.[118] When the coffee plantation failed, she went home with her life in ruins. Robert Langbaum in *The Gayety of Vision*, writes:

"She liked to tell how she asked her brother Thomas to finance her for two years while she found something to do. There were only three things, she told him, she could do better than average. She could cook; . . . she could take care of mad people; she could write. They settled on writing, and she produced *Seven Gothic Tales* two years later. The story is amusing," says Mr. Langbaum, but it doesn't really do, for "it has become apparent since her death" that there were "four soft-covered notebooks apparently bought in Nairobi" and "another kind of notebook, hardcovered, bought in Copenhagen" in which she had jotted notes and fragments of stories.

At any rate she published her first book at 49. Three years later came *Out of Africa*, then after five more years *Winter's Tales*. During the Occupation she published *The Angelic Avengers* under the pseudonym Pierre Andrezel, and Mr. Langbaum says you may have it. Then, in her seventies, Isak

Dinesen published in rapid succession *Last Tales, Anecdotes of Destiny,* and *Shadows on the Grass. Ehrengard* was published posthumously in 1963.[119]

A great lady, an inspired teller of her own tales, a traveler, possessed of a learned and seraphic mind, her health was extraordinarily frail—but she was not stopped. After an operation on her spine, she wrote *Last Tales* by dictation, lying on her back on the floor; and she was a writer given to doing a story 15 times over.

Mr. Langbaum, a professor of English at the University of Virginia, writes that after *Last Tales* and *Anecdotes of Destiny* were published in 1957 and 1958, "a number of literary people in this country, myself included, came to feel that Isak Dinesen had now produced an *oeuvre* and was ripe for serious critical consideration." He says he undertook his study to express his admiration for her work, to find the reasons why we like it, and to suggest that she is an important writer. He will show the high quality of her stories, he says, by explaining them.

He has accomplished his three aims usually by way of, but at moments in spite of, his method. His explication is stimulating because it is so learned, so remarkably allusive; this reader likes it better when it is far-flung than when it sticks too close. His analysis stays with each story episode by episode, point by point, sometimes it seems line by line—yet of course the analysis is not the story. It is like the negative of the positive of a time-exposure of a flying snow-crystal. I admire his study and have learned from it, and at the same time I found it fantastical—perhaps fittingly so.[120]

"In the beginning was the story," says Isak Dinesen's character, the Cardinal, talking about Genesis. "But you will remember . . . that the human characters in the book come forth on the sixth day only–by that time they were bound to come for where the story is, the characters will gather!"

The meaning of the story, "The Roads Round Pisa," he says, is in the title. "The truth is in Pisa, the heart of life is there. But the story that reveals the truth is played out on the roads round Pisa. . . . The point is that you don't get at the truth about the world or yourself by going straight to it. You get at it by seeming to move away to an esthetic distance. You get at it through artifice and tradition—by assimilating your particular event to a recurring pattern, your particular self to an archetype."

Mr. Langbaum calls *Seven Gothic Tales* in the long run "a great book about Europe." He goes on to say that this is "because Isak Dinesen's experience of Africa stands behind it; and Europe stands, in the same way, behind every word of *Out of Africa.* . . . For the imagination works by just such a reconciliation of opposites."

"The Deluge," in *Seven Gothic Tales*, he thinks her best story "because it is her wittiest. It combines the greatest number of her characteristic themes, and the most widely opposite effects. The wit fuses all these into a story that manages at every point to be both tragic and comic."

I find Mr. Langbaum brilliant throughout in his appreciation of his subject's wit, her lyric intensity, her highly organized and highly complicated artistry; in his treatment of the themes she carries farthest—the mysteries of identity, the vicariousness of experience, the polarities of experience, the myths of fall and redemption, her employment of characters as agents of destiny, her devices of the mask and marionette. How close he seems to come to her when he says, "Her wit is amazing in that it exalts and magnifies and never diminishes its object," and he remarks on "the quality of an amorous exchange between souls that is characteristic of [her] greatest conversations." What a delight to learn from him that the nom de plume Isak means "laughter."

She told Mr. Langbaum that she used the word "tale" not in the sense Hans Christian Andersen did, but in the sense Shakespeare did in *A Winter's Tale*, or "in the naive view of a child or primitive who sees a story as neither tragic nor comic but as marvelous." He says, "Isak Dinesen works by condensation rather than by the novelist's expansion." She writes "without the remotest reference to psychology and anthropology. [She] seems to contain and avoid our knowledge, to have access to it through some older source."

She is "dealing with the way in which relative or human motives are unconsciously at the service of absolute or divine intention. . . . [In] her latest two volumes of stories . . . the best . . . come closest to being perfect fables or myths or parables." Indeed, she typically "offers the form she is using, the story, as the solution to the problem posed in the story." "Her stories are fantastic in the way wit is—in the jubilant freedom with which possibilities are stretched and ideas combined."

"Not by the face shall the man be known, but by the mask," one of her characters says. "Because," as Mr. Langbaum points out, "You do not find out who you are by . . . looking into a mirror, but by putting on a mask." This allows you to play out your unrealized potentialities . . . to step from a human story into God's story." Also, "An identity is a work of imagination."

And, "The end of life is not safety but self-realization." Finally, "The lie becomes truth because they represent a truth deeper than the obvious one." "'What an overwhelming lesson to all artists! Be not afraid of absurdity; do not shrink from the fantastic. Within a dilemma, choose the most unheard-of, the most dangerous solution. Be brave!'" says the Cardinal in "Deluge," having already spoken of "the tremendous courage of the Creator of this world." The author points out that Isak Dinesen "considers tragedy to be fulfillment. It is in fulfilling one's destiny that one meets a completely tragic end, which is why traditional tragedy is a triumph, not a failure."

There is space here only to suggest what erudite and far-ranging and always explicit references Mr. Langbaum makes on every page. When a character says, "Keep always in your heart the divine law of proportion, the golden section," he is here with the reference: the 1469 treatise by a friend of Leonardo's, "De Divina Proportione," which in turn calls to his mind a theory of Jung's, and then is applied to Isak Dinesen's diagrammatic construction of plot. To speak of only the religious references, he has had to be familiar not only with the Bible but with theologies from Roman Catholic to Unitarian; with not only the Christian God but with the Greek gods and the Wendish.[121]

As his author writes stories within stories, so Mr. Langbaum has set her work as a whole into the cluster of traditions, mythologies, affinities and archetypes in which he feels it belongs. Indeed I think he has honorably explored all the roads round Isak Dinesen.

When she brings it off he is so pleased, so proud of her—perhaps a little proud with her in explaining her victories. Does he become the least bit possessive? She ventures to introduce Ibsen as a character in a story—he wishes she hadn't. He toys with the thought of transposing Parts IV and V in her autobiographical *Out of Africa*. He finds the origin of one of her stories in Kierkegaard: and "though she did not consider herself an existentialist and disclaimed any extensive understanding of existentialist philosophy," nevertheless "it is safe to say that [she] is an existentialist. . . ." Safe for whom?

This reader is chilled by Mr. Langbaum treating *Out of Africa* as he would as if it were fiction, although he can then say some penetrating things about this superb book. He feels it in place to comment as a literary critic of Isak Dinesen about Karen Blixen's living of her life, since "Isak Dinesen . . . made her life a part of her *oeuvre*. . . . It is because [she] had courage—both courage in the ordinary sense and the existential courage to be one's self and to follow the logic of one's own nature—that her life and work are all of a piece: that she was able to write stories distinguished by the courage that in art we call style, and to create for herself a life and personality as audacious, extravagant, surprising and, yes, as shocking, too, as her stories."

Isak Dinesen was amused to think of herself as a Scheherazade.[122] And what if, instead of only holding death over her head night after night, the Sultan had waited until she had an *oeuvre* and then, taking the voice of the critic, had put it to her: "Now, how would you like me to tell you what you have just said?" Whatever Scheherazade might have answered, we have the Sultan's interpretation.

But Mr. Langbaum has produced a fascinating study of this fascinating and enigmatic writer. "One admires before one knows why," he says at the beginning. I suspect that his own first response to her stories was "That's beautiful!"—before it was "That's important." He has demonstrated that they are important, and also acclaimed them for being marvelous. "Marvelous" is the relevant and better word, is it not?

Martha Graham: Portrait of the Lady as an Artist
By LeRoy Leatherman

MOVEMENT NEVER LIES
Sewanee Review Summer 1967: 529–33

Martha Graham, we read here, has said she learned her first dancing lesson from her father—a doctor. He had learned it from observing the behavior of his mental patients: *movement never lies.* From the beginning, says LeRoy Leatherman in his informative and beautifully mounted *Martha Graham: Portrait of the Lady as an Artist,* "Martha aimed for . . . ways of moving that would communicate varieties of human experience which the art of the dance had never before attempted . . . and ultimately for dramas that would be acted through movement alone."

An American from away back—Miles Standish is an ancestor—this bold and down-to-earth innovator is "a peculiarly American genius of whom Americans know very little." Before she was grown, she had gone with the Denishawn Company, dancing as a Japanese boy. (This was her role on stage; off stage she was being their bookkeeper.) She did an Apache number with Charles Weidman in the *Greenwich Village Follies,* taught after that at the Eastman School, where, said Rouben Mamoulian, who hired her, she came upon the scene "like John the Baptist." But when, in 1926, she gave her first performance as an independent artist, it was on the stage of a Broadway theater, the Forty-Eighth Street, and it has always been the theater, not the studio, that she has made her boundaries inside, performed in, created for.

Mr. Leatherman goes so far as to call Martha Graham not a choreographer but a dramatist. He is equipped to speak. Since for twelve years he has been variously associated with Miss Graham as her company manager, personal manager, and the director of her School, we may take this as official—or if not quite that, then as an opinion due respect. Since also Mr. Leatherman is a novelist, he is further equipped for translating story and movement onto the page without having his head go round. He has written what must have been, nevertheless, a difficult book to write: a book about the one artist from whose works *all* words, all "intellectualizations," have been specifically and warmly banned by the subject of the book. Yet he has done his job well: a sensitive portrait emerges; he has insight and wit; and where, in his world, he must be the only one who is standing still, he has kept his equilibrium as well as his firm affection.

The Graham ideas come from where all original and undeniable ideas in art come from—within; perhaps they are intense forms of human insight. She must mediate alone. But her work "begins to be cooperative the moment she hands her script to the composer and it becomes increasingly so until, by curtain time on opening night, a hundred or so people are involved."

Her script must be indescribable: "deliberately open and evocative," it is yet a working sheet; and for the composers she sends her scripts to, they do work: Aaron Copland, Henry Cowell, Norman Dello Joio, William Schuman, and others. When the music arrives, she never questions a note or asks for changes (she is not overly fond of music for its own sake); what she has to do is get "the pattern of the composition in her sinews." Once she's done that, she ties the handles of her studio doors together with a strip of red jersey, "and everyone on the premises knows what that means. From now on, no one unasked enters until the knot is untied."

Of her set designers, it is Noguchi with whom she has always worked best.[123] He did *Appalachian Spring, Cave of the Heart, Night Journey, Seraphic Dialogue, Clytemnestra, Alcestis,* and *Phaedra,* among others. "There is a perfect understanding by each of the other's art, a perfect agreement about the use and power of symbols and about the design and use of stage space." These are of course the fundamentals of her work. Noguchi makes her a tiny model that he can bring her in a shoe box. But they neither one can foresee quite everything from this: the finished set for *Seraphic Dialogue* (the shining, abstract structure in tubes which was to suggest Joan of Arc's cathedral, and which might have been made by Merlin out of Tinker-toys) would, Noguchi thought, fit into a good big suitcase; it somehow requires five crates "and some mechanical genius to erect."

Mr. Leatherman's book, of necessity loosely organized though explicitly worded, takes us from the beginning of a Graham work, which may, or may not, start with a script—*Clytemnestra* (which Mr. Leatherman considers her highest achievement) was achieved without a script—up to curtain rise on opening night. He supplies an account both affectionate and touching of the final hectic weeks before an Opening, and shares with us the cries heard from the great artist through the pandemonium: "Why did I ever get myself into this? Cancel the season." "I haven't had a minute to work on myself. Clear the building. Get the company out of here, they've rehearsed enough. I've got to have some time alone." "I cannot think about that now." There's no time to eat or think about food, and besides "It is better always to eat the same thing." "Money? Money's nothing. If we *need* it, we'll have it." "Don't *push* me!" And, "I'm being nibbled to death by ducks!"

Then, on the night, the lone meditation to which she has returned for a last hour over with, she waits in the wings transformed. Before, in the weeks of work, "she was in her own eyes a drudge; now she is ready for the conquering . . . alert for the cue and the wash of light to bring her out to be Clytemnestra or Phaedra or Alcestis or Judith . . . or the comical, but most moving and understandable, artist in *Acrobats of God*."

"She started, and her art starts," he writes, "with basic facts, on the ground; the floor, equivalent to the hard, resistant but cultivatable earth, is her element as surely as the ballet dancer's element is clear empty air." The drama she then builds he sees as essentially Greek: it must "move, purge and elevate the spirit." "Martha's best works are always models of poetic density, economy, and compression. She can convey more in twenty-five minutes than most playwrights can manage to do in three acts." I think he can say *that* again. When she works with history, myths, the ancient tragedies, "there is no guessing . . . how she will re-mold them." What is certain is the originality of her insight and of her approach. "She will . . . take full liberty with the events . . . but she never violates her source and never debases it. In fact she elevates her protagonists by bestowing upon them . . . a richer humanity." "She has never, as she says, been interested in anything small." Rather, her work is "an affirmation of man. Her art insists upon the meaningfulness of human experience, even the darkest."

"Dancing, she is an actress; 'choreographing', she is a dramatist." This is interesting, it is descriptive, and certainly the distinction matters, but does it matter a great deal, one may wonder, by what name we call a truly original artist of the first water? The unique might just as well go free of all tags. The Graham genius is, past argument, itself. Rather than hover over its definition, let us seize the day and testify to its force.

She is an artist whose work is inseparable from her life, whose art and whose being are one, as this book well brings out. In the presence of such integrity as hers the audience feels it like a blaze. Furthermore, to those of us who have filled her theaters since the early days of what she now calls her "long woolen period," the excitement of her work has been increasing with time; it has performed its own drama of change and growth.[124] It is as though her theater itself were a moving boat on a river, and we on the bank were running beside it to keep up with it and to celebrate with it where it is going. Not only are the performances new experiences, but the river is uncharted, no telling how deep, full of the dangers of a strong, unpredictable current; and the boat itself is homemade, as was the Ark, and like it based on a personal idea, a loyal company, and help from above. Martha Graham has acknowledged the impracticalities and impecunities and the dangers of her life's work with exhilaration, with many a joyous manoeuvre, many an astonishment clapped upon our eyes.

And in invention and in performance, she is consistently working in the line of magic and legend from which her characters spring. She calls up a spell and she uses it. We follow what she is doing on her stage because we are under enchantment; we are its subjects, or should I say its calculated objects? Circe had other plans for people, but were her working methods very different?[125]

Martha Graham, a strong-minded genius, whose new season this spring introduced her hundred and fortieth and her hundred and forty-first new work, has no plans of leaving the stage to begin with, and no intention at all of leaving it her notations. She has had an enormous influence on the dance, but she will not pass on her secrets: this would mean putting them into abhorred words. She abhors also reviving a work; Clytemnestra can not go back to being the Bride of *Appalachian Spring*. No film has successfully recorded her. Her art belongs to us who see her now. Its indelibility is offered only to the memory of lucky people.

There is no other way. An art in which the spirit of the artist is translated into the body, the dance belongs to the living present in which it moves. In fact, isn't its transience one of its awe-inspiring properties? If the same physical law applied to all the arts, we would need to have lived after 1787 and before 1791, and to have known the right people, and then not to have had a cold on the night of the invitation, to have heard *Don Giovanni* once.

Twenty-seven pages of stunning photographs lead off this book, twenty-seven pages more parade at the close, and dozens of others appear throughout its text. They are by Martha Swope, made during performances of the last five years; they are beautiful in themselves and invaluable as records. Included also is a complete chronological list of the dances composed by Miss Graham from 1926 through 1965, along with the names of the musical composers.[126]

The Little Man and the Big Thief
By Erich Kästner

Otto and the Magic Potatoes
By William Pène du Bois

Knee-Knock Rise
By Natalie Babbitt

FOUR REVIEWS BY EUDORA WELTY[127]

New York Times Book Review 24 May 1970, Part II: 4–5, 45

The Little Man and the Big Thief

Maxie Pichelsteiner, the hero of an earlier book, *The Little Man*, is a Bohemian gymnast and acrobat two inches high, who sleeps in a matchbox.[128] He is famous now, and his life story is being made into a film for television. He lives in his own house, Villa Glowworm, a gift from King Bileam the Nice, with everything made to his own scale down to a tiny dial telephone. (When he's on the ordinary telephone, he has to dash from earpiece to mouthpiece and back.)

Maxie lost his parents when he was only six, but he is fortunate in his friends. Professor Hokus von Pokus, the circus magician, has brought him up, teaching him Reading, Writing, and Arithmetic and another compulsory subject, Doing Nothing, which comes every day from three to four,

Sundays included. The warm-hearted trampoline acrobat Rosa Marzipan is equally devoted to his comfort.

Into this new adventure comes Miss Emily Simpson, Maxie's same size, wearing a tiny ponytail hairdo with a red velvet ribbon. It's a case of "instant friendship."

There's lots of excitement, plenty of speed and a satisfactory plot of wheels-within-wheels. Reappearing from the earlier book is the powerful villain Senor Lopez. He's the richest man in the world, with a castle and a vertical take-off jet. He's the kind of menace who collects odd people for oddity's sake and keeps them in "a kind of zoo for rare human beings." His earlier try for Maxie was foiled, but he will never give up, and, now under scrutiny by detectives, is being made the subject of a film himself—a documentary, which would run as a second feature with the movie about Maxie.

The spirit of the Continental circus, the techniques of today's film and television, and the old, old sense of magic in story-telling, are all together in this novel and the combination sounds perfectly natural.

" 'How much do I eat and drink in a day?' " (Maxie's being interviewed by the press.) " 'Approximately I should say I consume about a couple of square centimeters of brown bread, a knifepoint of butter, a teaspoonful of cocoa, a thimbleful of lemonade, one small button mushroom, one tenth of a new potato, two morsels of sausage. . . .'

" 'What! No cheese?' exclaimed the forward young miss.

" 'Oh, yes, yes. But only Swiss cheese. Lots of it, though! Every day twenty to thirty holes!' "

The book is about performers—but it's also about behavior and manners, the way people of any age and any size treat one another. Its touch is light and its world one of gaiety, but the story never says there's no sadness in experience.

In a press conference, a forward Miss, in the style of her kind, asks Maxie how he felt when his tiny parents were blown off the Eiffel Tower to their deaths. " 'Did you cry very much?' " Maxie in a flash jumps right into her beehive hairdo and starts pulling it to pieces for all he is worth. " 'There!' he said afterwards. 'And now I shall give you your answer. Yes, at that time I did cry, very much.' " Bravo for Maxie!

There is nothing sugary, no talking-down from Mr. Kästner toward his two-inch-high hero nor toward his young reader. Rather, he tells the story as though he's sharing in a common pleasure with them both, with an occasional remark addressed straight to the reader, "Have you ever tried to pack a conjurer's magic tails into a suitcase? No? Well, it takes at least an hour and a half." He tells the story, too, with its proper vocabulary; words like "confounded effrontery" are not left out.

And although nothing has been underlined, it's there for the young reader to observe for himself: in a human being, no matter if he is only two inches high, feelings may lie too deep for words, and actions may reach up to giant size in courage and high spirits.

Stanley Mack's illustrations are lively black-and-white drawings that will bear interested scrutiny. There's one that shows the Sergeant-Major and the Alsatian dog Pluto (both detectives) asleep side by side in identical positions, heads cushioned on arm and front leg respectively.

Otto and the Magic Potatoes

Clearly, unusual size is a sign of magic powers. Otto, the famous dog, a little over two-and-a-half stories tall and loved by everyone in the world, wins his famous medal for breeding in this his new adventure. He is kidnapped by a millionaire, Baron Backgammon, who likes to grow things as big as possible—particularly roses and potatoes. What bad luck it is that the sound of a gong causes the vast roses to shiver into fragments and that at a single prod, the potatoes weep so strenuously from every eye that they're literally reduced to tears, till there's nothing left of them but their skins, like collapsed tents. Since Otto's big, too, it seems only natural to the Baron that he should get hold of him, and try out a few scientific experiments on him to find the answer to his problem. In spite of Otto's master putting up a good fight, the Baron performs his experiments and tells why afterwards: "I had to find out, you see. He doesn't collapse, he doesn't empty out. He's big. He's perfect. THERE'S HOPE FOR MY ROSES! THERE'S HOPE FOR MY POTATOES! THERE'S HOPE FOR THE WORLD!"

The town catches on fire, then, and Otto runs to the rescue. He puts out the fire when the firemen fail, finding the tearful potatoes just the thing, and is awarded a medal from the villagers for his bravery.

The bland Baron had only wanted these monster roses and potatoes for the good of the people. "'GATEMEN, LOWER THE DRAWBRIDGES—AND CUT THEIR CHAINS!' Baron Backgammon shouted. 'My home is YOUR home!'"

Mr. du Bois's magnificent illustrations are, of course, the main reason for this story. They are executed with his usual bravura and have been supplied with a generosity splendid as that of the Baron himself—full color, double-page size, and irresistible.

Knee-Knock Rise

A little boy named Egan goes to visit relations in Instep, a village at the foot of a strange cliff called Knee-Knock Rise. On top of this cliff is a cloud of mist, and "from somewhere in that mist, on stormy nights when the rain drove harsh and cold, an undiscovered creature would lift its voice and moan. It moaned like a lonely demon, like a mad, despairing animal, like a huge and anguished something chained forever to its own great tragic disappointments."

Nobody knew what it was—nobody had ever gone to see and come back again, not in a thousand years. No wonder nobody in Instep sleeps well. All the same, there's a Fair held here every year and the inhabitants say, "Come and eat and dance; be entertained and spend your money; and—hear the Megrimum for yourselves." For the monster is a cause for local pride. "Megrimum" is a name calling up Grimm, mirage, maybe Moloch, but in essence it seems a sound-word for a power that's mainly all mouth, making a noise and reputed to devour.

Before the day of the Fair is over, Egan climbs the cliff to find out the secret for himself. Uncle Ott had disappeared before Egan's arrival—"Uncle Ott ran off up there and the Megrimum ate him," says his cousin Ada, and "she smiled rapturously." And once Egan reaches the top, who's there to greet him but Uncle Ott?

Uncle Ott, who's qualified in that he writes poems about Kings and Fools, says, "Boy, listen to me. There isn't any Megrimum. Never was. It's all been just a lot of nothing all these years." And he points into a cave. "It's only a natural spring. Sulphur. Nasty, but not unnatural."

Egan says, "They'll be glad when I tell them the truth. I did slay the Megrimum, in a way. Or at least I'll slay it now." He throws a rock into the spring and the moaning stops.

"There's always the possibility that they're happier believing," warns Uncle Ott.

Egan, safe down below again, waits to be called "a hero, or a savior," but nobody believes him. He begins to question his own experience. "Is there a Megrimum up there, or isn't there?" His Uncle Anson says, "I think it doesn't really matter. The only thing that matters is whether you want to believe he's there or not." And the chandler avows that the Megrimum is still there, all right, but "he's got his own ways." And then it storms again, and what is heard but another booming, another howling shriek, and the moaning once more?

This story is thoughtfully written and written to provoke thought. To an extent it will succeed. It does not, however, touch the feelings very deeply, beyond arousing uneasiness. There's a coldness about the treatment of the characters, who are not an altogether reassuring company to begin with. They represent attitudes. Egan is given more warmth and more reality than the others.

I felt a morbid quality in the insistent irony about the "intense satisfaction" the villagers took in the Megrimum, how "happily scared" they are to hear its moans. There's an almost punitive note, too, to the final revelations. "The only and lost and greatest terrible secret in the world" is "just a lot of megrimummery," says Uncle Ott, "just a hole in the ground."

The child reader will be aware that in the long run the Megrimum is symbolic. The story is about the mysterious, but more than that it's about belief in the mysterious. Do we believe in the Megrimum, or don't we? By placing the burden of final judgment on the child reader, the author may be wiser than she thinks. Children do know well some things that we have forgotten.

The drawings by the author are a good deal more serene than her story. Their gentle, flowing line has created lovely animals in particular; beside them, the human beings look curiously static.

No Flying in the House

By Betty Brock

FOR YOUNG READERS

New York Times Book Review 16 August 1970: 22

What child hasn't wondered, "Who are my *true* parents?" Annabel, 6, has honest cause for wonder, for she doesn't remember her parents and their whereabouts is a mystery.[129] She is being very well taken care of in Mrs. Vancourt's big, comfortable house, but the one who really mothers her is a little dog, only three inches high and three inches long, named Gloria. Gloria is wise, fiercely protective, she knows 369 tricks, and she can talk. In short, Gloria is a fairy.

The question is, is Annabel part fairy? *No Flying in the House* is the story of a little girl who can kiss her elbow and, after a few false starts, can fly around the room—and comes to believe that part-fairy is exactly what she is. She will be required to choose with which side, the human or the fairy, she will lead her life.

Pressure is brought to bear from all sides. There is a wicked fairy, of course, to oppose the good Gloria—a fairy cat, talented, hard and dangerous, named Belinda. The solid presence of Mrs. Vancourt, rich and well-intentioned but with no foolishness about her, is made-to-order contrast against fairies. "No flying in the house" is *her* edict. ("Vancourts do *not* fly.")

The quality of fantasy is unstrained. Betty Brock's short novel is gentle and imaginative, with a genuine atmosphere and a warm humor.

The book is especially commendable for the quality of its fairies. They're no saccharine, pastel-tinted mites coming when called and granting wishes, but beings of an inhuman race, glittering, intense, unpredictable, capable of fairy good and fairy evil, of going to pieces and coming back together again, of flying to the stars, or of shooting steam out of their ears if you trap them.[130]

Mrs. Vancourt is reliably obtuse about either children or fairies, but in the end she is changed by the wand—not that of the fairies, but the real wand of human affection. Fairy magic is wondrous but may be chill. Warmth comes only from the mortal side, from the human heart. Annabel chooses well.

Baby, It's Cold Inside

By S. J. Perelman

S. J. PERELMAN SHOULD BE DECLARED A LIVING NATIONAL TREASURE

New York Times Book Review 30 August 1970: 1, 25

It can do no harm to tell it now. At the age of 15, this reviewer fell hopelessly in love with S. J. Perelman. It was from afar, for I was sitting in Jackson (Miss.) High School, in Cicero class. While the others were studying "How long, O Catiline, must we endure your orations?" I was taking in "'Gad, Lucy, You're Magnificent!' Breathed the Great Painter," drawing and caption by S. J. Perelman, from a copy of *Judge* on my lap.[131] S. J. Perelman filled the whole copy of that now forgotten magazine every week — drawings, sketches, playlets. I didn't guess he was just a jump ahead of me in school himself at the time. I only knew what any child with a grain of prophecy would know—that here was one of the extraordinary wits of our time, who would come to be known, loved and feared by all. Well, it happened, and I didn't have to wait more than a minute.

What I predict now could really be put in the form of a nomination: that S. J. Perelman be declared a living national treasure. This would be a good time for it. He has a new book today, and we need the treasure.

"If I were to apply for a library card in Paris, I would subscribe myself as a *feuilletoniste*, that is to say, a writer of little leaves. . . I should like to affirm my loyalty to it as a medium. The handful of chumps who still practice it are as lonely as the survivors of Fort Zinderneuf; a few more assaults by television and picture journalism and we might as well post their bodies on the ramparts, pray for togetherness, and kneel for the final annihilation. Until then, so long and don't take any wooden rhetoric."

S. J. Perelman wrote this in 1958 in the preface to a collection made from 30 years' work, *The Most of S. J. Perelman*.[132] We didn't take his advice. But he's still holding the fort. Thirty-two new reports ring out today. The annihilation is all at the other end, and the glory is still his.

In *Baby, It's Cold Inside* you'll meet Shameless McGonicle (the Irish poet), Monsieur Trompemari and Monsieur Libidineux (lovers of Madame Perdant), Lascivio (a Filipino houseboy), Charlotte Russo (a shapely young colleen), Lothar Perfidissich ("noted Hungarian playwright and plagiarist"), "a Miss Haldeman-Julius, related to the book people" (a dinner companion), Umlaut, the Times theater critic, Urban Sprawl the architect, Miss Kathleen Mavourneen (selling cable-stitched sweaters, mittens and tamo'shanters in County Mayo), and Nards and Becks and Reedsworth Smiles (a trio of electricians). Also watch out for Crosspatch's (a luggage shop off St. James's), the Bon Ton Shoe Repair ("Hat Blocking Our Specialty, Crucifixion Our Portion"), and All-Gaul Airlines, and the dusty little bookshop on Fourth Avenue "where every prospect sneezes and only Mann, the owner, is vile."

Mr. Perelman has always taken aim at the same target. His aim is perfect, but human folly of course is deathless. It just changes shape. Once it was embodied in Hollywood ("I was radiant that night in blue velvet tails and a boutonniere of diamonds from Cartier's, my eyes starry and the merest hint of cologne at my ear-lobes. . . 'Have a bit of the wine, darling?' queried Diana solicitously, indicating the roast Long Island airplane with applesauce.")

Now: "You show an amazing knowledge of the body structure," says Dr. Prognose to his patient. "Very impressive in a layman." "I shrugged and said it was available to any student of Gray's 'Anatomy' or, for that matter, anyone with a TV set." He's been duplicating a test he witnessed on a commercial. "You've been glued to the tube studying your materia medica," says Dr. Prognose. This is from the sketch called "Turn the Knob, Doc, You're Obsolete."

Add to folly tourism. Gullible Joycean scholars in Dublin get what they ask for in "Anna Trivia Pluralized." In "Shamrocks in My Head" a buyer of a castle in Ireland ends up "composing a letter to the Irish Times about peasant brutality." The tourist in London runs into "Creative Humiliation Associates, Ltd." "Educational sort of thing. Equips all types of folk—clerks and shop assistants, hall porters, garage attendants, whomever—to protect themselves" against the customer. "We teach 'em the dynamics: wool-gathering, disdain, the snub direct and implied, *Schadenfreude*, the mechanics of sniggering, simple and compound exacerbation—the lot." The British traveler arriving over here has a bit of retribution dealt him in another sketch, "In Spite of all Temptations/To Belong to Other Nations," and an American vacationing in America doesn't have too easy a load to bear in "I Hate Spanish Moss."

Folk-art collecting gets brought down to size. In another study of snob culture, Mr. Gotrox, dressed as Jiggs down to the red sock feet, has made desperate efforts to raise his status as a qualified dog owner, so as to break down the refusal of Le Chien Chic to let him buy a dog—they show "an intensity, a pitiless zeal that reminded me of Savonarola," even after he'd taken a course in the great philosophers at the New School for Social Research.

The book has the brilliance we expect. If the insouciance of the early Perelman—"I had gone into a Corn Exchange bank to exchange some corn." "I have Bright's disease and he has mine"—is not as evident here, nobody could keep up *that* effervescence. (And if he could, he'd run into trouble today, with, at least, the Bright's Disease people.) In its place is a mood very much of its times, and all the more telling in its effects.

Folly is perennial, but something has happened to parody. Life has caught up with it. When Mr. Perelman wrote the superbly hilarious pieces of the thirties and forties, our misuse of the language was in its own vintage years, or so it seems in retrospect. The misuse had its natural place in the movie dialogue, the advertising pages and the sentimental fiction of the day. "There has never been a year like this for the giant double-flowering fatuity and gorgeous variegated drivel," Mr. Perelman wrote back then in "Caution—Soft Prose Ahead."

Now the misuse has proliferated and spread everywhere, and, to make it more menacing, it is taken seriously. Promoters of products, promoters of causes, promoters of self have a common language, though one with a small vocabulary. "Well, to be candid, there is a problem of a sort, psychological in nature, I should elucidate," says the patient in Dr. Prognose's office. "It involves a certain dichotomy, and to help you extrapolate its essence and form a viable rationale, I think I ought to sketch in the background first." To which Dr. Prognose replies, "You have a touch of susskind poisoning. Carry on, but watch your syllables."

The value of the *word* has declined. Parody is among the early casualties of this disaster, for it comes to be no longer recognizable apart from its subject. Parody makes its point by its precision and strictness in use of the word, probing to expose the distinction between the true and the false, the real and the synthetic. It's a demanding and exacting art, and there are few with the gift of penetration, and the temerity, let alone the wit and the style, to practice it. Right now, it's in danger of becoming a lost cause. The only writer I know who can save it is the author of this book. He stands alone. We already owe him a great deal for years of utter delight, but we owe him even more now.

Not for nothing is the new book called *Baby, It's Cold Inside*. Back of some of these pieces, and not very far, lies deep sadness, lies outrage. What an achievement Mr. S. J. Perelman makes today, that out of our own sadness and outrage we are brought, in these little leaves, to laugh at ourselves once more.

The Underground Man
By Ross Macdonald

THE STUFF THAT NIGHTMARES
ARE MADE OF
New York Times Book Review 14 February 1971: 1, 28–30

Curled up, with an insulted look on his upturned face, and wearing a peppermint-striped shirt, the fresh corpse of a man is disclosed in a hole in the ground. From the scene of the crime the victim's little boy is carried off, nobody knows why, by a pair of troubled teenagers. And at the same time, a deadly forest fire gets its start in these hills above Santa Teresa: whoever murdered Stanley Broadhurst must have caused him to drop his cigarillo into the dry grass. So opens the new novel by Ross Macdonald, *The Underground Man*. It comes to stunning achievement.

A Forest Service man looks into the killing to find out who was responsible for the fire; but Lew Archer goes faster and farther into his own investigation, for a personal reason. That morning, he had met that little boy; they fed blue jays together. He promises the young widow, the child's mother, to find her son and bring him back.

The double mystery of Santa Teresa cries urgency but is never going to explain itself in an ordinary way. For instance, it looks as if the victim himself might have dug the hole in which he lies. ("Why would a man dig his own grave?"—"He may not have known it was going to be his.") With the fire coming, Archer has to work fast. The corpse must be quickly buried again, or be consumed with his murder unsolved. This, the underground man of the title, waits the book out, the buried connection between present threat and something out of the past.

"I don't believe in coincidences," Archer says, as the investigation leads him into a backward direction, and he sees the case take on a premonitory symmetry. And it is not coincidence indeed, or anything so simple, but a sort of spiral of time that he goes hurtling into, with an answer lying 15 years deep.

He is to meet many strange and lonely souls drawing their inspiration from private sources. On the periphery are those all but anonymous characters, part of the floating population of the city, evocative of all the sadness that fills a lonely world, like some California versions of those Saltimbanques of Picasso's ("even a little more fleeting than ourselves") drifting across the smoke-obscured outskirts. They are the sentinels of a case in which everybody has something to lose, and most of the characters in this time-haunted, fire-threatened novel lose it in the course of what happens— a son, or a husband, or a mountain retreat; a sailing boat, a memory; the secret of 15 years or the dream of a lifetime; or a life.

Brooding over the case is the dark fact that for some certain souls the past does not let go. They nourish the conviction that its ties may be outlived but, for hidden reasons, can be impossible to outgrow or leave behind.

Stanley Broadhurst died searching for his long-lost father. The Oedipus story, which figured in Mr. Macdonald's *The Galton Case* and *The Chill*, has echoes here too.[133] But another sort of legend takes a central place in *The Underground Man*. This is the medieval tale of romance and the faerie.

It is exactly what Archer plunges into when he enters this case. Finding his way, through their lies and fears, into other people's obsessions and dreams, he might as well be in a fairy tale with them. The mystery has handed him what amounts to a set of impossible tasks: Find the door that opens the past. Unravel the ever-tangling threads of time. Rescue the stolen child from fleeing creatures who appear to be under a spell and who forbid him to speak to them. Meet danger from the aroused elements of fire and water. And beware the tower.

But Archer's own role in their fairy tale is clear to him: from the time he fed the blue jays with the little boy, he never had a choice. There is the maze of the past to be entered and come out of alive, bringing the innocent to safety. And in the maze there lives a monster; his name is Murder.

All along the way, the people he questions shift their stands, lie as fast as they can, slip only too swiftly out of human reach. Their ages are deceiving, they put on trappings of disguise or even what might be called transformations. As Archer, by stages, all the while moving at speed, connects one character with the next, he discovers what makes the sinister affinity between them.

"Robert Driscoll Falconer Jr., was a god come down to earth in human guise," the older Mrs. Broadhurst, mother of the murder victim, has written in a memoir of her father, and here her Spencerian handwriting went to pieces; "It straggled across the lined yellow page like a defeated army." Mrs. Crandall, the mother of the runaway girl, is "one of those waiting mothers who would sit forever beside the phone but didn't know what to say when it finally rang." Another character being questioned plays "a game that guilty people play, questioning the questioner, trying to convert the truth into a shuttlecock that could be batted back and forth and eventually lost." And the violence and malice of another character "appeared to her as emanations from the external world."

These people live in prisons of the spirit, and suffer there. The winding, prisonlike stairs that appear and reappear under Archer's hurrying feet in the course of the chase are like the repeated questionings that lead most often into some private hell.

And of course unreality—the big underlying trouble of all these people— was back of the crime itself: the victim was obsessed with the lifelong search for his father; oblivious of everything and everybody else, he invited his own oblivion. In a different way unreality was back of the child-stealing. "As you can see, we gave her everything," says the mother standing in her runaway daughter's lovely white room. "But it wasn't what she wanted." The home environment of the girl and others like her, Archer is brought to observe, was "an unreality so bland and smothering that the children tore loose and impaled themselves on the spikes of any reality that offered. Or made their own unreality with drugs."

The plot is intricate, involuted, and complicated to the hilt; and this, as I see it, is the novel's point. The danger derives from the fairy tales into which people make their lives. In lonely, fearful, or confused minds, real-life facts can become rarefied into private fantasies. And when intensity is accepted— welcomed—as the measure of truth, how can the real and the fabricated be told apart?

We come to a scene where the parallel with the fairy tale is explicit—and something more. It is the best in the book—I can give but a part.

"I made my way up the washed-out gravel drive. The twin conical towers standing up against the night sky made the house look like something out of a medieval romance. The illusion faded as I got nearer. There was a multi-colored fanlight over the front door, with segments of glass fallen out, like missing teeth in an old smile. . . . The door creaked open when I knocked."

Here lives a lady "far gone in solitude," whose secret lies hidden at the heart of the mystery. She stands there in "a long full skirt on which there were paint stains in all three primary colors." She is a painter—of spiritual conditions, she says; to Archer her pictures resemble "serious contusions and open wounds" or "imperfectly remembered hallucinations."

"'I was born in this house,' she said, as if she'd been waiting fifteen years for a listener." (And these are the 15 years that have done their worst to everybody in the novel.) "'It's interesting to come back to your childhood home, . . . like becoming very young and very old both at the same time.' That was how she looked, I thought, in her archaic long skirt—very young and very old, the granddaughter and the grandmother in one person, slightly schizo."

"There were romantic tears in her eyes" when her story is out. "My own eyes remained quite dry."

Fairy tale and living reality alternate on one current to pulse together in this remarkable scene. The woman is a pivotal character and Archer has caught up with her; they are face to face and there comes a moment's embrace. Of the many brilliant ways Mr. Macdonald has put his motif to use, I believe this is the touch that delighted me most. For of course Archer, this middle-aging Californian who has seen everything in a career of going into impossible trouble with his eyes open, who has always been the protector of the weak and the rescuer of the helpless, is a born romantic. Here he meets his introverted and ailing counterpart—this lady is the chatelaine of the romantic-gone-wrong. He is not by nature immune, especially to what is lovely or was lovely once. At a given moment, they may brush close. As Archer, the only one with insight into himself, is aware.

Time pressing, time lapsing, time repeating itself in dark acts, splitting into two in some agonized or imperfect mind—time is the wicked fairy to troubled people, granting them inevitably the thing they dread. While Archer's investigation is drawing him into the past, we are never allowed to forget that present time has been steadily increasing its menace. Mr. Macdonald has brought the fire toward us at closer and closer stages. By the time it gets as close as the top of the hill (this was the murder area), it appears "like a brilliant omniform growth which continued to grow until it bloomed very large against the sky. A sentinel quail on the hillside below it was ticking an alarm." Then, reaching the Broadhurst house, "the fire bent around it like the fingers of a hand, squeezing smoke out of the windows and then flame."

Indeed the fire is a multiple and accumulating identity, with a career of its own, a super-character that has earned itself a character's name—Rattlesnake. Significantly, Archer says, "There was only one good thing about the fire. It made people talk about the things that really concerned them."

What really concerns Archer, and the real kernel of the book, its heart and soul, is the little boy of six, good and brave and smart. He constitutes the book's emergency; he is also entirely believable, a full-rounded and endearing character. Ronny is the tender embodiment of everything Archer is by nature bound to protect, infinitely worthy of rescue.

When Archer plunges into a case his reasons are always personal reasons (this is one of the things that make us so much for Archer). The little boy for as long as he's missing will be Archer's own loss. And without relinquishing for a moment his clear and lively identity, the child takes on another importance as well: "The world was changing," says Archer, "as if with one piece missing the whole thing had come loose and was running wild."

If it is the character of the little boy that makes the case matter to Archer, so it is the character of Archer, whose first-person narrative forms all Mr. Macdonald's novels, that makes it matter to us. Archer from the start has been a distinguished creation; he was always an attractive figure and in the course of the last several books has matured and deepened in substance to our still greater pleasure. Possessed even when young of an endless backlog of stored information, most of it sad, on human nature, he tended once, unless I'm mistaken, to be a bit cynical. Now he is something much more, he is vulnerable. As a detective and as a man he takes the human situation with full seriousness. He cares. And good and evil both are real to him.

Archer knows himself to be a romantic, would call it a weakness—as he calls himself a "not unwilling catalyst" for trouble; he carries the knowledge around with him—that's how he got here. But he is in no way archaic. He is at heart a champion, but a self-questioning, often a self-deriding champion. He is of today, one of ours. *The Underground Man* is written so close to the nerve of today as to expose most of the apprehensions we live with.

In our day it is for such a novel as *The Underground Man* that the detective form exists. I think it also matters that it is the detective form, with all its difficult demands and its corresponding charms, that makes such a novel possible.[134] What gives me special satisfaction about this novel is that no one but a good writer—*this* good writer—could have possibly brought it off. *The Underground Man* is Mr. Macdonald's best book yet, I think.[135] It is not only exhilaratingly well done; it is also very moving.

Ross Macdonald's style, to which in large part this is due, is one of delicacy and tension, very tightly made, with a spring in it. It doesn't allow a static sentence or one without pertinence. And the spare, controlled narrative, built for action and speed, conveys as well the world through which the action moves and gives it meaning, brings scene and character, however swiftly, before the eyes without a blur. It is an almost unbroken series of sparkling pictures.

The style that works so well to produce fluidity and grace also suggests a mind much given to contemplation and reflection on our world. Mr. Macdonald's writing is something like a stand of clean, cool, well-branched, well tended trees in which bright birds can flash and perch. And not for show, but to sing.

A great deal of what this writer has to tell us comes by way of beautiful and audacious similes. "His hairy head seemed enormous and grotesque on his boy's body, like a papiermâché saint's head on a stick": the troubled teenager's self-absorption, his sense of destiny—theatrical but maybe in a good cause—along with the precise way he looks and carries himself, are given us all in one. At the scene of evacuation from the forest fire, at the bottom of a rich householder's swimming pool "lay a blue mink coat, like the headless pelt of a woman." A sloop lying on her side, dismantled offshore, "flopped in the surge like a bird made helpless by oil." The Snows, little old lady and grown son: "The door of Fritz's room was ajar. One of his moist eyes appeared at the crack like the eye of a fish in an underwater crevice. His mother, at the other door, was watching him like a shark."

Descriptions so interpretive are of course here as part and parcel of the character of Archer who says them to us. Mr. Macdonald's accuracy of observation becomes Archer's detection—running evidence. Mr. Macdonald brings characters into sudden sharp focus too by arresting them in an occasional archetypical pose. The obsessed Stanley is here in the words of his wife: "Sometimes he'd be just sitting there shuffling through his pictures and his letters. He looked like a man counting his money." And Fritz in the lath house, where Archer is leaving him, complaining among his plants: "The striped shadow fell from the roof, jailbirding him."

The Saddest Story:
A Biography of Ford Madox Ford

By Arthur Mizener

THE SADDEST STORY

New York Times Book Review 2 May 1971: 1, 14, 16, 18

What the reader hopes most to see in a biography is the work of the intelligent scholar who also feels an affinity for his subject. For Ford Madox Ford—who had greatness, who did so much for the cause of letters, who was intuitively kind to other writers everywhere but to whom unkindness has often been done in return—for Ford, in particular, his reader would hope he would fall into good hands.

Mr. Mizener's work has taken him, not surprisingly, six years. He has read and considered everything Ford ever wrote in his incredibly productive life. He has put his longest and most probing scrutiny, of course, into *The Good Soldier* and the four novels of *Parade's End*, but, we must believe, he has skimped nowhere, left nothing out.[136] Yet for all his intelligence and his devotion to the task, the book, as I see it, falls short. A little more imagination might have made all the difference.

Ford's heritage was a double one, and, indeed, his life was almost always under a double pressure of some kind, forces pulling him in opposite directions. His father, Francis Hueffer, was German, Catholic, a London music critic and composer; his mother, Kathy Brown, was the daughter of one of the formidable Pre-Raphaelites, the painter Ford Madox Brown. He himself grew up with a double alarm sounding in his ears: one, that he was "a patient but exceedingly stupid donkey" (this was his father talking) and the other, that he was expected to be nothing less than a genius (that was from Grandfather Brown). But perhaps the admonition that reached his deepest heart was something else his grandfather told him: "Fordy, never refuse to help a lame dog over a stile. . . . Beggar yourself rather than refuse assistance to anyone whose genius you think shows promise of being greater than your own." Ford not only remembered this; he acted upon it times without number.

Of course, he lived very much in the imagination—to the point of hallucination sometimes when he read (as a child he could see, could *watch*, Captain Kidd; after he was 40, as a World War I soldier in France, he looked up from *The Red Badge of Courage* and saw around him on the battlefield soldiers dressed in blue, not khaki). He was also uncompetitive, deeply un-self-confident; in fact, he showed as a child both the strengths and the weaknesses that would stay with him all his life. And, of course, he began in his cradle filling the capacious, wonderful and romantic memory that did him both service and disservice in his life and art.

Ford soon developed, as is well known, a tender susceptibility toward women and a deep need for them. At 21 he eloped with a 17-year-old girl, Elsie Martindale. When some years later he tried to persuade her to divorce him so that he could marry Violet Hunt, she would not, and the affair breaking into print made a scandal that left its scars on all involved. The long, exhausting and bitter ordeal (in telling which Mizener goes to equally exhaustive lengths) damaged Ford severely.

Violet was the oddest soul, a lady writer who was somewhat in vogue at the time. Henry James had called her his "Purple Patch," but when the scandal broke he had to write to detach himself from her acquaintance, signing himself, "Believe me, then, in very imperfect sympathy, . . ." Ford had humbly thanked Violet for loving him, but then he almost never saw the last of her. She liked to track down her predecessors in love and move in on them, and she moved in on Elsie; and she kept up with her own successor with Ford, Stella Bowen, by peeping at her through a fence. With Stella Bowen, who had warmth of heart and sanity of mind, Ford had a daughter, and a life in France, and a garden. His later, and last, strong alliance was with Janice Biala, and in this country (where he had moved) she seems to have offered him strength and comfort. They remained together for the rest of his life. The touching, almost never realized hope of Ford's relationships with women seems all the way through to have been for domestic peace—"rest."

It is not surprising that from time to time Ford suffered with neurasthenia.

What he usually did for it was to run over to Germany to see his Tante Emma, who was an advice giver. Other, more drastic, treatments were visited on him, too; almost none of them ever helped. "I live," he said during the first of these illnesses, "in a state of hourly apprehension of going mad."

Mr. Mizener sees Ford's illnesses as "a product of the destructive clash between his dreams of glory and the actualities of his existence." Whatever they are called, Ford survived them, as he survived emotional crises, financial troubles, and all the complications of his literary life. In the last, at any rate, he held for a long while a central place.

Ford wrote 81 books during his life, 32 of them novels. "These books were the purpose of his existence," says Mr. Mizener in his Foreword, "the one commitment of his life that nothing—disaster, illness, despair—was allowed to interfere with. They are the meaning of his life and its most valuable product. Some of them are important books; some are imperfect . . . some are failures. But every one of them shows something about a human imagination perhaps not radically different from other men's but made to seem so by being revealed to us in unusual detail by these books, and every one of them helps us to understand the process by which Ford slowly learned to reveal his imagination."

Thus the biography opens with promise of the kind of criticism we would most wish to see. But this reader does not find its promise very well fulfilled.

Part of the trouble has to come from the writing. Mr. Mizener's is a rather coarse-grained prose without the compensating liveliness that sympathy can sometimes give. This is a typical Mizener sentence: "Gradually during the winter of 1913–14, Ford succeeded in inventing a conception of himself and his motives that explained his recent conduct in a way that satisfied his imagination." He is referring to the writing of *The Good Soldier*. The heaviness in his own style seems always to show most when he comes up against Ford's imagination; it seems to burden him. "The right cadence," so central in Ford's style and in his own test of good writing, is lacking in his biographer. A good ear would have helped the biographer and critic of Ford almost as much as a deeper feeling for the man and his work: perhaps the two qualities are related. This calls insistent attention to itself, for situated in among the paragraphs of Mizener are the many quotations from Ford. To read while they alternate is like being carried in a train along the southern coast of France—long tunnel, blinding view of the sea, and over again.

Mr. Mizener is fully able, by astute use of the rich help available to him, to present a good scene, and the book is full of them. There is, for example, the one in which we see Ford and Conrad, their collaborative novel *Romance* finished, taking it up to London in the train, Conrad reading the proof down on his stomach on the floor because the train was jolting, so deeply absorbed that when Ford tapped him on the shoulder to tell him they had reached Charing Cross, "he sprang to his feet and straight at my throat."

And we see Wyndham Lewis, "in an immense steeple-crowned hat and an ample black cape of the type that villains in . . . melodramas throw over their shoulders when they say 'Ha-ha!'" appearing to Ford for the first time, having marched upstairs to find Ford in the bathroom taking a bath; producing "crumpled . . . rolls" of manuscript from all over his person as if he were a sleight-of-hand artist, he announced himself a genius and proceeded to read them aloud.

The extraordinarily large population that filled Ford's life is lively here, too; and not many are of an undemanding presence in their own right. The book is thronging with vivid personalities, by no means all of them Pre-Raphaelites; it has to concern itself with the literary great of three generations. I think Mr. Mizener has handled this surge of people very well. The trouble is that when he comes to the great rock in the middle of them, the heart of his work, Ford himself, his powers seem to weaken.

He is at his best on Ford as editor. In *The English Review*, "the most obvious measure of Ford's editorial skill is perhaps the fact that, even today, none of these writers except [two] needs identifying." Ford published James, Galsworthy, Hudson, Tolstoy, Wells, Conrad, Hardy, Pound, Yeats, Forster, Joyce. London took Ford to its bosom, to its clubs, even; and shouts could be heard going up from restaurant tables, "Hurray, Fordie's discovered another genius. Called D. H. Lawrence!" It was electrifying.

"If Ford's commitment to the highest standards together with his complete lack of business sense pretty well assured financial disaster," says Mr. Mizener, "that same commitment, with the support of his remarkable powers of selection, made it certain that as long as the *Review* survived it would be a great magazine."

But Ford's creative power, which I think must be Mr. Mizener's trouble, is something else. It was a mountain with many springs running through, sources he could tap at different times, at different levels—some near the surface, some deeper. The most profound was hidden until he reached the age of 40, its existence perhaps unsuspected until he wrote the novel *The Good Soldier.*

To that Rosetta Stone of a novel Mr. Mizener gives full and earnest study, but he still seems to feel that the only safe way to approach the novel is with a dossier and a timetable and a firmly literal grip. It is, in fact, a dangerous way to approach *The Good Soldier*, full of traps.

Except for the timetable. It is interesting and useful (and how hard it must have been to make it!) as a parallel to the shifting times of the story. But Mr. Mizener's assumption that he must trace the characters to real people and by that means lay a finger on their fictional meaning has put him in trouble; to start with, he finds Ashburnham to be Ford's "Image of himself" and the narrator Dowell to be Ford and therefore his own author.

The fact is, Mr. Mizener never makes the essential leap of mind to discover the novel as a complete entity, a world in itself and quite freed of its author.

Mr. Mizener refers to Ford's revolutionary and brilliantly developed technique as "the defensive air" he adopted "about factual inaccuracy that would eventually become a whole theory of literary art, which he would call 'impressionism.'" "Thus Ford sought to make a virtue out of his habit of representing his memories and impressions of an experience rather than the experience itself." Mr. Mizener's apparent unwillingness or inability to see further into Ford's greatest achievement seems to me a most serious defect.

I believe Mr. Mizener treats the construction of *The Good Soldier* as a riddle, and if he can't get the answer, he'd like to get the best of it. Another reader, with better content, might see the novel as a prism suspended by a thread and turning on it. Set in motion—forward, backward—at the delicate control of the author, it turns its faces to us, and the present moment moves into time past or time future. In so doing, it constructs a pattern out of its own fractured light, reflections and shadows; they glance, criss-cross, pass through and modulate one another. Ford the Impressionist was breaking up human experience by his technique of the time shift in order to show the inner life of that experience, its essential mystery. The reader slowly learns the meaning of the novel from this pattern; we *watch* it being revealed.

But Mr. Mizener consistently treats the inventions of fiction as Ford's barefaced attempts to get away with something in his personal life by foisting these false versions upon the public. "This is the novel's improved version of Ford's involvement with Gertrud Schlabowsky," he says of *The New Humpty Dumpty*. In effect, he implies that all that's not "real life" is inferior to it, that fiction is at best secondhand life, that fiction is, in fact, not honest, for it has been stolen from life and is capable of being returned to its original state by reliable critics.

Does Mr. Mizener not recognize Ford's subjects? Pain, going-to-pieces, loneliness, courage, honor, horror, hope, most of all, passion—and *these* are real life; they do not need Gertrud Schlabowsky's identity to make them real.

When Mr. Mizener does admire, we know it only from a quote from somebody else. On *Buckshee* we hear from Robert Lowell: "In these reveries, Ford has at last managed to work his speaking voice, and something more than his speaking voice, into poems—the inner voice of the tireless old man, the old master still in harness, confiding, tolerant, Bohemian, newly-married, and in France." If only the biographer himself could ever give us an expression of feeling, something of his own! We are not sure, as it is, that he ever feels any more than he can say.

The biography is written entirely from the outside. The book is one whole, huge compilation of details from outside. And so it is voluminous without being generous, just as it is lengthy but short on tolerance. One original insight would have equalled the force of a dozen of these pages.

Ford's life was sad. The scandal over the divorce is pitiable and the more so because another time in history would have let it go by without a ripple. Ford was never lucky in his timing. But there was a worse scandal that was done to *him*, which no difference in times or manners could excuse. He came out of the war gassed and in trouble—his memory itself was threatened—to find himself forgotten on the literary scene. He suffered neglect and indifference, even scorn; he was quite callously hurt by a number of people to whom he had been good and for whom he always bore the best will in the world.

Mr. Mizener has this to say of that time: "During Christmas week he came to London for a party at the French Embassy for the English writers who had supported France during the war . . . and no one recognized him. He had expected as much. 'It was seven years,' he said with superb impressionistic inaccuracy, 'since I had written a word.'"

This may serve to suggest why, in this reader's opinion, Mr. Mizener's biography is in some fundamental respects an antagonistic work. If affinity between biographer and subject is impossible, at the very least there had better be personal tolerance.

Ford's vulnerabilities, which were scaled to the rest of him, too large to miss, appear to have the fascination of guilty secrets for Mr. Mizener. Ford's condescension, Ford's "Tory gentleman" notions, Ford's overestimation of some of his work and his fantasies about his reputation, Ford's confusion in money matters, Ford's handwriting—they all exasperate him. The assertions of grandeur came, however, from a man of painfully little self-confidence, very often of none at all. Surely Mr. Mizener might see in this not the lie but the connection. I think it is hard, too, to accept his interpretation of Ford's innumerable acts of generosity as vanity, as he sometimes presents them.

By all accounts of those who knew him, Ford was a man of an exceedingly sweet nature, utterly without malice, bearing no thought of a grudge, an uncondemning man. All his life, when he heard that a friend was in trouble, he *went*. Sometimes it was at a risk to himself. He sat up with other people's sick children, he got out a book of a woman's poems when money was needed to pay her funeral expenses. When fire destroyed an installment of a novel Conrad had written for *Blackwood's*, Ford found him a house nearby and worked along with him day and night to write it all over again.

Ford's lifetime broached three generations of writers and readers who were affected by him and his work. He could remember, as a little boy of three in his grandfather's house, pulling out a chair for Mr. Turgenev, and toward the other end of his life the young Hemingway was pulling out *his* editorial chair—and taking it. In between those times—and to a lesser extent up until his death—practically every writer of serious substance in Britain or America moved through his life and gained from his mind and presence. How generously Ford offered both! There is no sign that he ever gave out of kindness.[137]

Mr. Mizener calls Ford's life "The Saddest Story" because of what Ford might have done and didn't do. Ford did, undeniably, waste his gifts and fail to live up to his greatest powers. But it is, to say the least, unavailing to blame a man—and the man who had done, in spite of this, so much for the cause of literature—for what most certainly had to be a cause of pain and frustration to himself.

It has to be expected that a biographer who is unimaginative about a man's work will be unimaginative about his life, and vice versa; but if this is the saddest story, then, of all ways to write it, the unimaginative is the saddest way. Mr. Mizener, fairly, records in his Introduction that in the opinion of Janice Biala the book does Ford injustice.

At bottom, Mr. Mizener puts blame on Ford as a man who could never face the truth; and apparently, in one sense, that can fairly be said. But at the same time, Mr. Mizener's truth of harsh fact is not Ford's truth. Ford said that the novelist "is a sensitized instrument, recording to the measure of the light vouchsafed him what is—what *may* be—the Truth." Ford not only faced but found inner truths that confound such statements as Mr. Mizener's or show them to be beside the point of his fiction.

"An old man mad about writing." This brief self-portrait of Ford at the end of his life contains at once the soberest and the most inspiriting truth he could teach us.

The honor that is due him, I think this book pays in part. But a larger response is also due him; there are many who believe as this reader does that the response of love is the true and the right one.

Words With Music
By Lehman Engel

EVERYTHING WRITERS AND COMPOSERS OF MUSICALS NEED TO KNOW

New York Times Book Review 28 May 1972: 7, 10

The author of this book and its present reviewer grew up in the same home town.[138] One night, the magician came—Thurston; or was it Blackstone?—to the Century Theater, and waiting for the curtain to go up, the Jackson, Miss., audience was fairly wild. Near me, on the front-row balcony, little boys were swinging like monkeys from the railing. Then I saw, stepping down the aisle of the orchestra, a handsome, stylish little boy about my own age, 7 or 8, who showed nothing but aplomb. Escorting his party of three beautiful little girls to their seats, he took his own on the aisle, where he sat looking entirely self-contained. I thought: *that* little boy knows how the magician does it. He may even be in on it. My intuition was working ahead of time.

Lehman Engel knows how the magic is done, all right, and he is as completely in on it as any one man could possibly be. He has had a long and exceedingly versatile career in the theater world, after getting an early start as musical director for the Group Theater. He has been most visible as a conductor, in a multitude of shows ranging from *The Cradle Will Rock* to *Li'l Abner*, and every theatergoer in New York knows him from the back at least.

He is also known as a serious composer of orchestral and choral works; and there is the incidental music he's written for dozens of plays from

Murder in the Cathedral to *A Streetcar Named Desire*, and notably for the Shakespearean productions of Margaret Webster. He's also a conductor of symphony orchestras and choirs, the author of books on music for the theater, and a born teacher. For the last several years he has conducted his own Musical Theater Workshops in New York, Los Angeles, Nashville and Toronto, on a regular flying circuit. This book is dedicated to his students.

Words With Music is the Compleat Musical Manual, in which everything his young writers and composers need to know is set forth. What works and what doesn't work and why is made specific, and nothing has been come by, or is offered, at secondhand. The same virtues that will make it of lasting importance to them are what make it of interest to the general reader, who can take pleasure in the company of an expert writing with penetration on the subject he knows best. In doing so he conveys a world, and we are struck by his force of feeling for the theater itself; we respond to the contagious exuberance of a man who really knows and really loves what he's doing. And believes in it, because the musical at its best, he holds, stands in a unique position in the theater: it may quite possibly be the form that "most truly represents our time."

The musical is brought about only through collaboration. How is a work the least bit related to art ever accomplished that involves at the same time "writers, composers, lyricists, designers, musicians, singers, dancers, publicists, a light designer, a stage manager with assistants, and, not the least, one or two stars and a producer"? How is it even begun?

Mr. Engel will tell you. The chapter called "The Needs of the Musical" is 104 pages long, and is the heart of the book. To attain its best, the show must have its roots in feeling, and through its performance the audience must be caught up in that feeling and become involved. Always sensitive to this basic need, Mr. Engel converts it down the line to the specific.

The characters must be what they seem and what happens to them immediately understood (it's different in plays): particular people, in a particular time and place, in a particular situation. There should be romantic characters—"romantic," Mr. Engel beautifully says, means "that they contain the element that enables them to sing." There should be comedy. (Comedy, "an absolute essential," was in the pre-thirties "kept like a contagious disease far away from the pure young romancers," but now it's learned to spring out of character and situation rather than out of jokes.)

Music, of course, by expressing any dramatic need in song, furnishing the springboard for dancing and the background for pantomime and the spoken word, is "one of the least perishable of the theatrical elements." Comedy songs, Mr. Engel engagingly points out, are the most personal of all songs by reason of being songs of complaint, "more humorous when delivered in the first-person singular" because "the audience experiences something felt as opposed to something observed."

The need for particularity extends from the characters to the lyrics of the songs they sing, and the songs need to function as integral parts of the plot. Only then can be brought into focus the feeling that the show is all about and which the show must impart. In explaining how we have learned these needs, Mr. Engel furnishes a running history of the musical and sketches in its family tree. *Guys and Dolls*, for example, goes back to *The Beggar's Opera*—which, the author remarks, we have never topped for "style, humor, and workability."

The libretto, of course, is the thing. So far, we have had "no truly successful and lasting librettos that were original." Mr. Engel considers in detail half a dozen adaptations from plays, pointing out why some work (*My Fair Lady, Pal Joey*) and others don't (*Candide:* though it had a wonderful Bernstein score, its characters were not flesh and blood but philosophical concepts—atheatrical). He tells how some adaptations of masterpieces succeed and still don't matter (*Man of La Mancha:* "pure Woolworth") and how some failed exactly as they deserved (*Billy Budd:* "it discarded elements of the original which defined the core of the idea"). He suggests how *Caesar and Cleopatra*, which was made into a poor musical (*Her First Roman*) might have been made to work ("History is meant for alteration when it interferes with theater").[139]

An adaptation carries no guarantee of success even though made by the party closest to it: "The book by Truman Capote [*House of Flowers*] could not have been more ruined by anybody than by its author, who demonstrated beyond any possible doubt that he knew nothing about the requirements of a libretto."

It is *West Side Story* that he puts forward as a superb lesson in intelligent, meaningful adaptation. The parallel with *Romeo and Juliet* (which he supplies by act and scene) "is basic. Its change of time and place are clear and valid and of course strongly pertinent. Because it elides or deletes certain elements that were present in the original so successfully and with such excellent taste, it has been brought closer to our life and time and given a shape as a libretto which works and requires music."

He is not in agreement with those who hold that there is no American opera; there has been for some time, he believes—but not at the Met. "*Porgy and Bess* (1935) is by definition and in spirit an opera. It began on Broadway, has gone through revivals everywhere, and has succeeded in opera houses as a repertory piece all over Europe and the Middle East and here and there in Asia and in fact just everywhere *but* at the Metropolitan Opera House, which is located in the United States of America." (Mr. Engel himself opened *Porgy* in Ankara at the Turkish State Opera in 1968.) He sees *Carousel* and *West Side Story*, too, as "operas in the same sense that *Carmen* is." Finally, Mr. Engel thinks that those who want to create opera might do worse than take lessons from Broadway.

The musical as we've known it, which entered into its golden age in the forties, has already reached full development and is not likely to go further now without new forms, Mr. Engel believes. He sees as dead-end streets librettos with non-characters and non-plots and music that, "in spite of its wide and even frantic acceptance . . . has retrogressed. . . . Its harmonic spectrum, melodic profile, and rhythmic patterns are as limited as the music of Protestant hymnology a century ago, and its dynamic range is from loud to loudest." Rather than *Hair*, it is *Company* that gives him hope at the moment, with its new way of using romance, "a shift in emphasis."

He deplores the waste of time, talent, youth and money on worthless projects and passing fads. He's impatient with those who cast blame on "the theater" itself for our ineptitudes, the lack of the intelligence and courage to learn from experience. When he blows his safety valve, it's on a critic: Mr. Clive Barnes, who, holding the power of life and death over an opening, can damn a promising new show with faint praise.[140] When some new growth capable of development appears, we must recognize and encourage it, he says, reminding us that the tap root of any new form still has to reach down to human feeling to take its nourishment.

This book demonstrates that Mr. Engel's investigations and his carefully-come-by advice to his students have their own roots in feeling. His love for the theater extends to the admiration, respect, and a benevolence, too, for his fellows in all branches of that composite world. In that, or in any world, where weariness, contempt, greed, despair, cynicism have a better-than-even chance to corrupt the human sympathies, Lehman Engel is an incorruptible man. I ought to add that years have now passed and this is not a judgment from the balcony. After 40 years of friendship, I am here on firm ground.

The Life to Come and Other Short Stories

By E. M. Forster

A COLLECTION OF OLD NEW STORIES BY
E. M. FORSTER

New York Times Book Review 13 May 1973: 27–28, 30

"The Life to Come" is the title of a short story that was written 70 years ago by E. M. Forster and is receiving its first publication today. The author himself valued it: it "came more from my heart than anything else I have been able to turn out," containing "a great deal of sorrow and passion that I have myself experienced." But because the sorrow and passion had a homosexual nature, the story has gone unpublished. Upon Forster's death, not quite three years ago, it was bequeathed to King's College, Cambridge, along with his other unpublished papers: two novels in "substantial fragments" (in addition to *Maurice*), and stories, plays, poems, essays, letters, notebooks, diaries. Of the total work of Forster, who lived to be 91, the reading public saw during his lifetime no more than perhaps one-half. Now, "The Life to Come" is giving its title to one volume of what is being published in England as a new and "as nearly as possible" complete edition of E. M. Forster.

Oliver Stallybrass, who is editor of the Abinger Edition (so named for a place of long association with Forster's family) has included in this book all the completed stories that Forster did not include in *The Celestial Omnibus* (1911) and *The Eternal Moment* (1928). Of the 14, only two have been published before; the rest were rejected by magazines or withheld by the author. They range in date of composition from 1903 to 1958; seven were written after the publication of *A Passage to India*;[141] upon completing that novel, Forster said in a letter, "My patience with ordinary people has given out."

For the texts here, the editor has followed as scrupulously as he could Forster's "latest intentions"; the manuscripts he has found to be in an untidy state. The handwriting is puzzling, the punctuation slapdash—Forster so rarely remembered to close his quotation marks—and more than one version turns up of most of the stories, "The Other Boat" in variations Mr. Stallybrass had to label from (a) to (g). At least one story seems to have risen from the ashes. What writer could live with his unpublished pages and let them alone?

And "How dependent on approval!" Forster wrote of himself in his diary. Going unpublished, he tried out his stories on a circle of his friends. How much did they help matters, we wonder? While Lytton Strachey thought "The Life to Come" was good, T. E. Lawrence gave it a laugh. Goldsworthy Lowes Dickinson's disgust at a "Rabelaisian" story was enough to put Forster off his work on *Maurice*. The young William Plomer, allowed to read a story and not caring for it, was never shown another.

Forster, worshiper of sylvan places and the sunlit open, of freedom of every kind, felt obliged to keep his work put away in the drawer. But works of fiction—growths of the mind, the green shoots of feeling—need air and circulation to give them nourishment. They need the world. These stories often show cramp and strain, understandably for not having reached the good light of acceptance.

All the stories in *The Life to Come*, like the familiar ones, are fantasies. The form suited Forster's temperament and was flexible to his needs. The title story, laid in a savage country, tells of the mistaking by "the wildest, strongest, most stubborn of all the inland chiefs" of an erotic passion that he feels for a British missionary for the love of Christ. "Dr. Woolacott" is the story of an ill young man, who suffers from daydreams "of the kind forbidden"; in spite of Dr. Woolacott, "who treats everybody," he is in love with death and longs for its coming. But when he has received a portentous visitor at last, "he was left with a human being who had somehow trespassed and been caught, and blundered over the furniture in the dark, bruising his defenceless body, and whispering 'Hide me.'"

This story, too, meant much to Forster; and in it comes a touching passage in which the genius of all these stories might be musing:

"A violin had apparently been heard playing in the great house for the last half-hour, and no one could find out where it was. Playing all sorts of music, gay, grave and passionate. But never completing a theme. Always breaking off. A beautiful instrument. Yet so unsatisfying . . . leaving the hearers much sadder than if it had never performed. What was the use (some asked) of music like that? Better silence absolute than this aimless disturbance of our peace."

"Arthur Snatchfold" is less mysterious, a straightforward account of the "netting" of a jolly young milkman in a yellow shirt. It opens with a view of the conventional world characteristic of all these stories, here as a country house on a Sunday morning, "with so much ahead to be eaten, and so little to be said": *something is missing*, which has left the world empty or asleep or simply waiting. It appears at the turning point in "The Other Boat"—the best story in the book and, one is glad to note, the latest-written, dated 1958. Young Lionel, after an exhausting scene with his young native lover "Cocoanut" down in the cramped cabin of a P & O liner, has come up on deck "to recover his poise and his sense of leadership":

"The deck was covered with passengers who had had their bedding carried up and now slept under the stars. They lay prone in every direction, and he had to step carefully between them on his way to the railing. He had forgotten that this migration happened nightly as soon as a boat entered the Red Sea; his nights had passed otherwise and elsewhere. Here lay a guileless subaltern, cherry-cheeked; there lay Colonel Arbuthnot, his bottom turned. Mrs. Arbuthnot lay parted from her lord in the ladies' section. . . . How decent and reliable they looked, the folk to whom he belonged! He had been born one of them, he had his work with them, he meant to marry into their caste. If he forfeited their companionship he would become nobody and nothing. The widening expanse of the sea, the winking lighthouse, helped to compose him, but what really recalled him to his sanity was this quiet sleeping company of his peers."

But this recalling is the herald of the murder and suicide with which the story ends. Like most of the stories, it is carrying a heavy burden of emotion with nowhere to go. As Forster saw, the stories were homosexual daydreams; like all daydreams, they go rushing toward the sanctuaries of extremes, and can end only in violence.

According to Forster's biographer, P. N. Furbank, it was the facetious homosexual stories rather than these serious ones that caused him misgivings.[142] Mr. Stallybrass quotes Forster's diary entry for April 8, 1922: "Have this moment burnt my indecent writings or as many as the fire will take. Not a moral repentance, but the belief that they clogged me artistically. They were written not to express myself but to excite myself. . . . I am not ashamed of them. It is just that they were a wrong channel for my pen."

Without being able to account for their coming through the flames, Mr. Stallybrass has produced three for this book. "What Does It Matter? A Morality" is one, moving at slapstick speed, about a mythical kingdom with an *agent provocateur*, winking policemen, doors popping open onto mismatched lovers, a concealed microphone under the mattress. The old facetiousness dances like a skeleton.

Clearly, nothing has got away from Mr. Stallybrass, and I consulted Forster here, turning to what he had to say about the Chapman Edition of Jane Austen, a writer whom he loved as much as I love Forster.[143] Yes, he says, all scraps are for bringing forth, because they "throw light." Print anything, however trivial, that will help in the "final estimate." (And Heaven knows, it was having to keep his work away from view that had been the affliction of his life.)

And so we have "Three Courses and a Dessert: Being a New and Gastronomic Version of the Game of Consequences," an outstanding example of a scrap. It's a composite story written by four friends for a magazine called *Wine and Food*; it saw print in 1944 and never did anybody any harm. Forster contributed the fish course.

But one misses comedy (as distinct from glee), so familiar a part of his fiction—to see at once the reason for its absence: when the women went out of his stories, they took the comedy with them. (And they were also a cause of much of the beauty of his work; they afforded him a good deal of his irony; and he has not got a thoroughly good sounding board without them.) Those women allowed to remain can be got down in a phrase ("that vengeful onswishing of skirts . . .!") or by a tag ("She was one of those women who behave alternately well and badly.") Perpetua, in "The Torque," belongs to the familiar sisterhood of Forster old maids, though she is the only one he disposed of by reducing her to ashes with a bolt of lightning. (Her brother "duly mourned his distinguished sister and collected what could be found of her in an urn. But what a relief not to have her about!")

Central place is perhaps occupied by Lionel's mother, in "The Other Boat," not in person but seen in Lionel's thoughts: "Blind-eyed in the midst of the enormous web she had spun—filaments drifting everywhere, strands catching. There was no reasoning with her or about her, she understood nothing and controlled everything. She had suffered too much and was too high-minded to be judged like other people, she was outside carnality and incapable of pardoning it."

There are flaws in these stories, and they show; but they are never flaws of feeling. Herein lies their relationship with Forster's other stories.

None have attempted the broader proportions of "The Road From Colonus," nor do they reach that story's nobility. When the traveler in Greece, who had felt only that "something great was wrong" and, vowing that "I will pretend no longer," steps inside the hollow tree, it is to find that "from its living trunk there gushed an impetuous spring." What all these stories say in part is here said perfectly. Here, Forster is writing about all human desire, and its epitome in the defiance of one half-helpless old man: he would cling to life at its most meaningful point, just where he had found it, never willingly to let himself to be torn away.

It will be sad if the aspect of homosexuality, which kept Forster's stories from reaching print in his own day, turns out to be their only focus of interest for today's readers. It will be sadder if it reanimates the "re-evaluators," who, upon the debut of *Maurice*, a novel then aged 57, wanted to go at the whole of Forster's work on the basis of news freshly received by them concerning his private life.[144] Have we been as ready for Forster's honesty as we thought we were?

Forster, whose greatness surely had root in his capacity to treat all human relationships seriously and truthfully, has Clive in that novel speak of homosexual love as "a passion we can direct, like any other, to good or bad." And of course, the best realized of the homosexual stories dovetail perfectly into the best of all his work. Even the earliest and most ephemeral of them will be recognized as the frailer embodiments of the same passionate convictions that made for the moral iron in his novels.

What engaged Forster was not the issue of respectability vs. homosexuality, but that of respectability vs. Apollo. The weights in the balance are always spiritual life, spiritual death.

As for the light thrown by the present volume, it has given us more knowledge about a writing life of immense fidelity—it was to be the truth or nothing—that from its beginning was difficult and sad, though lit with comic glints. It is much along the lines of a Forster novel, which continues to unwind itself after his death and is now heading for its ironic conclusion.

Since "The Trustees of the Late E. M. Forster" have been listed as the author's copyright holders, two new publishers have been added to the American publishers of his lifetime: Norton brought out today's book and *Maurice;* and Liveright, in between, brought out *Albergo Empedocle and Other Writings,* edited by George H. Thomson, a sort of grab-bag of 1910–15 ephemera containing the one prize. The reader, noting in the American Introduction that *The Life to Come* corresponds to Volume 8 of the Abinger Edition—Mr. Stallybrass foresees 20 in all—wonders at this point how much more we can expect to see of the complete, and how we shall see it, and when.

The Abinger Edition will not be the measure of Forster's achievement except in pound-weight; the complete is not answerable to standards, is as blind to excellence as to the lack of it, and passion counts for exactly the same as punctuation, although the latter can be corrected. But the complete has its own excuse for being. Knowing that it is to exist, Forster readers here will find it hard to settle for the occasional parcel. We must hope.

If Forster himself could have the last word on the destination of his books, that word might well be "Eternity." He spoke of Eternity often and in familiar terms, and it was indeed upon her that he placed his reliance for that final estimate. And will there be a reader who won't see, in each of these books being launched, the paper boat in "The Longest Journey"? It is being lighted and set into the stream at last, taking the current, going under the bridge—to be watched, from wherever we stand, "still afloat, far through the arch, burning as if it would burn forever."

Pilgrim at Tinker Creek

By Annie Dillard

MEDITATION ON SEEING

New York Times Book Review 24 March 1974: 4–5

"I am no scientist," says Annie Dillard, "but a poet and a walker with a background in theology and a penchant for quirky facts." In *Pilgrim at Tinker Creek* she offers "what Thoreau called 'a meteorological journal of the mind.'"

The book is a form of meditation, written with headlong urgency, about *seeing*. A blind child the author happened to read about saw for the first time after cataracts had been removed from her eyes. "When her doctor took her bandages off and led her into the garden, the girl who was no longer blind saw 'the tree with lights in it.'" Annie Dillard had found the central metaphor for her book; it is the vision, the spiritual conception, that she will spend her days in solitude tramping the Roanoke creek banks and the Blue Ridge mountainside in search of for herself.

A reader's heart must go out to a young writer with a sense of wonder so fearless and unbridled. It is this intensity of experience that she seems to live in order to declare.

There is an ambition about her book that I like, one that is deeper than the ambition to declare wonder aloud. It is the ambition to feel. This is a guess. But if this is what she has at heart, I am not quite sure that in writing this book she wholly accomplished it. I don't say this, though, to detract from her declared intention in laying herself open to the experience of seeing. It is a state she equates with innocence: "What I call innocence is the spirit's unself-conscious state at any moment of pure devotion to any object. It is at once a receptiveness and total concentration."

But apparently it is an unself-consciousness that can be consciously achieved and consciously declared. And part of her conception of seeing is that in the act of doing it she is herself, in turn, being seen.

"I walk out; I see something, some event that would otherwise have been utterly missed and lost; or something sees me, some enormous power brushes me with its clean wing, and I resound like a beaten bell. I am an explorer, then, and I am also a stalker, or the instrument of the hunt itself. . . . I am the arrow shaft, carved along my length by unexpected lights and gashes from the very sky, and this book is the straying trail of blood."

What happens to that paragraph is what happens to her book. As the episodes begin, we can imagine an appealing young woman standing alert in a meadow, dressed in shirt and pants, holding her field glasses and provided with a sandwich: she is waiting to see, being very patient and still. By the chapter's end, we realize or suspect we are watching a dervish dancing. Receptivity so high-strung and high-minded has phases of its own. The author shows us that it has its dark side too.

"The world has signed a pact with the devil; it had to. . . . The terms are clear: if you want to live, you have to die; you cannot have mountains and creeks without space, and space is a beauty married to a blind man. The blind man is Freedom, or Time, and he does not go anywhere without his great dog Death. The world came into being with the signing of the contract. . . . This is what we know. The rest is gravy."

I honestly do not know what she is talking about at such times. The only thing I could swear to is that the writing here leaves something to be desired. "What's going on here?" is one of the author's refrains. "The creator loves pizzazz," she answers herself.

She is better at stalking a muskrat: "Stalking is a pure form of skill, like pitching or playing chess. Rarely is luck involved. I do it right or I do it wrong; the muskrat will tell me, and that right early. Even more than baseball, stalking is a game played in the actual present. At every second, the muskrat comes, or stays, or goes, depending on my skill." This is admirable writing.

So is her account of the polyphemus moth—first in its cocoon, then emerging, then crawling away in the presence of a roomful of schoolchildren. It has been directly experienced at what I should say is eye-level. Her account of the migration of the monarch butterflies, which makes the reader see what they looked like coming, how they went over, what they left behind them, what the author learned from the whole event, is precise and memorable.

She can also write straight narrative, showing what the book would have gained in point, direction, and shape from being given a little more of it. She takes us through a flood on Tinker Creek and I think she sees truly when she says: "Tinker Creek is out of its four-foot banks. . . . It looks like somebody else's creek that has usurped or eaten our creek and is roving frantically to escape, big and ugly, like a blacksnake caught in a kitchen drawer." She walks out into the flood on a wall and on the return trip meets a young boy who's going in the opposite direction. "The wall is one brick wide; we can't pass. So we clasp hands and lean out backwards over the turbulent water; our feet interlace like teeth on a zipper, we pull together, stand, and continue on our ways." There's grace and quickness of writing. It also marks the rare appearance, momentary as it is, of another human being in her book, and the closest any human being comes into the presence of the author.

Annie Dillard is the only person in her book, substantially the only one in her world; I recall no outside human speech coming to break the long soliloquy of the author. Speaking of the universe very often, she is yet self-surrounded; and, beyond that, book-surrounded. Her own book might have taken in more of human life without losing a bit of the wonder she was after. Might it not have gained more? Thoreau's wisdom had everything to do with the relationship he saw between nature and the community of man. She read Thoreau, including of course his own meteorological journal of the mind.

While spending her days stalking, the young author was spending her nights reading. She read everything she could get her hands on that would elucidate and expand what she was finding out for herself. She copied long passages into her journal, and many excerpts appear in her book—not only from Thoreau, Fabre, Darwin and so on, but from novelists, artists. (An odd bit, unattributed, is tantalizing me: Who said, "Gravity, to Copernicus, is the nostalgia of things to become spheres"?) Her search for a vision has been at firsthand and at secondhand; a dual search.

There remains something about her wishes which is not quite related to the human world. She remarks somewhere, "I am interested in Alice mainly when she eats the cooky that makes her smaller. I would pare myself or be pared so that I too might pass through the merest crack, a gap I know is there in the sky. I am looking just now for the cooky." (Contrariwise, she will need to be looking for a little bottle, tied around the neck with a paper label with the words "DRINK ME" beautifully printed in large letters. And eating the "little cake"—if this is what she means by a cooky—will only result in her having to say, "Goodbye, feet!")

Actually, and not unlike the characters Alice herself *meets* in Wonderland, the author is given to changing style or shifting moods with disconcerting frequency and abruptness. "Thanks. For the Memories." "This oft was thought, but ne'er so well expressed as by Pliny." "The cottage was Paradise enow." You might be reading letters home from camp, where the moment before you might have thought you were deep in the Book of Leviticus.

The relationship between the writer and the reader is fully as peculiar and astonishing as the emergence of the polyphemus moth. It too has got to leave the cocoon, has got to draw breath and assume every risk of being alive before the next step, real understanding, can take place.

But a writer writes as a writer sees, and while the eyes are rolled up, what appears on paper may be exactly what it sounds like, invocation. "Mystery itself is as fringed and intricate as the shape of the air in time." This is a voice that is trying to speak to me out of a cloud instead of from a sociable, even answerable, distance on our same earth. And if I ask, as I do too at times in this book, "What's going on here?" the author would be likely to invoke the voice again, and we'd be told as we were before: "The creator loves pizzazz."

She concludes her book by saying, "And then you walk fearlessly . . . like the monk on the road who knows precisely how vulnerable he is, who takes no comfort among death-forgetting men, and who carries his vision of vastness and might around in his tunic like a live coal which neither burns nor warms him, but with which he will not part. . . . The giant water bug ate the world. And like Billy Bray I go my way, and my left foot says 'Glory,' and my right foot says 'Amen': in and out of Shadow Creek, upstream and down, exultant, in a daze, dancing, to the twin silver trumpets of praise."

And that's the way Annie Dillard goes. Is the Pilgrim on her right road? That depends on what the Pilgrim's destination is.

But how much better, in any case, to wonder than not to wonder, to dance with astonishment and go spinning in praise, than not to know enough to dance or praise at all; to be blessed with more imagination than you might know at the given moment what to do with than to be cursed with too little to give you—and other people—any trouble.[145]

The Last of the Nuba
By Leni Riefenstahl

J'Aime Paris: Photographs Since the Twenties
By André Kertész

About Russia
By Henri Cartier-Bresson

AFRICA AND PARIS AND RUSSIA
New York Times Book Review 1 December 1974: 5, 22, 28

Of the three new photography books, lying on my desk, Leni Riefenstahl's *The Last of the Nuba* (Harper & Row, $18.95) is unique; and the making of it is a story.[146] Mrs. Riefenstahl, a well-known film maker and actress in Germany before and during the Hitler years (she directed *The Triumph of the Will* and *Olympiad*),[147] was seduced into going to Africa by reading Hemingway's *Green Hills of Africa*. A projected documentary on the slave trade served to get her there, but didn't point her to the tribe of perfect human beings still living in innocence and harmony that she came to find. On the day she was leaving, she chanced upon a photograph of a magnificent naked athlete riding the shoulders of another, with the caption: "A Nuba of Kordofan." She would have to come back.

To suppose that convictions of romantic affinity are killed off early in life is folly. It was 1962, and Mrs. Riefenstahl was 60, when she was able to return and follow up her Nuba clue. Attaching herself to a German expedition to the Congo, then finding the rest of her way by compass bearing, she drove her Land Rover high into the southernmost hills of Kordofan, until she came in sight of some very strange houses: they were circular and clinging to the side of the cliff like bird's nests. And there they were.

The affinity proved out. Mrs. Riefenstahl found in the Mesakin Nuba the people she'd been looking for and they shyly made welcome the first white woman they'd ever seen. There in the hut they built for her, during visits over the next 10 years, she put together out of her deep commitment this extraordinary picture record.

Her 126 photographs, many in color, have an absorbing beauty and a cumulative power. Following a 72-page introductory set of pictures, "Land and People," she groups the rest about the four big occasions on which their lives center: the harvest; the cattle camp called the *zariba*; wrestling; and death. She has photographed them all from their point of view.

She uses the light purposefully: the full, blinding brightness to make us see the all-absorbing blackness of the skin; the ray of light slanting down from the single hole, high in the wall, that is the doorway of the circular house, which tells us how secret and safe it has been made; the first dawn light streaking the face of a calf in the sleeping camp where the young men go to live, which suggests their world apart. All the pictures bring us the physical beauty of the people: a young girl, shy and mischievous of face, with a bead sewn into her lower lip like a permanent cinnamon drop; a wrestler prepared for his match, with his shaven head turned to look over the massive shoulder, all skin color taken away by a coating of ashes.

Moving details of their lives emerge from the photographs of their houses. They were built as they were in defense against the slave raider. The entrance hole, only 14 inches wide, which the Nuba "flick themselves through like . . . fish," is set five feet high in the wall to keep out snakes and scorpions. The main entrance to the walled-in cluster of houses, the only door that reaches the ground, has the shape of keyhole so the women coming in from the fields can walk through with those big loads on their heads. And the blue sheen we see on the inside mud walls is achieved by rubbing in graphite for a very long time with the ball of the thumb—the Nuba love beauty.

We see them at work on their stony land—they harvest millet, but there is no plough, no wheel. Tools are the axe, the knife, and the hoe. There are a few ancient guns, hereditary treasures, fired off mostly as salutes at wrestling matches and funerals. Hunting is often done with sticks, and can go on for hours without the luck of so much as a rabbit; old men die of the effort. Their diet is sorghum twice a day (the wrestlers at the cattle camp get all the milk); meat is rarely eaten, the cattle being slaughtered only in sacrifice at funerals.

It is in the *zariba* where the young men attain their maturity, in which the real meaning of life lies for them; and for the whole tribe this meaning is epitomized in the wrestling match. The Nuba's deepest emotions come into expression here, only exceeded at the funerals of the wrestler heroes. Mrs. Riefenstahl has made extraordinary photographs of these dramas of joy and grief, as always, seen from within.

Contemplating their photographs we might see in these people a magnificent unselfconsciousness and at the same time a tender self-regard—as paradoxical as if they wore clothes like us. Mrs. Riefenstahl's word for their nature as she came to know it is "introspective." We can see that by the way they make music for themselves. Every Nuba, though he owns little else, owns a lyre. Each makes his own. Each has his own songs, which he composes and plays, and the lyre is the first thing he reaches for when he wakes up in the morning. The Nuba, who also laugh a lot, enjoy singing about themselves, about one another. While Mrs. Riefenstahl was in residence, they sang about her. They love round dancing and at the full moon may dance the night away, to their own singing.

There is hardly any crime, "except for the traditional goat-stealing." Punishment for breaking taboos is not imprisonment but contempt; even the children point and scoff at the adulterer. In 1969, though, the Nuba "found out about money." Before, barter had sufficed: leaves of tobacco swapped to the Arabs for steel lyre strings. We gather that some of the innocent ways have suffered change. Leni Riefenstahl got there just in time.

But she made timeless photographs. They give us fresh comprehension of man in, as might be, his original majesty and acceptance of life, in his vanity and courage, his beauty, vulnerability, pride.

Nobody had ever seen that Nuba village; everybody has seen Paris. If his photographs of the Paris he loves are very often clichés in *J'Aime Paris: Photographs Since the Twenties* (Grossman/Viking, $22.50), it's hardly André Kertész's fault that thousands of amateurs have stood in his shoes to photograph the same barges in the Seine under the same leaning trees.

They have their own value, in their loving preservation of scenes now gone (Les Halles, for instance) and of now-vanished callings in life—the street venders and barrel organists, the *midinettes*, the *clochards*, the coal sellers, the camping Gypsies, the *saltimbanques*, the goat's milk man and his goats set up in business on a busy street corner. For this reason, though the collection is subtitled "Photographs Since the Twenties," the best are the ones that date the farthest back, when white-silk-stockinged girls in a bistro in Montparnasse were dancing with customers in caps and one long-aproned waiter, and the Moulin Rouge could be photographed lit up for "La Revue Mistinguette."

There are happy events recorded which memory may have forgotten ("Celebration in Montparnasse after the first futurist ballet," 1929) and some yet remembered people. We see Marie Laurencin photographed in a velvet suit seated at a spinet, playing to a silky Pekingese (I *think* it's a spinet, and *think* it's a Pekingese). And here's "the famous model Kiki" (1927), whose amazing face under the black bang is like a Benda mask that has at last given in and completed the smile.

Most of the views of the city are romantic—"The Seine from Lady Mendl's Apartment"; "Rue de Grennelle"—a caressing study of the facade of enchantment in its flaking away. But not all—not the Canal Saint Martin with the old fellow washing his feet in it. And very somber and powerful is his "Under Pont Notre Dame, 1925," in which for once we don't see through the arch of the bridge, and are not to make out either the men or the river, but only shapeless bundles of rags and rugs, conveying an extraordinary feeling of dampness and cold.

The photographs of most lasting interest seem to me the interiors, especially when selected detail is focused on and allowed its authority: the rack of waiting mail at the Café du Dome; the stout, short-haired working dog belonging to the guard of Notre Dame, at sit with nose laid to the ring-load of Cathedral keys; "An artist's studio, 1927," with batik coverlet, ballet poster, scattered espadrilles, bidet, and four live hens pecking.

In Atget's time exposures, it's as if the camera, having fixed on some street, would not let go until it had extracted some essence of Paris from it, which the photograph is still able to suggest is there.[148] Atget might have pursued the spirit of the place, M. Kertész the sentiment—in which I see nothing wrong. In photography, as in other arts, what one finds is often quite exactly what one seeks: Mrs. Riefenstahl too, pressing her Land Rover up the hill to the Nuba.

If his photographs of Paris are somewhat over-familiar, this will never trouble those for whom clearly the book was made—those who remember

M. Kertész's Paris with his same love, who will greet them with the right romantic gratification, all the more so for so many of them having been taken in the rain. A charming portrait, "Elizabeth and I in a cafe in Montparnasse. A self-posed, self-timed picture, 1931," closes this personal and loving book.

Cartier-Bresson has sought all over the world to put his shutter-finger precisely on the world's pulse and to reproduce its pattern in black and white for our eyes. The reviewer should be able, as I am not, to study side by side Cartier-Bresson's 19-year-old earlier book on Russia[149] and the one appearing today—*About Russia* (Viking, $18.95). The biggest change must surely lie in the faces: there doesn't seem to be a worried face on the whole map of Russia any longer. The young faces show only bright curiosity, the old only resignation, while the middle-aged are as broad as possible with satisfaction.

The 141 photographs are grouped geographically, in four parts: Leningrad, Moscow and the Federal Republic of Russia; The Republic of Estonia; the Republics of the Caucasus; and the Republic of Central Asia. Cartier-Bresson, who has given his book the peripheral title *About Russia*, declines to generalize about his pictures: "What I am trying to do more than anything else is to observe life . . . to note a number of significant facts, applying the strictest visual standards possible." As for their significance, the camera "questions and answers simultaneously."

His camera does. His subject and its moment are one, the composition undistractedly telegraphing its central fact, with its questions and answers adhering. There is no waste.

Here's a picture composed of (1) the rooftop—tall figure of Lenin, (2) two fashion models holding poses as untrembling as Lenin's, and (3) a photographer kneeling before the models in overcoat and beret in the act of clicking the camera—all on the vast stage of Hermitage Square in Leningrad. Cartier-Bresson's visual wit points up his observations like another source of light, human and portable.

They are his flawless black-and-whites, keyed to the most sensitive modulations, and in Russia how many grays he finds! All of them come into the small and beautiful "Village on the Shores of Lake Baika." Then he does without any grays at all in "Fishermen on a Frozen River," a double-page spread of infinite white cold, dotted with small, isolated, black silhouettes: 14 men and a dog.

Among the subjects: a standing sunbather, very white, with his feet on a newspaper, face to the wall of the fortress of Peter and Paul, apparently in strange communion with his own black shadow; museum goers: the towering statue of Tsarina Anna, spiky as some giant Iron Maiden, being gazed up at by a lad with open mouth; dancers at the plastics factory in practice for a competition,[150] in letters as large as the dancers' heads words of Lenin cover the wall beside them; washerwomen in Siberia dipping their clothes from a footbridge through a hole in the ice; a shepherd and his grazing flock in a Georgian meadow, some new iron and steel complex stretching the width of the sky behind him, like somebody else's mirage; a row of bundled up old women, bent over on their sticks, patiently waiting for something in the Cathedral at Pakov, above their heads an ancient painting of the Day of Judgment.

And the rows of housing complexes, rows of portraits of cosmonauts on hoardings, rows of tractors, rows of computers, rows of human beings lined up for public occasions! They allow Cartier-Bresson to point out that impressiveness in number is subject to the humor that lies in repetition. Lined up along the row of computers in the petro-chemical factory is, he shows us, a row of potted plants in metal stands in supervisory positions: we catch a little Gallic mockery along with the Russian reiterations.

The Russians themselves, although exhibiting in great variety, much substance and charm, strike this viewer as utterly devoid of the gifts that equipped Cartier-Bresson to take their pictures; in their pictures it is he who seems to have his worldly bearings, rather than they. One feels he has used these, his unerring equilibrium, his recognition of the comic, and indeed his world-traveler's experience of the profundity of long despair, almost without their knowing concurrence, to let them show and suggest what their real daily life is.

For the actions we see them engaged in never seem to have much more spontaneity than, say, the open-heart surgery Cartier-Bresson—who does get in everywhere—has photographed in an operating room in Georgia. Perhaps it would be thought just as inappropriate to all they do. It's good when he does come upon—and record—the lovely rare thing, such as dancing in the meadows at a picnic on Festival of Chemistry Day.

Best of all there is the father photographed on the shore of a lake in the mountains of Armenia, lifting up his little boy, who stands erect and smiling in his little fur hat in the palm of his father's hand. With its superb, giving gesture of one man's own pride, hope, promise, this is the photograph "about Russia" that most closely touches us.

Pictures and Conversations
By Elizabeth Bowen

AS IF SHE HAD BEEN INVITED
INTO THE WORLD
New York Times Book Review 5 January 1975: 4, 20

Spencer Curtis Brown, Elizabeth Bowen's literary agent and friend of many years, writes in his affecting and helpfully informative foreword to this collection about the circumstances surrounding the appearance of *Pictures and Conversations*. Miss Bowen, who died on Feb. 22, 1973, had talked over this book with him, and he prints here some notes she made for her publishers before she began it.[151]

She did not intend it to be an autobiography in the accepted sense. (It got its title from *Alice in Wonderland*.) It was not to follow a time sequence, and "it will be anything but all inclusive." Rather, "the underlying theme—to which the book will owe what it is necessary that a book *should* have, continuity—will be the relationship (so far as that can be traceable, and perhaps it is most interesting when it is apparently not traceable) between living and writing."

Instead of the "personal" (in the accepted sense) we were to be given the more revealing findings she herself could bring out of her life and her work, calling for the truer candor, the greater generosity—a work to do reader as well as writer honor.

Entering into her decision to write it was the unnervement factor. She had seen studies and analyses of herself and her work by others. "While appreciative of the honor done me and of the hard work involved, I have found some of them wildly off the mark. To the point of asking myself, if anybody *must* write a book about Elizabeth Bowen, why should not Elizabeth Bowen?"

Then she became ill. She wrote into her last year for as long as she could, and the last words she was able to speak were to Curtis Brown: "I want it published."

That wanting was an act of passionate good faith in the intuition of a lifetime, as I see it. (Here I must speak as her friend as well as her reader.)[152] She believed that what she had managed to set down in however small part would carry a strength to make known to her readers what was to have been the burden of the whole. Her fragment is all affirmation and she was right. Most of her readers will feel less pain in there being so little completed for the radiance of what is here: this is what would have filled the book we shall never see.

The book we do have fairly ripples with life.

We are meeting an enchanting little girl, the Elizabeth Bowen of age 7 recently transplanted from Ireland to England, in her prophetic relationship to the woman and the writer she was to become. We find it possible everywhere and time after time to make the jump.

The schools she was sent to nourished what was to become her life-long love affair with other people's houses, for, she says, "Never had I the misfortune to be educated in any building erected for that purpose." Digging, the leader of her schoolgirl companions, through walls and into foundations of some former rectory on speculation of secret passages, quite naturally turned into writing stories about houses a little later. "For all that," she says, "it was the foreground I stood upon that possessed me. Underfoot, it lost nothing by being *terra firma:* actual and tangible, it remained magic."

One is made aware in these pages of the scattering of seeds due for later flowering into *The Death of the Heart, The Little Girls, Eva Trout* and other fiction.[153] And well does one recognize this child. There is the same sense of expectation, the eagerness to join in, take part, that gives its special strength and delight to her writing. She was a prime responder to this world. It was almost as if she'd been *invited* here. Some great pleasure lay deep inside her great sophistication—and here she was, at the top of her form, arrived to do it honor: a romantic, of course—self-described. A romantic with a particularly penetrating power of observation, and a joyous sense of the absurd.

What she says about the Irish is as wonderful as what she has made dramatically clear in stories. All share in inborn traits: belligerence ("poles apart from aggressiveness," "your belligerent person tends to sail through life in excellent spirits"). The passion for virtuosity of all kinds. The ability to strike root wherever set down, a peculiarity of the Anglo-Irish—which of course she is. And there is writing: "To *that* we have taken like ducks to water." But, she goes on to say, "Possibly, it was England made me a novelist," because with the move, there was to be "a cleft between my heredity and my environment—the former remaining, in my case, the more powerful." "If you began in Ireland, Ireland remains the norm: like it or not." "What had to be bitten on was that two entities so opposed, so irreconcilable in climate, character and intention, as Folkestone and Dublin should exist simultaneously, and be operative, in the same life-time, particularly my own."

"I am not a 'regional' writer in the outright sense"—but she is another: "Since I started writing, I have been welding together an inner landscape, assembled anything but at random." Not people and places in their own identities, but people and places that experience called up in her became her stories and novels. They represent her reactions to experience, her "beholding afresh."

Her understanding of a wide range of relationships might easily have been rooted in what she describes in her childhood nature as "outgoing." Later on, her grown-up generosity might have been a form of concentration almost psychic, and in her writing this may have become the novelist's gift of quick perception, and a working tool. Fascination with the outside world, in retrospect, and through the intensity of writing fiction, becomes sharp scrutiny. A highly conscious ability to imagine herself in another's place is a writer's power too—in her case, to precipitate a highly complex plot and a full house of vivacious characters.

Pictures and Conversations was important to Elizabeth Bowen. Published, it is important to her readers, for, fragment that it is, it is whole in its essence, which survives interruption to the page. That relationship between her life and her art—and here I use, for her, the word she forbore to use for herself—she *has* divined in its spontaneous and still mysterious source and has traced it part way at least toward its broadening stream. What is here holds a particular blessing for those who loved Elizabeth, for they will not be able to read any sentence of it without being brought the cadence of her voice and the glow of her company.

As autobiography (in the Bowen sense), the chapters will fall into natural place beside the enchanting *Seven Winters* (for the first seven years of her life, the summers were spent in Bowen's Court, the winters in Dublin); the brilliant introduction to the republished *Early Stories;* and of course the book *Bowen's Court* here is the chronology, here in the house, the family, the native land, and the history: Elizabeth Bowen abides in that book, deeply in it, and while it was not designed to tell us of herself as apart from it, it joins in, all joins in together now.

There was to have been a new Bowen novel, too. We have its opening chapter. Entitled "The Move-In," it gets straight down to business with the arrival at a (somehow chosen) strange house of a carload of young people and a banging at the door. We are in at the systematic onset of outrage upon a house, of whose already existing, internal, outrages we are receiving hints in counterpoint.

There is not a safe square inch in any of this chapter of preposterous conversation for a single character to move. The dangers signaled in the setting (a sort of lodge at road's end, in the stuffy heat of a July evening growing dark) are the deep psychological tensions that this highly contemporary situation is rapidly and impartially connecting up into an alarm system which the first touch will let loose.

"The Art of Bergotte," written at the request of Peter Quennell for a symposium and never published before among Elizabeth Bowen's own works, treats again, in another form, of the relationship that springs into existence and persists in growth between a novelist and his characters. Here the author is of course Proust and his character Bergotte another author. In the Bowen confrontation, we are guided through the kind of dream-construction that fiction is, a house full of inter-connecting rooms and crossing passages, finally being stopped by its secret door.

"Notes on Writing a Novel" was a piece contributed to John Lehmann's *Orion II* in 1945. Later, Elizabeth Bowen says, she came not to like "their peremptory tone"—but to this reader it seems the natural tone for a writer firing off working directions to herself from the thick of things. They are probing, unadorned and succinct to the point where they could almost serve as passwords between writers. They have the currency today, as far as I can see, of pure gold. "Plot is the knowing of destination." Its object is "the nonpoetic statement of a poetic truth." Characters, she thought, pre-exist for the novelist. "They are *found.* They reveal themselves slowly to the novelist's perception—as might fellow-travelers seated opposite one in a very dimly-lit railway carriage." Among things this taught me that I found most startling: "Nothing physical can be invented."

Curtis Brown has included the "Nativity Play" against the suggestion of some that he not do so "because it is so different from the work expected from Elizabeth Bowen." This seemed to him "a most excellent reason for including it. Herself a many-faceted person, her gifts were many-faceted, too . . . and I think she would have liked to know it was in print."

It was written for her friends and neighbors near Bowen's Court, who wanted a nativity play to perform with organ, chorus and trumpets, narrators and actors, in Limerick Cathedral. The treatment is very much her own, and when I read it first, in Ireland, it seemed to me very Irish. I see now how she made skillful dramatic use of the Irish country people—in Mary and Joseph, the Shepherds, and the Children come to worship the Child—in contrast to the Three Kings in their scene in the royal tent, who are austere philosophers and speak as intellectuals ("We three, who have come to a standstill"); and in contrast again to *them* used the heavenly members of the drama, ranks of Angels and Smaller Angels.

Even behind the wish to make a gift to the neighbors may there have lain another impulse? Elizabeth told, in *Seven Winters*, of the frequent reminders during her infancy from her mother of the unseen presence of angels and of her Guardian Angel, and of the picture on her nursery walls of "The Herald Angels." "My mother wished me to care for angels: I did."

The Cockatoos
By Patrick White

LIFE'S POSSIBILITIES ARE THOSE VERY THINGS ONCE FELT AS DANGERS
New York Times Book Review 19 January 1975: 4, 37

These are six stories (a few are short novels) to do with lives often driven or hopeless, but what they are ultimately about is what might have been.[154] They bring together the possibilities and the impossibilities of human relationships. They happen in Australia, Egypt, Sicily, Greece, where they go off like cannons fired over some popular, scenic river—depth charges to bring up the drowned bodies. Accidentally set free by some catastrophe, general or personal—war, starvation, or nothing more than a husband's toothache—Patrick White's characters come to a point of discovery. It might be, for instance, that in overcoming repugnancies they are actually yielding to some far deeper attraction; the possibilities of a life have been those very things once felt as its dangers. Or they may learn, in confronting moral weakness in others, some flaw in themselves they've never suspected, still more terrifying.

The common barriers of sex, age, class, nationality *can* in uncommon hands operate as gates, which open (for White's characters) to experience beyond anything yet traveled, hope of which may have beckoned from earliest years and gone ignored, only haunting dreams and spoiling the day at hand. Passing us through these barriers is what Mr. White is doing in his writing.

All these stories are studies of ambiguities, of which the greatest is sex. In

"A Woman's Hand," a long-married couple, traveling after the husband's retirement find themselves rather peculiarly put back in touch with two old friends out of their respective pasts—a man for him, a woman for her—representing to each a different turn that had offered itself to their young lives. The wife's wifely solution is simple and disastrous (her bothersome guilt for her own inadequacy is set at rest if she can rearrange other people's lives): instead of letting these two make things awkward, why not marry the misfits off to each other?

This is the longest (86 pages) and in some ways the most sinister of Mr. White's stories treating of the realities and the unrealities of developing human relationships. It is highly symbolic, presided over by peacocks. (According to fable, a peacock's flesh is incorruptible, which made it a symbol of the Resurrection; here it assumes the meaning of liberation from captivity.) In this story, too, the irony lies most clearly in the fact that the true and guiding relationships of our lives—for whatever inhibiting reasons—may never achieve the reality credited the ones that are acknowledged and binding but remain superficial and daunting.

"The Full Belly," a short novel laid in Athens during the German Occupation, takes us deep into the humiliations and terrible intimacies of starving to death as a family: the excruciating pressures of competing unselfishness, the demanding self-sacrifice. Aunt Pronoë radiates a "kind of hectic gaiety" as they dine off boiled dandelions. Aunt Maro takes to her bed, declining ever to eat or drink again: "Remember the children. Who am I to deny them food?" The young boy in question is a musical prodigy, with his ticket to Paris still at the bottom of his handkerchief drawer; he goes on practicing ("play to me, Costika," says the determined martyr, "music is more nourishing than food") and sees everything "with a vividness which only sickness or hunger kindles." Away from the house, there are the temptations coming out of doorways and the cautionary sights lying in the gutters; one old woman greedy for a boy's hand in her bosom—she'd give him a fresh egg; the next old woman lying dead in her decent dress with her emptied purse beside her and her shoes already taken from her feet.

Hunger and shame merge into a single monster. A terrible scene in front of Aunt Maro on her dying day spoils her victory for her: the boy and Aunt Pronoë come to desperate grappling over the plate of sacrificial rice lying untouchable before the icon, struggling together, smashing the plate and losing it all; then Costa is down on the carpet. "If only the few surviving grains. Sometimes fluff got in. Or a coarse thread. He licked the grains. He sucked them up. The splinters of porcelain cutting his lips. The good goo. The blood running. Even blood was nourishment."

"Five-Twenty" is the time a certain car passes in the traffic line every afternoon. The scene is a front porch where sits an aging and childless married couple, a man, now an invalid in a wheel chair and imperious as ever, and his wife, a plain woman whose marriage has been one long deprivation of love, which she has taught herself to handle as best she can; she finds it easier now, being a nurse. She fastens on the 5:20 car as something to watch for and point out: it makes her day. Inevitably, the strands converge. It happens down on the garden path, after the husband leaves her a widow. A flower garden like hers, that's been overtended, and a love like hers, that's gone unnourished too long, may burst out alike into the overwhelming and monstrous.

The characters in most of these stories are men and women whose predicaments are rooted in their pasts, to whom fresh pressure is put by the predicaments of growing old. In "The Night the Prowler," we are plunged into the world of a 17-year-old girl whose state of being has everything to do with today. When Felicity is raped, she hadn't been afraid; she'd even hoped something real and revealing might be going to occur, but the rapist is a failure and pathetic. She sees that her conventional parents, in the shock of what's happened, think mostly of themselves and that the conventional boy she's been about to marry is relieved to get his ring back, and enters into a secret life of her own. Beginning by breaking in and wreaking havoc on a house near hers and like hers, she goes on the loose into the city night with its derelicts, drunks and hoods. She remains alone, roaming the park kicking at lovers, accusing and punishing all the world, shouting up at God "for holding out on me," calling out only to others like herself for guidance, so they can give each other "the strength to face ugliness in any form," which might offer some kind of revelation. She herself becomes the night the prowler. As we see her "whirling in the air above her head a bicycle chain she had won from a mob of leather-jackets," she is like some saint-to-be of the Troubled Young. This story, with all the rawness of today in it, is not without its old progenitors. Felicity's progress through the scarifying world of Sydney nightlife is also a path of self-mortification. She is divested of that pride too; when she comes in the final scene to an abandoned house and finds there a naked, diseased, dirty, solitary old man lying on a mattress at point of death, she has her revelation. It is a stunning story.

A middle-aged Australian couple is on holiday, in "Sicilian Vespers," when the husband gets stuck in their hotel with toothache. Ivy would will herself to feel the pain for him; she believes in the efficacy of love, but suspecting her husband (with his "honest un-Sicilian eyes") believes in it only theoretically. She doesn't confess it to him: "She did not want to damage his affection for her: it was too precious." She is held back in her life, too, by a ghost out of her girlhood riding with her still—father. There seems nothing for it but a deliberate act of adultery with a repugnant American (another hotel guest). In the Cathedral of San Fabrizio, she drags him from the crowd into a side chapel and down onto the marble floor.

If nearly all the stories do end up on the floor, it is, after all, the natural place for humiliation, degradation, lust, despair and hunger to reach their limit. "The Cockatoos" does not—it ends with a smell of cake.

A flock of wild cockatoos makes a descent upon a residential neighborhood, alighting first at one house, then another, arousing jealousies, coveting, intent to murder, and other things, even causing a husband and wife who haven't spoken for years in the same house to break silence—"trapped into comforting each other," they fall into bed "with laughing mouth on mouth." The characters are wayward, rather than driven. Passions fly thick and fast but in a neighborhood level, like the cockatoos themselves, selecting the house they'd like to visit and making their choice of feeding places, setting up no more than a neighborhood commotion.

"The Cockatoos," the only story here that's a comedy, is also the only one in which the sexual aggressor is a man. As Mick (the husband who doesn't speak to his wife) sits straddling the lady who lives down the street (it's Busby LeCornu, who waits for him every day leaning on her gate, and the only time he puts on a hat is to walk through it), they exchange these words—the subject of course, is the cockatoos:

" 'See here Busby . . . I didn't tell you about me birds to have you seduce um away from me.'

"She sighed from within the crook of her arm. 'I don't see why we can't share what doesn't belong to either of us.'

"He was already getting back into his clothes. 'The wife would be disappointed,' he said."

The Letters of Virginia Woolf, Volume II

Edited by Nigel Nicolson and Joanne Trautmann

THE LETTERS OF VIRGINIA WOOLF

New York Times Book Review

14 November 1976: 1, 10, 12, 14, 16, 18, 20

"Life would split asunder without letters," Virginia Woolf wrote in *Jacob's Room*, the high point in this period of her working life. During it—between 1912 and 1922—she wrote 600 of those saving letters. They are published now as Volume II in the projected six being edited by Nigel Nicolson and Joanne Trautmann.

By now, the traumas of her growing up—all those family deaths—are behind her (though never to be forgotten). So is the casting about for the kind of friends she can share her life with—now she knows. She has just married Leonard Woolf.

She writes Lytton Strachey from their honeymoon in Spain; they are walking, talking, and: "My God! You can't think with what fury we fall on printed matter, so long denied us by our writing! I read 3 new novels in two days: Leonard waltzed through the Old Wives Tale like a kitten after its tail."

They come home to Asheham, the house in Sussex—"the best place in the world for reading Shakespeare"—where:

"All the morning we write in two separate rooms. Leonard is in the middle of a new novel . . . but as the clock strikes twelve, he begins to write an article upon Labour for some pale sheet, or a review of French literature for the Times, or a history of Co-operation.

"We sew [sic] articles all over the world—I'm writing a lot for the Times too, reviews and articles and biographies of dead women—so we hope to make enough to keep our horses."

Two milestones were shortly passed in Virginia's life without her awareness, the publication of her first novel, *The Voyage Out*, and the move to Hogarth House. It was to aid in her recovery from this most severe period of insanity that Leonard cast about for a plaything "sufficiently absorbing to take her mind off her work."

"Have you heard about our Printing Press?" Virginia writes to Margaret Llewelyn Davies. "We're both so excited that we can talk and think of nothing else, and I think there's a chance of damaging the Webb influence irretrievably (which is my ambition in life)."

The hand-press, bought in a shop off the street, fitted onto the Woolf's dining room table, and they were teaching themselves how to work it from a 16-page pamphlet that came with it. (A school of printing in Fleet Street had turned them down: they were the wrong age and the wrong class— middle in both, as Leonard wrote in *Beginning Again*.

"We want to start on something very short and very sublime," Virginia writes Lady Robert Cecil. This is exactly the way we want the story of the Hogarth Press told. "I see that real printing will devour one's life," she writes Vanessa, and later goes on: "After 2 hours work at the press, Leonard heaved a terrific sigh and said, 'I wish to God we'd never bought the cursed thing!' To my relief, though not surprise, he added, 'Because I shall never do anything else.' You can't think how exciting, soothing, ennobling and satisfying it is. And so far we've only done the dullest and most difficult part— setting up notice."

"We find we have only 50 friends in the world—and most of them stingy," she writes Lady Ottoline Morrell.[155] "Could you think of any generous people?" She enlists Vanessa's help with the covers. The binding equipment turns up from Cousin Emma Vaughan, though she, with her obsessive concern for German prisoners, naturally had to offer it to a camp of these first.

"Two Stories"—Leonard's "Three Jews," Virginia's "The Mark on the Wall," with woodcuts by Dora Carrington—was printed in an edition of 150 copies, of which the stingy friends bought only 135. In 1918, "Prelude," a 60-page book—was printed on a bigger machine, borrowed, and bound with their own hands in an edition of 300 copies. It had been rejected by all publishers up to now, but Virginia thought Katherine Mansfield "had a much better idea of writing than most." In May 1919, the Hogarth Press was to issue three bound books together: Virginia's "Kew Gardens," John Middleton Murry's "The Critic in Judgment," and Eliot's "Poems"; and Virginia was breaking off a letter with "I must go now and boil some glue."

The Hogarth Press, Asheham and the circle of Bloomsbury—form the real background of the letters. World War I was going on, but we are grateful (knowing that she was to be lacerated by the next world war) to find Virginia comparatively immune. She was spared the great personal losses so many of the English suffered: Leonard was exempt for physical reasons, as were a number of their friends; others were conscientious objectors—two of them, not by chance being Duncan Grant and David Garnett, were farmed out with Vanessa at Charleston. When air raids over London and Sussex got to be a habit, so did the Woolfs' sitting in the cellar; mainly this was boring, with only the servants to talk to. The pinch was noticed when it came to butter and tea and the importing of good paper for the Press.

We are in Bloomsbury when it was young, when the creative juices were running high and there was a heady current of daring in the air. Seen through the eyes of one who helped make it, Bloomsbury is restored to us briefly here, a society every bit its own, brightly conscious of itself, civilized, unsentimental, liberally disposed, not only led by, but thrilled by, their intelligence, young artists and writers wandering in and out of one another's houses in a sort of home-made state of grace. We see the Bloomsburies themselves in their own earliness, before they take on the blur of time and reminiscence:

"Nessa left the room and reappeared with a small parcel about the size of a large slab of chocolate. On one side are painted six apples by Cezanne. Roger [Fry] very nearly lost his senses. I've never seen such a sight of intoxication. He was like a bee on a sunflower."

Mr. Nicolson's policy of editing the letters is to include everything. There is no order but the chronological. The effect is one of profusion like a spacious Edwardian flower bowl being constantly added to out of the advancing garden, useful little zinnias stuck in with the great peonies, spires of delphinium, and the night stock as they come into bloom. The method is appropriate to Virginia Woolf. Side by side may be letters helping Vanessa find a cook, paying her respects to Thomas Hardy for his whole lifetime, sharing whatever she's reading with Lytton ("I read the book of Job last night—I don't think God comes well out of it"), supplying Vanessa with a new list of names for her coming child ("I like a name that has the look of a clear green wave"), asking money for a fund for Eliot so he can get out of the bank, reassuring a young man she's never met, David Garnett, who's apologized for his escapade of breaking into Asheham with a few of his friends, while the Woolfs were away, and making away with the food: "As a matter of fact, we are not at all annoyed—It seems a very sensible thing to do . . . it's a relief to find it was you. . . . Leonard is reading your poems [in manuscript], and says they are the best return you could make for the raid."

Mr. Nicolson in his introduction remarks, "She gives only part of herself to anybody." Moved primarily by natural courtesy, one imagines, she used her gift of the light touch more often than not. But these beautiful, spontaneous letters never underestimate the seriousness of experience, or betray her sense of its magnitude. What she gives in her letters comes from her awareness of the other person, the part of herself, it seems to me, that matters in the other's circumstances. This sensitivity in giving is Virginia Woolf's particular mark: it can guide her to speak from an extraordinary depth of candor. To Saxon Sydney-Turner, friend of her brother Thoby who had died young, she can write:

"I've a feeling that I want somehow to give you back or that some one else should give you back what you lost in Thoby. For I've often thought that you were the one person who understood about him—I mean that his death meant almost more to you and me than to anyone, and I think we shared together some of the worst things. I know anyhow that you helped me then—and often I've known that we both kept him with us, though we did not talk of him."

Just before a violent period of her illness was coming on, she wrote to Margaret Llewelyn Davies about being ill before in a letter that seems to all but lay bare the very mystery of what she suffers. "And I wanted to say that all through that terrible time I thought of you, and wanted to look at a picture of you, but was afraid to ask! You saved Leonard, I think, for which I shall always bless you, by giving him things to do. It seems odd, for I saw you so little, but I felt you had a grasp on me, and I could not utterly sink. I write this because I do not want to say it, and yet I think you will like to know it."

Mr. Nicolson relates that Virginia and Leonard, after the first months, did not often sleep together. He sounds confident, if one wants to stop there. The tenderest letter in the book, the most directly declaring, is a brief one written to Leonard after they had been married for four years, on one of the rare occasions when they were separated.[156]

Be that as it may, what her readers have always known from her writing is that a need for intimacy lies at the very core of Virginia Woolf's life. Besides the physical there are other orders of intimacy, other ways to keep life from splitting asunder. Lightly as it may touch on the moment, almost any letter she writes is to some degree an expression of this passion, of which the eventual work of art was *The Waves*.

So richly present is Vanessa Bell in these letters written to her and about her (Vanessa's outnumber the rest) that it seems odd to realize we never hear her speak in her own voice (obviously, not at all like Virginia's), never read her side of the correspondence, when even her handwriting is brought close to our eyes—with "the quality of a great sheep dog paw—a sheep dog which has been trotting sagaciously through the mud after its lambs all day long." This painter sister was closer even than a sister; Virginia would now and then speak of herself as Vanessa's child, "your first-born." It is possible that Virginia was seeking the maternal in everyone she loved, Leonard included; but in Vanessa she found it.

There's a touching corollary. "I like myself as a child," she writes Vanessa; the letter comes from Cornwall, scene of their childhood visits, where the lighthouse, of *To the Lighthouse*, stands. She writes Saxon, too: "I think how I was a nice little girl here, and ran along the top of the stone walls, and told Mr. Gibbs after tea that I was full to the chin. . . . Do you like yourself as a child? I like myself, before the age of 10, that is—before consciousness sets in." (Compare this with Mrs. Vallance's thoughts in the starlit garden in *Mrs. Dalloway's Party*, the little sequence recently published, but written in these days.)[157]

Vanessa really wanted to hear nothing from her but the latest gossip, Virginia was fond of telling her. "Let me see what I have in my bag for you." Samples:

"I got her [Violet Dickinson] to tell me a series of death bed scenes of the Lyttleton family—the poor old Bishop Arthur L. was pestered to death by them. 'Now you're practically dead, Arthur, you *must* collect yourself and tell us what you see. Don't you feel anything like immortality coming on?'"

"Janet Case still more or less bedridden . . . though she was writing an article upon illegitimacy in Sweden for a newspaper. Downstairs, Emphie was playing very badly on the violin to a party of wounded soldiers. The house is crowded with photographs of old pupils, deceased parents and the

Elgin Marbles . . . Does this convey any of the spirit of Hampstead to you?"

"I think there is a good deal of the priest, it may be of the eunuch, in [Logan Pearsall Smith] . . . He thought it very delightful to extract the flower of Urn Burial, 6 words long, and print it by itself in an exquisite little volume, to carry in the breast pocket, like a scent bottle. He has several of these sentences always on his person, and reads them aloud in a high nasal chant. . . ."

It is most often when she shoots darts at the aristocracy that malice appears; and springing from a rather exceptional insight, it still has a quiver to it. "The other day," she tells Vanessa, "we went to tea with Nelly Cecil, and met old Beatrice Thyme, who is more like a sunburnt tinker who has just had a mug of beer than ever, notwithstanding the death of her mother and nephew. She was as black as a rook, with one very large Bumble Bee, carried out in pearls and sapphires, attached to her throat. She is going to live in lodgings over St. Johns Wood post office, in order to economise; she uses margarine instead of butter, and wears no underclothes. She spends all her time reading family letters, and tying them up in bundles, as they are too many to burn, and all perfectly dull. Nelly is going to economise by living in Henry James' flat. It is wonderful how entirely detached from sanity the aristocracy are; one feels like a fly on a ceiling when one talks to them."

Vanessa sometimes provides the subject herself of gossip around London, but criticism of her is not to be tolerated from holier-than-thou Cousin Dorothea Stephen. Virginia sent her this letter:

"Your view that one cannot ask a friend who has put aside the recognised conventions about marriage to one's house because of outsiders and servants seems to me incomprehensible. You, for example, accept a religion which I and my servants, who are both agnostics, think wrong and indeed pernicious. Am I therefore to forbid you to come here for my servants' sake? . . . I could not let you come here without saying first that I entirely sympathise with Vanessa's views and conduct. If after this, you like to come . . . by all means do; and I will risk not only my own morals but my cook's."

The reckless moment—it lasted hardly longer than that—when Virginia and Lytton Strachey were engaged to marry is forgotten now and they have settled into what Cyril Connolly has called "a Solomon-Sheba relationship," which was to last until Strachey's death. Her letters to him, brilliant as they are, are the only ones in which we might see a touch of self-consciousness. Virginia didn't write drafts for letters, but she may have taken a little more trouble with Lytton's, to make them flash in his face.

When he sends her an essay for his forthcoming *Eminent Victorians*, she writes him of her admiration for ". . . how you weave in every scrap—my God what scraps!—of interest to be had, like (you must pardon the metaphor) a snake insinuating himself through innumerable golden rings—(Do snakes?—I hope so.)"

She needed a little time to adjust to his fame, which blazed up when the book appeared. "I think fame has changed him, as love might," she writes to Vanessa. "He is immensely appreciative, even tender; jumps up and seizes withered virgins like Vernon Lee, and leaves them gibbering with ecstasy." A little later, "He's doing a grand season, with Cunards, Asquiths, and all the rest; completely happy; still, he assures us his soul is untouched; and I think it probably is."

An envy she recognizes in herself, mocks, but continues to feel enters into this and into other letters. But she had something to be envious about in other writers: not their work, but their time, She had reason for envy, in the unfairness of life which robbed her, with abominable suffering, of years of the work she passionately wanted to do, as well as of the children she and Leonard had both wanted to have. (And in reading the letters, we cannot do her the disservice of ignoring what falls between them when the continuity breaks off and the gap appears like a black fissure in bright landscape.)

Recovery was always slow. She wrote to E. M. Forster, in 1922:

"Writing is still like heaving bricks over a wall . . . I should like to growl to you about all this damned lying in bed and doing nothing, and getting up and writing half a page and going to bed again. I've wasted 5 whole years (I count) doing it; so you must call me 35—not 40—and expect rather less from me. Not that I haven't picked up something from my insanities and all the rest. Indeed, I suspect they've done instead of religion. But this is a difficult point."

Virginia Woolf did not use a letter to a friend as a vent for her constant preoccupation with her writing in progress. Her self-discoveries, analyses, her elations and fears, her devastating suffering over every one of her books in turn, all went into the privacy of her diaries, which she had started during this period and was to keep up for the rest of her life. But a passing remark makes a flash in the air sometimes ("I daresay one ought to invent a completely new form [of the novel]" she says to the beginning David Garnett).

It is significant that when she most generously and ardently spoke her mind on writing itself, it was to the young. The marvelous letter she wrote to Gerald Brennan, a young man, new friend, whose letter she was answering on Christmas Day, 1922, comes just at the last of this book. It reads in part:

"One must renounce, you say . . . Ah, but I'm doomed! . . . It is not possible now, and never will be, to say I renounce. Nor would it be a good thing for literature were it possible . . . The human soul, it seems to me, orientates itself afresh every now and then. It is doing so now. No one can see it whole, therefore. The best of us catch a glimpse of a nose, a shoulder, something turning away, always in movement. Still, it seems better to catch this glimpse, than to sit down with Hugh Walpole, Wells, etc., etc., and make large oil paintings of fabulous fleshy monsters complete from top to toe . . . I mean, life has to be sloughed: has to be faced: to be rejected; then accepted on new terms with rapture. And so on, and so on; till you are 40, when the only problem is how to grasp it tighter and tighter to you, so quick it seems to slip, and so infinitely desirable it is.

". . . One must renounce, when the book is finished; but not before it is begun. . . . I was wondering to myself why it is that though I try sometimes to limit myself . . . to the things I do well, I am always drawn on and on, by human beings, I think, out of the little circle of safety, on and on, to the whirlpools; when I go under."

Selected Letters of
William Faulkner
Edited by Joseph Blotner

SELECTED LETTERS OF
WILLIAM FAULKNER
New York Times Book Review 6 February 1977: 1, 28–30

William Faulkner's wife and daughter had said he "would not have wanted such a volume. His personal letters were never remotely intended for publication," and Faulkner himself had written (to Malcolm Cowley): "I don't like having my private life and affairs available to just any and everyone who has the price of the vehicles it's printed in." Thus Joseph Blotner writes in his Introduction to this volume. "So a book of selected Faulkner letters was a logical next step."

The logic has shifted from Faulkner's to Blotner's, but while I suppose we can have little doubt that this fierce guardian of his privacy would have abominated the publication of his letters, we can doubt too that he would have been much surprised at its being done anyway. Publishing personal letters of a genius gone to his grave is a human act of man. And plainly, in Blotner's case, even a reverent act.

Therefore it is good to have the book done by an editor and a publisher who cared about Faulkner the man as well as Faulkner the artist. It's been assembled with taste, the responsible, devoted, and thorough job we would expect from Faulkner's biographer.

Jill Faulkner Summers gave Blotner access and permission to publish letters in her possession, a number of which he'd drawn upon or already published in the biography. Some recipients of letters withheld theirs, in whole or in part. Mr. Blotner doesn't say what proportion of the existing body of letters this absence represents, or name any of their recipients, if indeed he knows all these facts himself. In the letters published, a row of dots indicates where something is omitted, though without a clue of how much—a sentence or half the letter; we aren't told whether it was the recipient or the editor who has cut it. (Blotner says he has excised some things.) "The editor and biographer must take what he can get," he says. The letters are in chronological order, but not numbered, and not bracketed in any way; there is no sectioning by period of time of life or place—it's Oxford to New Orleans to Paris, Hollywood, New York, Stockholm, Egypt, Virginia and all the rest, and home again, from page 3 to page 465, all without an extra one-line space between.[158] If this plan lacks something in imagination, still it is uninterfering.

Faulkner's letters are not "literary" but they are very much letters about writing. They are the letters of a man living in the midst of his own world and his own society and kin, a man who was ardently and all by himself trying to do the thing he most passionately wanted to do, and by necessity earn the family living by it. The greatest number of the letters we have are those to his publishers and agents. "Yours to hand," he customarily begins them. Intimacy was no part of them; they were factual business letters, as telegraphic as an S.O.S., which they often were. We cannot miss the sound of desperation so often underneath: these were letters of life-and-death, about the wherewithal to survive, to keep alive his genius; he was so pressed that he often sent them off without signing them.

In 1932 to his agent Ben Wasson: "I hope to hell Paramount takes Sanctuary. Dad left mother solvent for only about 1 year. Then it is me."

In 1934 he is working on two novels, and writing one short story each month, trying to sell to the Post. "As I explained to you before," he writes to Harrison Smith, "I have my own taxes and my mother's, and the possibility that Estelle's people will call on me before Feb. 1 and also my mother's and Dean's support, and occasional demands from my other two brothers which I can never anticipate . . . Then in March I have . . . insurance and income tax. . . ."

To his agent Morton Goldman, in 1935: "The man who said that the pinch of necessity, butchers' and grocers' bills and insurance hanging over his head, is good for an artist, is a damned fool."

From the start Faulkner could look at his work, and thought an artist ought to, with the objectivity of (as he liked to say) a carpenter who'd built a henhouse. What he *thought* and *felt*, had worked in anguish to convey, must make its appearance in the work itself—it was the hen in the henhouse. But he had to look at all he wrote with recognition of its earning possibilities. "By God I've got to."

He stepped up his pace to two short stories a week—"I don't know how long I can keep it up"—and prophesies that his insurance premiums "will be difficult to meet and perhaps even impossible, unless I should produce a book which the movies would want—which God Himself could not promise Himself to write."

Through all this, when a publisher's comprehension of his problems was so vital, Faulkner's editors at Random House met these letters with unfaltering willingness to advance him money against the future. Faulkner appreciated his luck, which brought him in the course of time to Smith, Robert K. Haas, Saxe Commins, Bennett Cerf, and Albert Erskine. In Hollywood, where he'd go to buy himself time, he wrote the Harold Ober: "If they [Warners] had any judgment of people, they would have realized before now that they would get a damn sight more out of me by throwing away any damned written belly-clutching contract and let us work together on simple good faith and decency, like with you and Random House." Ober, it ought to be said, must have been the most understanding of agents, as well as the most patient.

By 1940, Faulkner writes: "But maybe a man worrying about money can't write anything worth buying." To Haas he says, "I had planned after finishing THE HAMLET, to try to earn enough from short stories by July 1 to carry me through the year, allow me six months to write another novel. I wrote six . . . the sort of pot-boilers which the Post pays me $1,000.00 each for, because the best I could hope for good stories is 3 or 4 hundred . . . but only one of them has sold yet. Now I have not only wasted the mental effort and concentration which went into the trash, but the six months . . . as well as the time since March 15, which I have spent mortgaging my mares and colts one at a time to pay food and electricity and washing and such, and watching each mail train in hopes of a check. Now I have about run out of mules to mortgage."

Then he replies to Harold Ober in 1941 that no, he has no carbon of the story he'd sent. It was a story rewritten from a novel under way and sent "first draft and in haste because I need some money badly."

"In hopes that Post will take it and I can get a check next week, I am trying to make the revision desired from memory, without waiting to get back your copy. If it does not fit, please return your copy, and this revision AIR MAIL and I will get it back the same day. Please sell it for something as soon as you can. I am in a situation where I will take almost anything for it or almost anything else I have or can write."

The Post found the rewrite acceptable and it appeared in May 1942. It was "The Bear."

But threats of oblivion were increasing, and it was during the course of his being rescued from it that Faulkner put down the best things he ever said about his writing in a series of letters to Malcolm Cowley. The correspondence between the two men, later good friends, who had then never met, began in 1944 when Cowley put to Faulkner his idea of a Viking *Portable Faulkner*, to be compiled and edited by him. The story, like all of Faulkner's life, is well-known now, but it remains wonderful. Had it not been for the reemergence of Faulkner's work in the triumphant organization Cowley made of it for this volume, and Cowley's fresh literary insight, which called forth Faulkner's composition of the Compson genealogy called "Appendix/Compson 1699–1945," all Faulkner's work, already out of print then, might be worse than only out of print now—it might be half forgotten.

"I would like the piece," Faulkner initially writes Cowley, "except the biography part. You are welcome to it privately, of course. But I think that if what one has thought and hoped and endeavored and failed at is not enough, if it must be explained and excused by what he has experienced, done or suffered, while he was not being an artist, then he and the one making the evaluation have both failed."

Then to the letter that's the masterpiece: "I'm trying primarily to tell a story, in the most effective way I can think of, the most moving, the most exhaustive. But I think even that is incidental to what I am trying to do . . . I am telling the same story over and over, which is myself and the world . . . I am trying to go a step further [than Thomas Wolfe] . . . I'm trying to say it all in one sentence, between one Cap and one period. I'm still trying, to put it all, if possible, on one pinhead. I don't know how to do it. All I know to do is to keep on trying in a new way. . . . Life is a phenomenon but not a novelty . . . Art is simpler than people think because there is so little to write about. All the moving things are eternal in man's history and have been written before, and if a man writes hard enough, sincerely enough, humbly enough, and with the unalterable determination never never never to be quite satisfied with it, he will repeat them, because art like poverty takes care of its own, shares its bread."

On April 28, 1946, he has the book: "Dear Cowley: The job is splendid. Damn you to hell anyway. But even if I had beat you to the idea, mine wouldn't have been this good. By God, I didn't know myself what I had tried to do, and how much I had succeeded."

We have to fillet this story from where it lies embedded in the chronological pages, spread over a section 51 pages long. It's alongside letters like the kind one to Miss Lida, his mother-in-law, about the flowers in California, their likeness to and difference from the flowers in Mississippi, just because it comes next—telling us something about Faulkner's character but holding us up when we want the next letter to Cowley. The letters, the best in Blotner's book, can better be read in Cowley's own 1966 *Faulkner-Cowley File*, where they appear, along with the other side of the correspondence, in uninterrupted sequence, and where, read thus, they can move you to tears.

But there are values in the chronological order of a special kind, too. When you read the letters above, of all Faulkner has taught himself about what he's doing, you can remember those he wrote back in 1925, when he walked over Europe in the greatest exuberance, planning to make his reputation abroad. He writes his mother, "I have just written such a beautiful thing that I am about to bust—2000 words about the Luxembourg gardens and death."

There are of course other letters in this book, but I have reported mostly on those that have to do with Faulkner's writing, because Mr. Blotner says in his Introduction that "The main purpose of this collection is to provide a deeper understanding of the artist, to reveal as much as possible what one can see in the letters about his art—its sources, intentions, and process of creation. . . ." Those letters that directly speak of his work are marvelous, and so are others that say things obliquely. They make clear that it remained the gift—not its cost in the work or its anguish—but the gift he had that came first with him.

He writes to the novelist Joan Williams in 1953: ". . . And now, at last, I have some perspective on all I have done. I mean, the work apart from me, the work which I did, apart from what I am. . . . And now I realise for the first time what an amazing gift I had: Uneducated in every formal sense, without even very literate, let alone literary, companions, yet to have made the things I made. I dont know where it came from. I dont know why God or gods, or whoever it was, selected me to be the vessel. Believe me, this is not humility, false modesty: it is simply amazement."

Neither was it self-centered. Faulkner's marked sensitivity to others, to their pain, their needs of affection, encouragement, moral support, might have been taken for granted from the evidence of his work. What might not have been so easily guessed was that their gifts as artists brought about a profound response in him.

In the occasional—even rare—letter to a literary peer, his feeling for, appreciation of the writer's gift—not shop talk—is almost sure to be the subject. Just as it is to a young unknown black poet whose manuscripts Faulkner read and helped him with: "Put the passion in it, but sit on the passion. Dont try to say to the reader what you want to say, but make him say it to himself *for* you. I will edit the second one and send it to you when I get it right . . . Your idea in both is all right." ("All right" emerges in Faulkner's letters as his strongest, surest term of praise.) He apparently fell in love with Joan Williams, but the very touching letters to her all carry the current of a continuing wish to encourage her talent—she was in her twenties, just beginning to try to break away from the constrictions of family and write. He gave her his handwritten manuscript of *The Sound and the Fury*—a different sort of present from a bunch of roses.

Faulkner's letters show honesty, fairness and largeness of mind, genuine consideration for others, and compassion; also exhilaration and also despair. They pull no punches. They are in turn funny, sad, angry, desperate, tender, telegraphic, playful, quick in arithmetic and perfect in courtesy, unhappy. But these qualities, in one combination or another, can be found in the letters of a lot of human beings who didn't write *The Sound and the Fury*, "Spotted Horses" and "The Bear." It would deny the author's whole intent, in a lifetime of work and passion and stubborn, hellbent persistence, to look for the deepest revelations he made in his letters.

No man ever put more of his heart and soul into the written word than did William Faulkner. If you want to know all you can about that heart and soul, the fiction where he put it is still right there. The writer offered it to us from the start, and when we didn't even want it or know how to take it and understand it; it's been there all along and is more than likely to remain. Read that.

The Never-Ending Wrong

By Katherine Anne Porter

POST MORTEM

New York Times Book Review 21 August 1977: 9, 29

As this is being written, the Governor of Massachusetts has issued a proclamation calling for a memorial day on Aug. 23, the anniversary of the elec-
trocution of Sacco and Vanzetti in the Charlestown Prison for a holdup and
murder, and his legal counsel has cited "the very real possibility that a
grievous miscarriage of justice occurred with their deaths." It has taken the
law exactly 50 years to acknowledge publicly that it might have made a
mistake. But after that same 50 years, the renowned short-story writer and
novelist Katherine Anne Porter has written a book, *The Never-Ending
Wrong*, also to be published on Aug. 23; and it seems to her that she still
believes and feels today the same as she believed and felt at that time, on
that scene.

This book of 63 pages, a "plain, full record of a crime that belongs to
history" as she states in a foreword, was not intended to establish the guilt
or innocence of Nicola Sacco and Bartolomeo Vanzetti, but rather to examine the guilt or innocence of those on the outside, all those gathered there,
like herself, to see the final scene played out.

"I did not know then and I still do not know whether they were
guilty . . . but I had my reasons for being there to protest the terrible
penalty they were being condemned to suffer; these reasons were of the
heart, which I believe appears in these pages with emphasis."

Her own participation was outwardly of little substance—a matter of
typing letters Sacco and Vanzetti wrote to their friends on the outside, of

showing up in the picket line and going through the motions of being arrested, jailed and bailed out. She knew herself to be largely in the dark about what was really going on. Questions rose out of personal feeling— deeply serious questions. She made some notes. This book, their eventual result, is a searching of a personal experience, whose troubling of the heart has never abated and whose meaning has kept on asking to be understood. The notes of that time have been added to, she says, "in the hope of a clearer statement," but the account is "unchanged in feeling and point of view."

The picket line in which she marched included the poets and novelists Edna St. Vincent Millay, John Dos Passos, Michael Gold, Grace Lumpkin, Lola Ridge.[159] "I wouldn't have expected to see them on the same street, much less the same picket line and in the same jail."

By today's standards, the conduct of these exercises was almost demure. "I never saw a lady—or a gentleman—being rude to a policeman in that picket line, nor any act of rudeness from a single policeman. That sort of thing was to come later, from officers on different duty. The first time I was arrested, my policeman and I walked along stealing perplexed, questioning glances at each other; . . . neither of us wished to deny that the other was a human being; there was no natural hostility between us."

She made notes:

"*Second day:*

"He (taking my elbow and drawing me out of the line; I go like a lamb): 'Well, what have you been doing since yesterday?'

"I: 'Mostly copying Sacco and Vanzetti's letters. I wish you could read them. You'd believe in them if you could read the letters.'

"He: 'Well, I don't have much time for reading.'"

On the day they were all aware that the battle was lost, she said to him, "I expect this will be the last time you'll have to arrest me. You've been very kind and patient and I thank you." "Thank *you*," he replied.

They were bailed out by the same kind soul every time they were put in jail. Edward James, Henry James's nephew, invariably appeared and put up the money for all of them, even those who did not wish to be bailed out, "getting us set free for the next round."

But, it appeared, Sacco and Vanzetti did not trust their would-be rescuers. "Many of the anxious friends from another class of society found [it] very hard to deal with, not to be met on their own bright, generous terms in this crisis of life and death; to be saying, in effect, we are all brothers and equal citizens; to receive, in effect, the reserved answer: No, not yet. It is clear now that the condemned men understood and realized their predicament much better than any individual working with any organization devoted to their rescue." They "knew well from the beginning that they had every reason to despair, they did not really trust these strangers from the upper world who furnished the judges and lawyers to the courts, the politicians to the offices, the faculties to the universities, who had all the money and the influence. . . ."

What they may not have known, says Miss Porter, was that "some of the groups apparently working for them, people of their own class in many cases, were using the occasion for Communist propaganda, and hoping only for their deaths as a political argument. I know this because I heard and I saw."

It was a certain Rosa Baron who made this clear through her own words to Katherine Anne Porter, who had expressed the hope that even yet the men might be saved. This "grim little person" headed Miss Porter's particular group during the Boston demonstrations, and what Miss Porter remembers most vividly through the 50 years of time are Rosa Baron's "little pinpoints of eyes glittering through her spectacles at me and her shrill, accusing voice: 'Saved? Who wants them saved? What earthly good would they do us alive?'"

"In the reckless phrase of the confirmed joiner in the fight for whatever relief oppressed humanity was fighting for, I had volunteered 'to be useful wherever and however I could best serve,' and was drafted into a Communist outfit all unknowing."

The account of her experience is clear and has the strength of an essence, not simply by virtue of its long distillation. It is clear through candor, as well. Miss Porter says of herself at this time:

"I was not an inexperienced girl, I was thirty-seven years old; I knew a good deal about the evils and abuses and cruelties of the world; I had known victims of injustice, of crime, I was not ignorant of history, nor of literature; I had witnessed a revolution in Mexico, had in a way taken part in it, and had seen it follow the classic trail of all revolutions. Besides all the moral force and irreproachable motives of so many, I knew the deviousness and wickedness of both sides, on all sides, and the mixed motives—plain love of making mischief, love of irresponsible power, unscrupulous ambition of many men who never stopped short of murder, if murder would advance their careers an inch. But this was something very different, unfamiliar."

"There were many such groups, for this demonstration had been agitated for and prepared for many years by the Communists. They had not originated the protest, I believe, but had joined in and tried to take over, as their policy was, and is. . . ."

Being used! The outrage she had found unbearable for the men on trial in court she realized was also the outrage being inflicted on those who had tried to help them, and on others more vulnerable than picketers in their line.

Through Miss Porter's eyes we see their wives, Rosa Sacco and Luigia Vanzetti, being marched through the streets at the head of a crowd massing at a rally, on the night before the scheduled execution.

". . . and the two timid women faced the raging crowd, mostly Italians, who rose at them in savage sympathy, shouting, tears pouring down their faces, shaking their fists and calling . . . 'Never you mind, Rosina! You wait, Luigia! They'll pay, they'll pay!' It was the most awesome, the most bitter scene I had ever witnessed."

But the crowd assembled to await the execution itself was in contrast "a silent, intent assembly of citizens—of anxious people come to bear witness and to protest against the terrible wrong about to be committed, not only against the two men about to die, but against all of us, against our common humanity. . . ." The mounted police galloped about, bearing down on anybody who ventured beyond the edge of the crowd and rearing up over their heads.

"One tall, thin figure of a woman stepped out alone, a good distance into the empty square, and when the police came down at her and the horse's hoofs beat over her head, she did not move, but stood with her shoulders slightly bowed, entirely still. The charge was repeated again and again, but she was not to be driven away." Then she was recognized as Lola Ridge, and dragged to safety by one of her own; the strange, poignant, almost archetypical figure Miss Porter describes must remain indelible.[160]

After that night was all over, the picketers themselves were given a trial; that is, "simply our representatives" (Edna St. Vincent Millay was one) "were tried in a group in about five minutes." The judge "portentously, as if pronouncing another death sentence, found us guilty of loitering and obstructing traffic, fined us five dollars each, and the tragic farce took its place in history."

The aftermath was numbness, silence; disbanding and going home. Miss Porter writes: "In all this I should speak only for myself, for never in my life have I felt so isolated as I did in that host of people, all presumably moved in the same impulse, with the same or at least sympathetic motive; when one might think hearts would have opened, minds would respond with kindness, we did not find it so, but precisely the contrary."

Katherine Anne Porter's fine, grave honesty has required of her, and she has given it to this account, a clarity of statement, a respect for proportion, an avoidance of exaggeration, a watchfulness against any self-indulgence, and a regard for uncompromising accuracy.

But the essence of the book's strength lies in its insight into human motivations, and the unique gifts she has brought to her fiction have been of value to her here as well—even in the specific matter of her subject. The theme of betrayal has always run in a strong current through her work. The worst villains of her stories are the liars, and those most evil are the users of others. Elements of guilt, the abandonment of responsibilities in human relationships, the betrayal of good faith and the taking away of trust and love are what her tragic stories are made of. Betrayal of justice is not very different from the betrayal of love.[161]

And a nation is a living human organism. Like a person, a nation sometimes needs years to comprehend the full scope and seriousness of some wound that has happened to it or some act it has brought itself to perform. Though an experience in its history may have hurt it deeply, left a scar and caused it recurring discomfort and bad dreams, yet only slowly may its meaning grow clear to the sufferer.

"The never-ending wrong," says Miss Porter, "is the anguish that human beings inflict on each other," which she pronounces at the end "forever incurable." And she finds that "The evils prophesied by that crisis have all come true."

As no concerned citizen can argue, this book she has written out of her own life is of profound contemporary significance.

Essays of E. B. White

By E. B. White

DATELESS VIRTUES

New York Times Book Review 25 September 1977: 7, 43

"As a writing man," E. B. White says in one of these essays, "The Ring of Time," "I have always felt charged with the safe-keeping of all unexpected items of worldly or unworldly enchantment, as though I might be held personally responsible if even a small one were to be lost."

This collection, chosen by himself, grouped under heads of "The Farm," "The Planet," "The City," "Florida," "Memories," "Diversions and Obsessions" and "Books, Men, and Writing" has managed in many ways to carry out that charge.

The pieces range over something like four decades; there are 31 (8 have never appeared in book form), chosen as "the ones that have amused me in the rereading, along with a few that seemed to have the odor of durability clinging to them," he writes in a foreword.[162]

So we come back in this volume to the timeless story of his two young geese—the sisters Liz, the laying fool, and Apathy, who laid three eggs, then quit, and the old gander and the young gander—a story funny, fierce and sad. We are happily back with some of the author's friends we don't want to forget. Here's Mr. Strunk, the author of *The Elements of Style*, delivering his oration on brevity to the class: "Rule Thirteen. Omit needless words! Omit needless words! Omit needless words!" And here's Fred the dachshund in his act of birdwatching, "propped luxuriously against a pillow, as close as he could get to the window, his great soft brown eyes alight with expectation and scientific knowledge. . . . Spotting a flicker or a starling on the wing, he would turn and make a quick report. 'I just saw an eagle go by,' he would say. 'It was carrying a baby.'"

We can have a reunion with the St. Nicholas League of our youth—motto: "Live to Learn and Learn to Live"—a thinning crowd of whose graduates still carry on in the world of arts and letters today. It receives an affectionate tribute from the author, who won his Silver Badge and Gold Badge as an essayist from the start, although his honorable mention was for a drawing called "The Love of a Mother Rabbit."[163]

"Farewell, My Lovely!"—"my lovely" is the Model T Ford—takes many of us back, and it's a joyride, but nostalgia is not its destination. It is a celebrating piece, and what it celebrates is man's pristine relationship with his car. There was no automatic transmission or automatic anything else in the Model T; in sole charge was the owner with a crank in his hand, the throttle waiting for his finger, the low-speed pedal for his opening stomp.

"The driver of the old Model T was a man enthroned."

"The last Model T was built in 1927, and the car is fading from what scholars call the American scene—which is an understatement," says Mr. White, "because to a few million people who grew up with it, the old Ford practically *was* the American scene."

It had, in fact, a domestic status. It demanded the care of some creature of farm life. "A Ford was born naked as a baby, and a flourishing industry grew up out of correcting its rare deficiencies and combatting its fascinating diseases." The Jiffy patching kit came "with a nutmeg grater to roughen the tube before the goo was spread on. Everybody was capable of putting on a patch, expected to have to, and did have to."

Man could handle its habits. When you Got Results with your crank, as it was called, "Often if the emergency brake hadn't been pulled all the way back, the car advanced on you the instant the first explosion occurred and you would hold it back by leaning your weight against it. I can still feel my old Ford nuzzling me at the curb, as though looking for an apple in my pocket."

The odor of these pieces is not the stale one of nostalgia, but the fresh one of evocation. It is thus that he calls up those summers when his father took the family to camp on a lake in Maine:

"Summertime, oh, summertime, pattern of life indelible, the fadeproof lake, the woods unshatterable, the pasture with the sweetfern and the juniper forever and ever, summer without end. . . . It seemed to me, as I kept remembering all this, that those times and those summers had been infinitely precious and worth saving."

In this collection, Mr. White has made such scenes as the summers of "the American family at play" fadeless for us. The fact that the essays are not presented with chronological order in mind is its own evidence that indelibility of memory is not something attached to dates, is not dependent on the grudging mercies of change. It has to do with the meaning at the core of remembered experience. The losable item.

In his fine piece on traveling by railroad, he writes: "If our future journeys are to be little different from flashes of light, with no interim landscape and no interim thought, I think we will have lost the whole good of journeying and will have succumbed to a mere preoccupation with getting there. I believe journeys have value in themselves, and are not just a device for saving time—which never gets saved in the end anyway."

The writing is itself dateless as a cloudless sky, because the author has dateless virtues. For one, he sees so well. We owe the beauty of the reports from Maine, of land and sea, of season and hour, and particularly of animal and bird, to his remarkably accurate eye. (He also, of course, has an accurate inner eye, out of which he looks at man.)

Describing a physical act in the happening can daunt or even stop many a writer, but E. B. White brings before our eyes a boy carrying a two-handled cauldron of boiling stew down the swaying vertical ladder, from the galley of a ship going to Alaska during a storm at sea. It's a double triumph for E. B. White—first carrying the cauldron down without spilling it (for he was the boy) and then describing it by some equally tricky feat of balance and daring. (As he says, he writes by ear.)

He also brings a coon down a tree at twilight: here, the result is poetic:

This performance "has a ritualistic quality, and I know every motion, as a ballet enthusiast knows every motion of his favorite dance. The secret of its enchantment is the way it employs the failing light, so that when the descent begins, the performer is clearly visible and is a part of day, and when, ten or fifteen minutes later, the descent is complete and the coon removes the last paw from the tree and takes the first step away, groundborne, she is almost indecipherable and is part of the shadows and the night. The going down of the sun and the going down of the coon are interrelated phenomena; a man is lucky indeed who lives where sunset and coonset are visible from the same window."

One of the biggest losable items was a city. "Here Is New York," written in 1948, Mr. White brackets among the essays in this collection that "have been seriously affected by the passage of time and now stand as period pieces." "The last time I visited New York," he writes in his 1977 Foreword, "it seemed to have suffered a personality change, as though it had a brain tumor as yet undetected."

The piece brings us the band playing in the Mall in Central Park on a summer night, the listeners "attentive, appreciative," while the strollers passing to and fro "behave considerately respecting the musical atmosphere." "It is a magical occasion, and it's all free."

Harlem is "a racial unit," like the other units of the city he enumerates, happy in remaining intact. "The Bowery does not think of itself as lost; it meets its peculiar problem in its own way. . . ." "In the slums are poverty and bad housing, but with them the reassuring sobriety and safety of family life." He speaks of "the nightly garden party of the vast Lower East Side—and on the whole they are more agreeable-looking hot-weather groups than some you see in bright canvas deck chairs on green lawns in country circumstances. It is folksy here. . . ."

"The city has to be tolerant," he concludes, "otherwise it would explode in a radioactive cloud of hate and rancor and bigotry. If the people were to depart even briefly from the peace of cosmopolitan intercourse, the town would blow up higher than a kite. In New York smoulders ever race problem there is, but the noticeable thing is not the problem but the inviolate truce." And "The city at last perfectly illustrates . . . the perfect demonstration of non-violence."

Indeed, what New York was once able to do, able to promise and bestow, able to seem and to be, constituted a feat, and had the breathtaking quality of a feat. Mr. White might almost have been summing it up in a symbolic way in his description, in another essay, of the young bareback rider he watched working out in the winter quarters of John Ringling North's circus in Sarasota. Just as he thought "It is a miracle that New York works at all. The whole thing is implausible," of the young rider circling her ring in "the balance of the performance" seeming superior to the laws of gravity, he thought—he knew—"She will never be as beautiful as this again."

E. B. White wrote of New York as a lover, not as a prophet, but he always had that gifted eyesight. He saw the loved object in the motion of time, and he noted along with the glow the shadows and some foreshadows.

We know now that the future itself is a losable item on this planet. "I would feel more optimistic about a bright future for man if he spent less time proving that he can outwit Nature and more time tasting her sweetness and respecting her seniority." This is Mr. White in his garden, in a spring when the nuclear test bans were being broken: "The character of rain has changed, the joy of watching it soak the waiting earth has been diminished, and the whole meaning and worth of gardens has been brought into question."

He finds pertinence and timeliness in Thoreau—it is *Walden*'s hundredth birthday: "In the brooding atmosphere of war and the gathering radioactive storm, the innocence and serenity of his summer afternoons are enough to burst the remembering heart, and one gazes back upon that pleasing interlude—its confidence, its purity, its deliberateness—with awe and wonder, as one would look upon the face of a child asleep."

What joins all these essays together is the love held by the author for what is transitory in life. The transitory more and more becomes one with the beautiful. It is a love so deep that it includes, may well account for, the humor and the poetry and the melancholy *and* the dead accuracy filling the essays to the brim, the last respects and the celebrations together.

There is a melancholy running through nearly all these pieces, at times surfacing, at other times running deep like Alph the sacred river.[164] It is not the kind of melancholy that leaves us in the end depressed. This may be due to the lyric quality irrepressible in Mr. White's writing, it may be due also to its prevailing sanity. Also to the author's recognition of nonsense, which occurs in the world and shows up in his writing as naturally as melancholy runs alongside humor. We welcome the appearance of his wanton parenthesis as we would a bird that alights on the windowsill. (Wanton parenthesis sounds like a bird's name, might be a bird seen by one of Mr. Forbush's tipsters for the "Birds of Massachusetts" celebrated in an essay.)

Finally, Mr. White is our best authority on humor, in addition to being its practitioner, and his essay "Some Remarks on Humor" is durable by double rights. It deserves to stand for many more years ahead, not least because it hitches humor to truth-telling. Rereading it this time, though, I paused at the end, where Mr. White agrees with Mark Twain that "we never become really and genuinely our entire and honest selves until we are dead. . . . People ought to start dead, and they would be honest so much earlier." I didn't really agree with these experts. It's by living on, it seems me now, that the way of real honesty lies. The realest possible honesty is come by, attained, earned if you like, by continuing. I'd put up these essays in evidence. Honesty is of human birth: it must breathe, and keep restoring itself. It seems to do quite well in the salty air of Maine.

Selected Stories

By V. S. Pritchett

A FAMILY OF EMOTIONS

New York Times Book Review 25 June 1978: 1, 39–40

This great and fascinating writer is about the age of our century and has written short stories most of his way through it.[165] With their abundance, they are of equally remarkable variety: Where would one look for the typical Pritchett story? But one always finds this—that any Pritchett story is all of it alight and busy at once, like a well-going fire. Wasteless and at the same time well fed, it shoots up in flame from its own spark like a poem or a magic trick, self-consuming, with nothing left over. He is one of the great pleasure-givers in our language.

Pritchett himself has said that the short story is his greatest love because he finds it challenging. The new collection makes it clear that neither the love nor the challenge has let him down.

As ever, the writing spouts with energy. Dialogue, in constant exchange, frisks like a school of dolphin. These are *social* stories: Life goes on in them without flagging. The characters that fill them—erratic, unsure, unsafe, devious, stubborn, restless and desirous, absurd and passionate, all peculiar unto themselves—hold a claim on us that is not to be denied. They demand and get our rapt attention, for in their revelation of their lives, the secrets of our own lives come into view. How much the eccentric has to tell us of what is central!

Once more, in the present volume, the characters are everything. Through a character Pritchett can trace a frail thread of chivalry in the throatcutting trade of antique collecting. Through a character he finds a great deal of intrigue in old age. The whole burden of "The Spree" is grief and what his character is ever to do with it. Paradox comes naturally to Pritchett, and he has always preferred, and excelled in, the oblique approach; and I think all these varying stories in today's book are love stories.

One is called "The Diver." Panicking as his initiation into sex confronts him in the middle-aged French-woman lying "naked and idle" on her bed—who mocks him with "You have never seen a woman before?"—the young English boy is surprised by his own brain beginning to act: He hears himself begin answering her with a preposterous lie. He is into another initiation—he is becoming a story writer as he stands there quaking. "It was her turn to be frightened." All being squared, the woman back in her earlier character of "a soft, ordinary, decent woman," that is when his heart begins to throb. "And everything was changed for me after this."

Of these 14 stories—chosen from four volumes published over the last nine years—"The Diver" is not the only one here to suggest that, in times of necessity or crisis, a conspiracy may form among the deep desires of our lives to substitute for one another, to masquerade sometimes as one another, to support, to save one another. These stories seem to find that human desire is really a *family* of emotions, a whole interconnection—not just the patriarch and matriarch, but all the children. All kin, and none of them born to give up. If anything happens to cut one off, they go on surviving in one another's skins. They become something new. In fact, they become storytellers.

In "Blind Love," when Mr. Armitage employs Mrs. Johnson, two people have been brought together who have been afflicted beyond ordinary rescue. Mr. Armitage is blind; Mrs. Johnson has a very extensive and horrifying birthmark. Beneath her clothes, "She was stamped with an ineradicable bloody insult." When she was young and newly married, her husband had sent her packing for the horror of its surprise, for her having thus "deceived" him. Now, "as a punished and self-hating person, she was drawn to work with a punished man. It was a return to her girlhood: Injury had led her to injury." In the love affair that grows out of this doubleness, blindness and deceiving are played against each other, are linked together—as though each implied the other. How much does each really know? We watch to see what hurt does to vision—or *for* vision; what doubt does to faith, faith to doubt. These two magnetized people have selves hidden under selves; they have more than one visible or invisible skin. After they reach and survive a nearly fatal crisis of ambiguous revelation, the only possible kind, we see them contentedly traveling in tandem. "She has always had a secret. It still pleases Armitage to baffle people." But they are matched now in "blind love": They depend on each other altogether.

"The Marvelous Girl" is a double portrait. One side is blind love, love in the dark. The obverse side is a failed marriage in clear view. (It failed because "even unhappiness loses its tenderness and fascination.") A husband, from the back of a large audience, can see his wife seated on a stage in the glare of the light and the public eye, "a spectator of his marriage that had come to an end." She looks "smaller and more bizarre." When the lights suddenly go out in the auditorium, the darkness "extinguished everything. It stripped the eyes of sight. . . . One was suddenly naked in the dark from the boots upward. One could feel the hair on one's body growing and in the chatter one could hear men's voices grunting, women's voices fast, breath going in and out, muscles changing, hearts beating. Many people stood up. Surrounded by animals like himself he too stood up, to hunt with the pack, to get out."

On the stairs he comes by accident up against his wife: "He heard one of the large buttons on his wife's coat click against a button on his coat. She was there for a few seconds: It seemed to him as long as their marriage."

Still in the dark, and like a dream, comes his discovery—it is his pursuit— of "the marvelous girl." And afterward, when the lights come on again, "they got up, scared, hot-faced, hating the light. 'Come on. We must get out,' he said. And they hurried from the lighted room to get into the darkness of the city."

We read these stories, comic or tragic, with an elation that stems from their intensity. In "When My Girl Comes Home" Pritchett establishes a mood of intensification that spreads far around and above it like a brooding cloud, far-reaching, not promising us to go away. We are with a family in England 10 years after the last World War as they face the return of a daughter, gone all this time, who is thought to be a prisoner of the enemy. Hilda, "rescued" at last from Japan, where she had not, after all, been tortured and raped but had done very well for herself, brings on a shock as excruciating as it is gradual when her shifting and cheapening tales begin to come out.

The youngest boy muses: "We must have all known in our different ways that we had been disturbed in a very long dream. We had been living on inner visions for years. It was an effect of the long war. England had been a prison. Even the sky was closed, and, like convicts, we had been driven to dwelling on fancies in our dreary minds. In the cinema," he says, and that cloud begins to reach overhead, "the camera sucks some person forward into an enormous close-up and holds a face there yards wide, filling the whole screen, all holes and pores, like some sucking octopus that might eat up an audience rows at a time . . . Hilda had been a close-up like this for us when she was lost and far away."

In the shock of reunion, the whole family—several generations and their connections—sees appearing, bit by bit, the evidence that all of them have been marred, too, have been driven, are still being driven and still being changed by the same war. Alone and collectively, they have become calloused as Hilda has been and, in some respect of their own, made monsters by their passage through an experience too big for them, as it was too big for Hilda—for anyone.

"Hilda had been our dream, but now she was home she changed as fast as dreams change," the boy tells us. "She was now, as we looked at her, far more remote to us than she had been all the years when she was away."

Finally, it is not Hilda's errant life in Japan but the "rescue," the return to the family circle, that wrecks her imperviousness. It wrecks the life at home, too. When the young narrator finds himself alone at the end with Hilda, "I wanted to say more. I wanted to touch her. But I couldn't. The ruin had made her untouchable."

None of the stories is livelier than these new stories of Pritchett's written of old age. Old bachelor clubman George is militant, astringent, biting, fearsomely grinning, in training with his cold baths, embattled behind his fossilized anecdotes, victoriously keeping alive ("he got up every day to win") on the adrenalin of outrage and of constituting himself a trial and a bore to everyone. But afraid. Afraid not of the North wind but of the East wind, afraid not that the Arch Enemy will get him but that the building will be sold out from under him.

" 'O God,' he groaned loudly, but in a manner so sepulchral and private that people moved respectfully away. It was a groan that seemed to come up from the earth, up from his feet, a groan of loneliness that was raging and frightening to the men around him. He had one of those moments when he felt dizzy, when he felt he was lost among unrecognizable faces, without names, alone, in the wrong club, at the wrong address even, with the tottering story of his life, a story which he was offering or, rather, throwing out as a lifeline for help."

What wins out over George is not the East wind or the Arch Enemy but the warm arms of a large, drinking, 40-year-old woman with a kind disposition and a giggle for his indignation, who "drops in" ("What manners!") out of his past that he had thought safely sealed behind anecdotes. She was the woman the old man had admired once "for being so complete an example of everything that made women impossible."

It is thus that he faces "the affronting fact that he had not after all succeeded in owning his own life and closing it to others; that he existed in other people's minds and that all people dissolved in this way, becoming fragments of one another, and nothing in themselves. . . . He knew, too, that he had once lived, or nearly lived."

Of all the stories of desiring, and of all the stories in this collection, "The Camberwell Beauty" is the most marvelous. It is a story of desiring and also of possessing—we are in a world of antique-shop keepers—and of possessing that survives beyond the death of desiring. It is a closed world, one that has its own hours, its own landscape inside nighttime warehouses, its edges the streets beneath the sodium lights. It has its own breed of people, its own language, its codes and spies and secrets and shames, jealousies, savageries, fantasies. And like some fairy tale itself, it has its own maiden, carried off and shut up and, you and I would think, wanting to accept rescue, but provided with a bugle to play if this should threaten.

"It broke my heart to think of that pretty girl living among such people and drifting into the shabbiness of the trade," says the young man—he is also of the trade—who discovers her and loses her when an old man named Pliny carries her off for himself and shuts her up in his shop. The boy cannot forget how she had written her name in the dust of a table top and left it unfinished: "I S A B—half a name, written by a living finger in the dust."

The young man is left "with a horror of the trade I had joined." He abhors "the stored up lust that seemed to pass between things and men like Pliny." It is not long before "the fever of the trade had come alive in me: Pliny had got something I wanted." The end is unescapable—for all, that is, who are connected with the trade.

"The Camberwell Beauty" is an extraordinary piece of work. Densely complex and unnervingly beautiful in its evocation of those secret, packed rooms, it seems to shimmer with the gleam of its unreliable treasures. There is the strange device of the bugle—which, blown by Isabel, actually kills desire. All the while the story is filled with longing, it remains savage and seething and crass and gives off the unhidable smell of handled money.

Most extraordinarily of all, it expresses, not the confusion of one human desire with another, not sexuality confused with greed, but rather the culmination of these desires in their *fusion*.

"How unreal people looked in the sodium light," the defeated boy thinks as he walks in the street at the story's end. Or by the light of their obsessions.

Each story's truth is distilled by Pritchett through a pure concentration of human character. It is the essence of his art. And, of course, in plain fact, and just as in a story, it is inherent in the human being to create his own situation, his own plot. The paradoxes, the stratagems, the escapes, the entanglements, the humors and dreams, are all projections of the individual human being, all by himself alone. In its essence, Pritchett's work, so close to fantasy, is deeply true to life.

The Collected Stories of Elizabeth Bowen

By Elizabeth Bowen

SEVENTY-NINE STORIES TO READ AGAIN

New York Times Book Review 8 February 1981: 3, 22

It is not unusual for a period of neglect to follow upon a good writer's death. Elizabeth Bowen, the Anglo-Irish author of nine distinguished novels, six collections of superb short stories and five other books of criticism, memoirs and other nonfiction, died in 1973. Certainly she will command a perpetuity of readers, many of whom have followed and loved her work for 50 years.[166] But her books have not been easy to come by since her death. For this one feels she would have been sorry; her turn of mind was always toward the young, especially the writers to come, and she would have particularly liked her books to take their chances with them. And in their behalf, it could be asked: What writer now coming after her could fail to be nourished by her work, exhilarated by her example? She wrote with originality, bounty, vigor, style, beauty up to the last. Her old publisher and friend Alfred Knopf does an important service for Elizabeth Bowen's readers everywhere in bringing out this present volume of *Collected Stories*.[167] Angus Wilson provides it with an appreciative introduction, generous with personal feeling, valuable for its knowledge of her life and the changing times in which she wrote. He is well situated to give a critical perspective from which to view her work today.

The appearance of all 79 stories in one volume makes several new pleasures possible. The famous stories we know in their own right are seen here in the context of their original book editions. To see anew these bright stars set among their own constellations, to read again "Mysterious Kôr" in company with "Summer Night," "The Happy Autumn Fields," "Ivy Gripped the Steps" and "The Demon Lover" is to experience in its full force that concentration of imaginative power which was hers.

We can gain, too, a truer perception of its nature. Her work was in very close affinity with its time and place, as we know. She recalled, in a preface to her *Early Stories* when they were republished 25 years later, that her story "Daffodils" "overflowed from uncontainable pleasure in the streets of St. Albans on one March afternoon." The lyric impulse was instinctive with her.

In "Her Table Spread," we're at a dinner party in a remote Irish castle overlooking an estuary on a rainy night; in the estuary is the rare sight of a visiting English destroyer. The heiress Miss Cuffe, 24 but "detained in childhood," is "constantly preoccupied with attempts at gravity, as though holding down her skirts in a high wind." And now the destroyer will possibly land, and the officers, uninvited as they are, might still quite naturally call upon the castle. They are momently expected by Miss Cuffe. There is irrepressible excitement, rocketing hilarity at the dinner party. Candles blaze in the windows, there are wet peonies on the table, through the windows can be seen the racing lantern—Miss Cuffe is out there waving signals—and now the piano is playing: the visiting English concert pianist—this was to have been the occasion to allow *him* to meet the heiress—has been asked for a Viennese waltz. At moments notes can be heard through the gales of sympathetic conversation. A whole welcoming world is being made out of that wet, lonely, amorous Irish night.

They are all asleep at the end, even the bat in the boathouse; while the rain goes on falling on the castle, and below in the estuary the destroyer, still keeping to itself, is steaming its way slowly out to sea.

As it ends the story can be seen to be perfect, and the perfection lies in the telling—the delicacy, the humor, above all the understanding that has enveloped but never intruded upon it, never once pricked the lovely, free-floating balloon.

Elizabeth Bowen's awareness of place, of *where she was*, seemed to approach the seismic; it was equaled only by her close touch with the passage, the pulse, of time. (Not only what o'clock it was: She used to say, "I am the same age as our century," a fact she enjoyed.) There was a clock in every story and novel she ever wrote; those not in running order were there to give cause for alarm. Time and place were what she *found* here. Her characters she invented, in consequence.

The lyric impulse itself, which goes loose in the world, is anywhere and everywhere; any lucky human being may be its instrument. Elizabeth Bowen, however, was—and was from the start—a highly conscious artist. Being alive as she was in a world of change affected her passionately. The nature and workings of human emotions magnetized her imagination; with all her artist mind she set forth to comprehend, and thus capture, human motives—men's, women's and children's. Time and place that she was so aware of, sensitive to, conveyed to her: situation. Human consciousness meant urgency: drama. Her art was turned full range upon a subject: human relationships.

Writing did not take for Elizabeth Bowen the direction or the form of "self-expression." From the first, she wrote with enthrallment in the act of writing itself. The imaginative power to envision a scene—acute perception, instinctive psychological insight, in an intensified form—was her gift. It became the greatest gift of an artist who was profoundly happy to give the rest of her life to fathoming it.

The passage of time has deactivated "The Needlecase." There are no longer "fallen women," so designated, whose doom it was to earn their living by sewing dresses for other women in other women's houses, poor souls, taking their meals upstairs from a tray. The story dates, and is only mentioned because it constitutes the exception in the 79. The others don't date and will not; their subjects are major.

"The Disinherited" is one of a number of Bowen stories of the dislocations arising from social and psychological disturbance. Davina, young, rebellious, without money, living off an aunt and cadging money from the baleful chauffeur, leads a life of mortification and uncertainty. "Had she had sphere, space, ease of mind, she might have been generous, active, and even noble." She and the young wife of a university professor from the raw new housing development, unlikely friends, team together for an evening, borrowing money from the rude chauffeur, driving through the uncertain autumn night under the strain of lost maps, changed plans, undelivered messages, toward a supposed party. Stood up at the first rendezvous, the two women eventually blunder into the right but unfamiliar house, which is not prepared for their coming:

Lying on the settee at an angle to the fire, "an enormous, congested old lady slept with her feet apart, letting out stertorous breaths. Her wool coatee was pinned over the heaving ledge of her bust with a paste brooch in the form of a sailing-ship, and at each breath this winked out a knowing ray. Her hands, chapped and knouty, lay in the trough of her lap. Half under her skirts a black pair of kitchen bellows lay on the marble fire-kerb. There was not much more furniture in the room.

" 'That is Mrs. Bennington, who takes care of me. She's so nice,' " says Oliver, their host.

This story of a long and misspent evening, in which everything is at cross purposes, miscarries, is misdirected, and every intention seems as lost to the world and as in the way as old Mrs. Bennington, is a turning kaleidoscope of shifting, fragmented lives. The startling moment when Prothero, the chauffeur, comes into view seated before the table in his quarters and writing a letter gives us the interlocking piece. Nothing so far has come up in the story as true, as straightforward and brutally lined out, as plain and simple and never to be changed or subject to change, as Prothero's letter addressed to a woman named Anita, which is the full account of how and why he murdered her. At the end of his long day he writes the letter and then burns it in the stove; he writes it every night and burns it. "So his nights succeeded each other." What interlocks the fragments is the cause of their being—it is the bursting power of despair.

Prothero's letter is an example of the extraordinary tour de force of which Elizabeth Bowen was capable. Her imaginative power to envision a scene is almost hallucinatory here; it makes one feel that she might have put herself within the spell of its compulsion. I think it is a fact that she knew out of her experience how close great concentration could come to the hallucinatory state. That a story *has* a life of its own she would be the first to grant.

How closely she brings "The Disinherited" home to us today! She published it first in 1934.

Her sensuous wisdom was sure and firm; she knew to its last reverberation what she saw, heard, touched, knew what the world wore in its flesh and the clothing it would put on, how near the world came, how close it stood: in every dramatic scene it is beside us at every moment. We see again how pervasive this knowledge was through her stories.

And firmly at home in the world, Elizabeth Bowen was the better prepared to appreciate that it had an edge. For her, terra firma implies the edge of a cliff; suspense arises from the borderlines of experience and can be traced along that nerve. Her supernatural stories gave her further ways to explore experience to its excruciating limits, through daydream, fantasy, hallucination, obsession—and enabled her to write as she did about World War II.

In the unsurpassable "Mysterious Kôr," her most extraordinary story of those she wrote out of her life in wartime London, the exalted, white, silent, deserted other city of Kôr occupies the same territory as bombed-out London through the agency of the full moon at its extreme intensity. In "The Happy Autumn Fields" a direct hit in an air raid has opened a woman's house and displaced the present as she lies on her bed; it lets in instead a walking party of her family of 50 years ago on a momentous day in bright fall in a different country; young twin sisters, her ancestors, cement their lives together with a pledge of love promised to be undying. The bomb victim transfers her life.

Of all the stories, it is "Summer Night" that I return to. Not only Emma, bidding her husband good night, driving stockingless through the Irish evening to an assignation with her lover; not only her little daughter Vivie at home, jumping frenzied up and down on her bed like a savage with snakes chalked all over her; but all the characters in "Summer Night" might be in nothing but their skins, exposed to the night.

Aunt Fran, wrapping the savage in an eiderdown, instructs her to kneel and say her prayers. Then in her own room, "the room of a person tolerated," the woman makes her outcry at last: "It's never me, never me, never me! . . . I'm never told, never told, never told. I get the one answer, 'nothing.' " "There are no more children: the children are born knowing," thinks the despairing woman. "And to wrap the burning child up did not put out the fire. You cannot look at the sky without seeing the shadow, the men destroying each other. What is the matter tonight—is there a battle? This is a threatened night." (And war is indeed raging, of course, across the water.)

Emma arrives at her lover Robinson's house; she must wait—he has callers; they see her car. There is Justin, the tormented abstainer from life, starved for talk, who will find no other way out of his urgency than by writing a letter after he gets home to tell Robinson, who is never likely to read it, "The extremity to which we are each driven must be the warrant for what we do and say." (It had been a mistake, of course, to ask him before leaving that unpremeditated question, "What is love like?") Robinson is a solid, ordinary, coarse-grained, incurious man. Justin's sister Queenie knows this. Her deafness is not a barrier to her awareness of what goes on between people in a room. The night has carried her back to her girlhood, to the chaste kiss of her one and only love. The serene, unhearing, aging lady at the story's end is drifting to sleep on her pillow: "This was the night she knew she would find again."

This unforgettable story, the most remarkable of a group of longer ones, is an example of the sheer force of the Bowen imagination. What other writer could have *propelled* the whole of "Summer Night" from its rushing headlong start to its softly subsiding conclusion, like a parachute let down to earth gently folding in its petals? The turmoil of all these passionate drives, private energies that in their own directions touch yet never can merge or become one together, is yet all magical; their passions become part of the night sky and part of the world in wartime.

All carries its momentum; this is the truth that seems to emerge. Time is *passing*. Places are *changing*. This is what speed is. There is suspense everywhere, all the time: we are living in its element, racing to keep up with being alive. And in the end there is no rest or help for anything but what lies in the acceptance of love.

That the collection richly reconfirms the extraordinary contribution Elizabeth Bowen has made to English letters alleviates the pain one feels at their neglect since her death. Their vitality is their triumph. Read them again. You may even, like me, discover that there is one you have never read before, though I thought I knew her work. "A Day in the Dark," her last story, is the last one in the book. It is a growing girl's story of the accidental way in which one learns the name of the deepening feeling that one has come to live with. An old lady tauntingly remarks to her, "Oh, I'm sure you're a great companion to him." What she has felt for her uncle is love. "There was not a danger till she spoke." Like many another of these stories, it is its own kind of masterpiece.

The Oxford Companion to Children's Literature

Edited by Humphrey Carpenter and Mari Prichard

INNOCENCE, SIN AND J. D. SALINGER

New York Times Book Review 19 August 1984: 3, 17

Humphrey Carpenter, a writer, broadcaster and biographer (of Tolkien, C. S. Lewis and others) and Mari Prichard, a writer and teacher, took over *The Oxford Companion to Children's Literature* after its original editors, Peter and Iona Opie, had begun preparation on it. The Opies (Mr. Opie died in 1982) were of course the preternatural gatherers: tirelessly over 30 years they searched out and brought or subdued into print every existing scrap of song and game and bit and tag of folklore that childhood offered. Now they were gathering its literature and were already "advanced" in the new work. The editors have dedicated the book to the memory of Peter Opie.[168]

So it is not surprising whose spirit presides over it rather than that of Sir Paul Harvey, the editor of *The Oxford Companion to English Literature*. In that Companion, Mr. Carpenter and Miss Prichard say, "inclusion of a particular book or author is in itself an indication of merit. . . . This method was one we found did not serve us. The popular and the classic are especially hard to keep separate in the field of children's literature, and a book might often rate more space as a phenomenon than it could for literary merit."

By the Opies' day, the editors say, "Children's books became the focus of countless courses, conferences, centers of study, and works of scholarship. It might be said that the subject reached maturity." (Could it also be said that the heart of a reader sinks?) The Companion has been carried out as the Opies probably themselves designed it: "a reference book dealing equally with both English and American children's books and authors, and including articles on traditional materials, illustrators, characters from cartoons, films, radio and television, and the recurrent subjects of children's reading-matter." The editors have expanded this to include "very brief summaries of the state of children's literature in all languages, countries, or continents for which we could find reliable information readily available. And while specifically educational writing and publishing was outside our brief, we decided to deal with early examples of the main categories of school-book, and with some of the educational ideas that affected the juvenile literature of their time." This is exactly what happened.

The editors go on to say that "since the length of entries for particular works could not do the work of criticism for us, we have often had to be more explicit in our judgments, and have made brief comments on what seem to us the qualities or failings of many of the authors and books included."

Yet the length of the entries, which greatly varies, does in effect stand for an estimation, a comparison, when for instance Enid Blyton, of the Noddy books ("the most commercially successful British children's author of the 20th cent.") gets 178 lines; Walter de la Mare gets 60 ("His writing . . . defies classification"). As for their judgments, the editors tell us, they have benefited from the advice sought from librarians, educationalists, historians of children's literature, publishers and booksellers. The resulting focus is sharpest, over all, on "reputation." "Reputation" tells us what is "popular." These editorial evaluations can hardly escape merging into those of the publishing industry. The Enid Blyton entry reports, as many entries do, explicitly on the author's income, which "by the late 1950s was reportedly over £100,000 per annum." "Her output . . . by the late 1940s totalled more than 30 books a year, and was keeping a whole host of London publishers busy." It continues: "What all agree on, both friends and detractors, is that she had outstanding business acumen and knew how to make the very most out of what talent she had." In contrast, take Andrew Lang, whose entry concludes: "For all his huge output and great success, Lang never accumulated any wealth, and up to the end he wrote in order to make a living." (So, children, which would you rather be?)

Certainly the debt owed by literature to publishing is boundless and always will be. Beginning with John Newbery, London bookseller, "acknowledged to be the first British publisher of children's books 'to make a permanent and profitable market for them,'" such men—generally from publishing families that often lasted for generations—have given courage, daring and sometimes selfless nobility to their calling. But this doesn't mean that the history of writing books and the history of publishing and selling them can be told as the same story. If it can, it had better be called the Companion to the Publishing of Children's Literature.

The desolation of those earliest books designed for children! There were always dolorous schoolbooks. Henry VIII's royal proclamation that Lily's Latin grammar, and no other, should be taught in schools "remained in effect for two centuries." In the 17th century, Latin was still being taught as a spoken language, to be used in conversation in class; a child learned how to say, in Latin, that he desired to be taught it, even if it meant he had to be flogged. Noah Webster's *American Spelling Book* carried a frontispiece of Noah Webster looking so frightful that it was known as the Porcupine Edition. But how much kinder were the schoolbook's lessons than those taught by Mrs. Sherwood in *The Fairchild Family*.

When the Fairchild children quarreled, "their father 'whipped their hands' with a rod, and 'made them stand in a corner of the room, without their breakfasts.' That evening he takes them to a gibbet where there hangs the body of a man who killed his brother in a quarrel: 'the body had not yet fallen to pieces, although it had hung there some years . . . The face of the corpse was so shocking that the children could not look upon it.'" The Companion quotes the *Dictionary of National Biography:* " 'Most children of the English middle-class born in the first quarter of the 19th century may be said to have been brought up on *The Fairchild Family*." Mr. and Mrs. Fairchild "take every opportunity presented by domestic life to draw religious lessons for the children, who are taught that since the sin of Adam and Eve 'all their children, who have been born in their likeness, are utterly and entirely sinful: so that of ourselves we cannot do a good thing, or think a good thought. . . . There is no such thing as being saved, except by the Lord Jesus Christ, through his death: nothing you can do yourselves can save you.' "

Of course the Companion is a reference book, with listings in alphabetical order, but you realize as you browse that it's putting together in your head, and aligning it, the whole history of children's literature. You see clearly how the crushing darkness of the Fairchild books and their kind was disrupted by the blaze of newness that came with *Alice's Adventures in Won-*

derland.[169] In *Alice*, Lewis Carroll "revolutionized children's literature with its fantastic plot and brilliant use of nonsense. Characters . . . had never before been created for the amusement of children, without any moral purpose whatsoever," and the editors quote the children's book historian Harvey-Darton's words: "It was the coming to the surface, powerfully and permanently, the first un-apologetic appearance in print, for readers who sorely needed it, of liberty of thought in children's books."

Certainly this tide of moral tales rose up in opposition too to the fairy tale. The imagination had to be fought the same as sin. Or maybe it *was* sin. Children got their hands for the first time on the fairy tale by way of the sensational chapbooks. *Tom Thumbe, His Life and Death* crept in among *The Wandering Jew, Mother Shipton, Mother Bunch's Closet Newly Broke Open*, and *The Life of John Knox*—each about 20 lines long. But the Brothers Grimm, Hans Andersen and the wonderful undertakings of Andrew Lang reached them at last.

Fairy tales were of course oral creations; they were a long time coming into print at all. (The very earliest Cinderella of all was Chinese—in a ninth-century book of folk tales.) What may or may not be surprising is that fairy tales were not designed for children. The Companion tells what high fashion they were in 17th-century France. Madame de Sévigné wrote of a visitor's sharing with her salon "the sort of story that was now entertaining the ladies of Versailles: it involved a green isle, a most beautiful princess with fairies breathing continually upon her, a prince of delights, and a journey in a crystal globe. The tale took a full hour to tell."

Fairy tales are the oldest of sources for stories, and the search for sources obviously means nearly everything to the editors in preparing this reference book. They make the same search for the sources of fiction and poetry. Where did the author get his idea?—or more often the word is "incentive." The most plausible answer to them is a previously existing book by another author. It is one thing for editors to say, as they do correctly as far as it goes, that Lewis Carroll parodies Isaac Watts's songs in *Alice*. But they also suggest this: "Blake undoubtedly knew the poetry of Isaac Watts, and his 'Songs of Innocence' may possibly have been a consequence of Watts's suggestion that 'some happy and condescending genius' should one day produce a great work on the model of his own *Divine Songs*."

The source of fact is helpful as a source, but is sometimes insufficient. Was there a real King Arthur? I liked the editors doing their best for King Arthur: "The fact that a number of people born in Celtic . . . areas of the

British Isles in the late 6th and early 7th cents. were named Arthur, a name not previously recorded in Britain, suggests that some national figure called Arthur existed at that time, or shortly before." And there's a consolation, if not: "Arthur was still a figure of some importance in Tudor times; Henry VII called his first son Arthur, so that if this prince had not died in 1502, there would have been a real King Arthur."

(There can also be an incentive for *not* writing. Why didn't Milton go on with the Arthuriad he contemplated? Because "he abandoned this plan in favor of *Paradise Lost.*")

The horrors of the fiction written about the youth of today are the fault of J. D. Salinger; he is blamed in full for starting the "teen-age novel," which is their category for *The Catcher in the Rye.*[170] This category is, in their view, "a modern phenomenon. Until the middle of the 20th cent. children who grew out of juvenile books were expected to read popular classics, such as the works of Dickens and Scott; before graduating to more demanding adult novels." All in one, they blame Salinger and condescend to Dickens—a condescension they repeat elsewhere.

Humorists, I believe, receive more put-downs than other authors. E. B. White's *Stuart Little* is called "brilliant in its way" but "too eccentric for the doyenne of American children's librarians, Anne Carroll Moore, who tried to persuade White not to publish it. (She also disliked *Charlotte's Web.*)" The doyenne's effort might have been intimidating to another *librarian*, but fortunately for the life of the book, Mr. White is a writer. (And so is Charlotte.)[171]

Edward Lear gets a demerit for his limericks because he didn't really try: "For the most part he did not attempt to produce a surprising or comic rhyme in the last line, but merely repeated the last word of the first line."[172]

What is original is perhaps the real suspect. Source unknown.

The handsome volume is copiously supplied with 137 illustrations well selected from the wide range of books and publications. The cover bears an Edmund Dulac watercolor illustration from Cinderella, in color. Inside you find work from Bewick to Sendak. And artists of course are written up in the text as well as the authors.

Lear, who was both, is given disappointing treatment on both counts. Writing of *The Owl and the Pussy-Cat*, the editors mention only its 20th-century illustrations; his own, the original ones, are ignored. Most importantly, Lear's work is all one, verse and drawings the two halves of the same creation. The drawings of Lear's described elsewhere in the book are called "distortions." Of John Tenniel there's a long account, but it takes on the personal terms that simply suggest the editors don't like him: He was blind in one eye, he married but there were no children and his wife died two years later; he would not use live models or draw from nature; and "the excellence of his published drawings owes much to the wood engravers who interpreted them." Randolph Caldecott too is given generous space; much of it has to do with the money involved in publishing. For illustrating a certain trio of books, "Caldecott received a royalty of one penny per copy, which was very high considering that the books sold at only one shilling." A suggestion of what the editors would like to be able to tell their readers about artist's work may lie in what they say about the illustrations of *Outside Over There:* "The book is Sendak's eeriest and most disturbing work; he offers no explanation of its significance."

But the *pictures* are here in the book, ample in size and well reproduced. Without any need of editorial help, they speak for themselves.

Columns and columns and columns have been devoted to chapbooks, tracts, primers, catechisms, Sunday School stories, boys' stories, girls' stories, pony stories, doll stories, Nonconformist poems, moral tales, cautionary tales, courtesy books, books of instruction, manuals in trades. There are travelogue story books: *Three Vassar Girls in England* came from us as a tit for tat to Mrs. Trollope. But not only these, not only *books*. Literature covers television and radio, comic strips, Punch and Judy shows, pantomimes, puzzles. All that can be catalogued is here. At what point can the reader ask the Companion. is this category really necessary? Is "full-time hack writer" necessary? Or Blue Peter, a twice-weekly television magazine program intended for children between five and 12 years old, broadcast from the BBC since 1958?

The extravagant attention the editors pay Walt Disney and his employment of children's tales and stories is perhaps the prime example of their position on the importance of what is "phenomenal." He is given space for his own statement: "Be commercial. What is art, anyway? It's what people like. So give them what they like. There's nothing wrong with being commercial."

But there's something better, to which children's literature has given itself naturally—works of art, of imagination and taste that sprang from and were nourished by fairy and folk tales, myths, Mother Goose. There are operas and ballets performed on stage, television and film—*The Sleeping Beauty, Cinderella, The Firebird, Alice in Wonderland.*

Like every worthwhile reference book, the Companion provides a lovely grab bag of small treasures:

¶ The most notable feature of E. Nesbit's *The Children's Shakespeare* was that the illustrations showed all the characters as children, excepting King Lear.

¶ When *The Babes in the Wood* was made a pantomime, Robin Hood and his Men came in at the end and rescued the children from death.

¶ When *Chatterbox* magazine appeared as a protest to the penny dreadfuls, J. M. Barrie, an early subscriber, went out into a field, dug a hole, and buried all of his hoard of penny dreadfuls.

¶ "Among those dressed in Fauntleroy outfits in Britain were the infant Compton Mackenzie and A. A. Milne. . . . On the stage the part of Cedric was usually played by a girl, though a New England production in the early 1900s featured the ten-year-old Buster Keaton in the title role."

Clearly, no expense, no drudgery of research and selection and compiling, were spared in the preparation of this volume. And now—to whom will it be a companion? The librarians, the collectors, the rare book dealers, the thesis writers—yes, all of these from now on. But hardly for the children. It *is* a reference book, but if a book concerns children, it should be theirs to consult. One hoped for a book they could read and live with that would nourish their love for reading.[173] Perhaps it's my failure to recognize it in the Companion, but I felt the absence of some central love of literature that would have warmed the whole.

Appendix A
Books Reviewed by Eudora Welty
Alphabetical by Author

Amorim, Enrique. Trans. Richard L. O'Connell and James Graham Luján. *The Horse and His Shadow*. New York: Charles Scribner's Sons, 1943.

Babbitt, Natalie. *Knee-Knock Rise*. Illus. by the author. New York: Farrar, Straus & Giroux, 1970.

Baker, Dorothy. *Our Gifted Son*. Boston: Houghton Mifflin, 1948.

Biddle, George. *Artist at War*. New York: Viking Press, 1944.

Bowen, Elizabeth. *The Collected Stories of Elizabeth Bowen*. New York: Alfred A. Knopf, 1981.

———. *Pictures and Conversations*. New York: Alfred A. Knopf, 1975.

Brock, Betty. *No Flying in the House*. Illus. Wallace Tripp. New York: Harper & Row, 1970.

Colette, Sidonie Gabrielle. *Short Novels of Colette*. New York: Dial Press, 1951.

Collis, Maurice. *The Land of the Great Image*. New York: Alfred A. Knopf, 1943.

Carter, Margery Allingham. *The Galantrys*. Boston: Little, Brown, 1943.

Cartier-Bresson, Henri. *About Russia*. New York: Viking Press, 1974.

Crane, Aimee. *G. I. Sketch Book*. New York: Penguin Books, 1944.

Derleth, August, ed. *Sleep No More*. New York: Farrar & Rinehart, 1944.

Dillard, Annie. *Pilgrim at Tinker Creek*. New York: Harper's Magazine Press/Harper & Row, 1974.

Dinesen, Isak. *Last Tales*. New York: Random House, 1957.

Du Bois, William Pène. *Otto and the Magic Potatoes*. Illus. by the author. New York: Viking Press, 1970.

Engel, Lehman. *Words With Music*. New York: Macmillan, 1972.

Faulkner, William. *Intruder in the Dust*. New York: Random House, 1948.

———. *Selected Letters of William Faulkner*, ed. Joseph Blotner. New York: Random House, 1977.

Appendix A

Forster, E. M. *The Life to Come and Other Short Stories.* New York: W. W. Norton, 1973.
———. *Marianne Thornton: Domestic Biography.* New York: Harcourt, Brace, 1956.
Fredenthal, David, and Richard Wilcox. *Of Men and Battle.* New York: Howell, Soskin, 1944.
Gilbert, Enrique Gil. Trans. Dudley Poore. *Our Daily Bread.* New York: Farrar & Rinehart, 1943.
Guareschi, Giovanni. *Don Camillo and His Flock.* New York: Pellegrini & Cudahy, 1952.
Guterman, Norbert. *Russian Fairy Tales.* Illus. Alexander Alexeieff. New York: Pantheon, 1945.
Hale, Nancy. *Between the Dark and the Daylight.* New York: Charles Scribner's Sons, 1943.
Hamilton, Patrick. *The West Pier.* Garden City, N. J.: Doubleday, 1952.
Harris, Bernice Kelly. *Sweet Beulah Land.* New York: Doubleday, Doran, 1943.
Heard, H. F. *The Great Fog and Other Weird Tales.* New York: Vanguard Press, 1944.
Jenkins, Dorothy H., and Helen Van Pelt Wilson. *Enjoy Your House Plants.* New York: M. Barrows, 1944.
Johannesson, Eric O. *The World of Isak Dinesen.* Seattle: U of Washington P, 1961.
Kästner, Erich. *The Little Man and the Big Thief.* Illus. by Stanley Mack. New York: Alfred A. Knopf, 1970.
Kertész, André. *J'Aime Paris.* New York: Grossman/Viking Press, 1974.
Kroll, Harry Harrison. *Waters Over the Dam.* Indianapolis: The Bobbs-Merrill Company, 1944.
Langbaum, Robert. *The Gayety of Vision: A Study of Isak Dinesen's Art.* New York: Random House, 1965.
Leatherman, LeRoy. *Martha Graham: Portrait of the Lady as an Artist.* New York: Alfred A. Knopf, 1967.
Macaulay, Rose. *The World My Wilderness.* Boston: Little, Brown, 1950.
Macdonald, Ross. *The Underground Man.* New York: Alfred A. Knopf, 1971.
Macken, Walter. *The Green Hills and Other Stories.* New York: Macmillan, 1956.
McDermott, Francis, ed. *The Western Journals of Washington Irving.* Norman, Okla.: U of Oklahoma P, 1944.
Mizener, Arthur. *The Saddest Story: A Biography of Ford Madox Ford.* New York and Cleveland: World Publishing Co., 1971.
Morris, Edita. *Three Who Loved.* New York: Viking Press, 1945.
Oxford Companion to Children's Literature, eds. Humphrey Carpenter and Mari Prichard. New York: Oxford U P, 1984.
Perelman, S. J. *Baby, It's Cold Inside.* New York: Simon & Schuster, 1970.
———. *Crazy Like a Fox.* New York: Random House, 1944.
———. *The Most of S. J. Perelman.* New York: Simon & Schuster, 1958.

———. *Westward Ha! Around the World in 80 Clichés.* Illus. by Al Hirschfeld. New York: Simon & Schuster, 1948.

Perrault, Charles. *French Fairy Tales.* Illus. Gustave Doré. New York: Didier, 1945.

Peters, Fritz. *The World Next Door.* New York: Farrar Straus, 1949.

Porter, Katherine Anne. *The Never-Ending Wrong.* Boston: Atlantic-Little, Brown, 1977.

Pritchett, V. S. *Selected Stories.* New York: Random House, 1978.

Riefenstahl, Leni. *The Last of the Nuba.* New York: Harper & Row, 1974.

Russell, John. *Henry Green: Nine Novels and an Unpacked Bag.* New Brunswick, N. J.: Rutgers U P, 1961.

Salinger, J. D. *Nine Stories.* Boston: Little, Brown, 1953.

Sansom, William. *Fireman Flower and Other Stories.* New York: Vanguard, 1945.

———. *South.* New York: Harcourt, Brace, 1950.

———. *The Stories of William Sansom.* Boston: Little, Brown, 1963.

Saxon, Lyle, Edward Dreyer, and Robert Tallent, eds. *Gumbo Ya-Ya, A Collection of Louisiana Folk Tales.* Boston: Houghton Mifflin, 1946.

Shipton, Clifford K. *Roger Conant, A Founder of Massachusetts.* Cambridge, Mass.: Harvard U P, 1945.

Steedman, Marguerite. *But You'll Be Back.* Boston: Houghton Mifflin, 1942.

Stewart, George R. *Names on the Land: A Historical Account of Place-Names in the United States.* New York: Random House, 1945.

Summers, Hollis. *City Limit.* Boston: Houghton Mifflin, 1948.

Undset, Sigrid. *True and Untrue and Other Norse Tales.* Illus. Frederick T. Chapman. New York: Alfred A. Knopf, 1945.

Wagenknecht, Edward, ed. *Six Novels of the Supernatural.* New York: Viking Press, 1944.

Warner, Sylvia Townsend. *A Garland of Straw.* New York: Viking Press, 1943.

Wescott, Glenway. *Apartment in Athens.* New York: Harper & Brothers, 1945.

West, Jessamyn. *The Witch Diggers.* New York: Harcourt, Brace, 1951.

White, E. B. *Charlotte's Web.* New York: Harper & Brothers, 1952.

———. *Essays of E. B. White.* New York: Harper & Row, 1977.

White, Patrick. *The Cockatoos.* New York: Viking Press, 1975.

Whitehead, Henry S. *Jumbee and Other Uncanny Tales.* Sauk City, Wis.: Arkham House, 1944.

Woolf, Virginia. *Granite and Rainbow.* New York: Harcourt, Brace, 1958.

———. *A Haunted House and Other Short Stories.* New York: Harcourt, Brace, 1944.

———. *The Letters of Virginia Woolf Volume II 1912–1922.* Eds. Nigel Nicolson and Joanne Trautmann. New York: Harcourt Brace Jovanovich, 1976.

Appendix B

The Eye of the Story: Selected Essays and Reviews

Bowen, Elizabeth. *Pictures and Conversations*. New York: Alfred A. Knopf, 1975. 269–76.

Dinesen, Isak. *Last Tales*. New York: Random House, 1957. 261–63.

Faulkner, William. *Intruder in the Dust*. New York: Random House, 1948. 207–11.

———. *Selected Letters of William Faulkner*, ed. Joseph Blotner. New York: Random House, 1977. 212–20.

Forster, E. M. *The Life to Come and Other Short Stories*. New York: W. W. Norton, 1973. 227–34.

———. *Marianne Thornton: Domestic Biography*. New York: Harcourt, Brace, 1956. 221–26.

Macdonald, Ross. *The Underground Man*. New York: Alfred A. Knopf, 1971. 251–60.

McDermott, Francis, ed. *The Western Journals of Washington Irving*. Norman, Okla.: U of Oklahoma P, 1944. 177–81.

Mizener, Arthur. *The Saddest Story: A Biography of Ford Madox Ford*. New York and Cleveland: World Publishing Co., 1971. 241–50.

Perelman, S. J. *Baby, It's Cold Inside*. New York: Simon & Schuster, 1970. 238–40.

———. *The Most of S. J. Perelman*. New York: Simon & Schuster, 1958. 234–38.

Stewart, George R. *Names on the Land: A Historical Account of Place-Naming in the United States*. New York: Random House, 1945. 182–89.

White, E. B. *Charlotte's Web*. New York: Harper & Brothers, 1952. 203–06.

White, Patrick. *The Cockatoos*. New York: Viking Press, 1975. 264–68.

Woolf, Virginia. *Granite and Rainbow*. New York: Harcourt, Brace, 1958. 190–92.

———. *The Letters of Virginia Woolf Volume II 1912–1922*. Eds. Nigel Nicolson and Joanne Trautmann. New York: Harcourt Brace Jovanovich, 1976. 193–202.

Notes

1. The 19 September 1942 *Saturday Review of Literature* was a special "Deep South" issue edited by David Cohn of Greenville, Mississippi, containing pieces by Cleanth Brooks, Robert Penn Warren, Phil Stone, Howard Odum, and others. For a discussion of the issue see Introduction.

2. Peter Breughel, the Elder, Flemish painter of the sixteenth century. Welty is perhaps reminded of Breughel's *Children's Games* (1560), one of many crowded panoramic landscapes. See also note 76 for *The Witch Diggers*. Painting was among Welty's subjects at Mississippi State College for Women (1925–27), and she often uses painterly language to describe a writer's style.

3. Symbols, Welty says, "must come about organically, out of the story" (Peggy Whitman Prenshaw, *Conversations with Eudora Welty*, Jackson: U P Mississippi, 1984, 84). Of the symbols in her own writing, she says, "They occur naturally; they are organic. If they're a part of the story, they come readily to hand when you want them, and as often as you want them, and you use them with a proper sense of proportion, and with as light a touch as possible" (Prenshaw 52). The Harris review is only Welty's second, but she clearly identifies the particular weaknesses in the writing.

4. Welty's first collection, *A Curtain of Green* (1941), contained 17 stories; her later collections had only seven or eight stories each.

5. *Between the Dark and the Daylight* was Hale's fifth book, all edited by Maxwell Perkins for Scribner's. Her third novel, *The Prodigal Women* (1942) had been a financial and critical success.

6. This is the earliest of Welty's reviews for which an extant typescript is preserved in the Welty Collection at the Mississippi Department of Archives and History. For a full description of the collection see Suzanne Marrs, *The Welty Collection* (Jackson: U P Mississippi, 1989). Hereafter cited, for example, as MDAH WC18, Marrs 68. The fourteen editorial changes from Welty's typescript are mostly deletions to

tighten and shorten the review. The translator's name is moved from the first paragraph to the headnote. The following paragraph preceding Welty's concluding sentence was cut to fit the review onto the page with three others under the title "The Latest Works of Fiction":

"At first glance the exotic quality of the book may make it alien to our dull demands—think of our usual 'novel of the soil.' Lushness startles you, but it will reward you. The women are like fruits, flowers, jaguars, and yet from the moment of their arrival at the settlement that has been made ready for them, when 'from under the parasols in the middle of the boat came the incessant chatter of women: laughter delicate as the singing of birds, little chirps and cries, dreamy talk,' they are wholly of the common humanity too. There is no dim, farsighted quality in the men or in their plan. Their hope is bound up in the immediacy of perception, and the power of their bodies to directly respond. The vigor and thrust of this book are fundamental things" (MDAH WC18, Marrs 68).

7. In her first paragraph, Welty uses her favorite words, *love, passion,* and *power* to summarize the essence of the novel. For a discussion of the words, *imagination, love, communication,* and *passion* in selected nonfiction by Welty see Michael Kreyling, "Words into Criticism: Eudora Welty's Essays and Reviews," *Eudora Welty: Critical Essays,* ed. Peggy Whitman Prenshaw (Jackson: U P of Mississippi, 1979) 411–22.

8. The following paragraph was cut from the typescript for the published review:

"This novel is presented almost completely to the eye—like a dance. We see action instant, unhesitating, forthright, graceful, without words—far too quick and complete for words—before a backdrop ever-present and completely clear and vivid. There are the serious, decorative principals, the suffering comic figure of the old mother wandering on and off, the chorus of gauchos when the stage is darkened and a little red fire glows out, the dramatic, symbolic figure of the stallion towering over all" (MDAH WC18, Marrs 68).

9. A carbon typescript, apparently an early version, includes a third paragraph and a continuation of the second-to-last paragraph that are not in the published review. Much of the information in these excised portions is included elsewhere in the review, suggesting that the typescript may be an early version that was subsequently revised by Welty. The typescript includes six other descriptive phrases or quotations that are later deleted, probably by the *NYTBR* editor, including the following sentence at the end of the second-to-last paragraph: "The sights of festivals and processions, of ballets and coronations, of the elephants 'stuffing their mouths in a glad greedy way' or war-elephants whirling swords in the trunks in the sunset glow—all is given us in a full light; we can see, and trustingly, in this book, to our heart's content" (MDAH WC18, Marrs 68).

10. The unfulfilled possibilities of the meeting of the king and the friar and their failure to profit from the opportunity must have reminded Welty of her story "A Still Moment" (1942) in which three historic characters, itinerant Methodist preacher

Lorenzo Dow, bandit James Murrell, and artist John Audubon, meet on another famous pathway, the Natchez Trace, for a brief and equally futile moment. There are further similarities between Collis's novel and Welty's story.

11. Welty is well aware of the power of fairy tales. She had just published *The Robber Bridegroom* (1942), a fantasy of folklore, fairy tale, and mythology on the Natchez Trace, and *The Wide Net* (1943), stories also set along the Natchez Trace filled with dream, illusion, folk and fairy lore.

12. Carter's Mr. Campion mystery novels were published under the name Margery Allingham. *The Galantrys* was published as Carter's *Dance of the Years* in England the same year.

13. Daily *New York Times* reviewer Orville Prescott also complains that "characters may speak for the author, but not the author for the characters," 13 Oct. 1943: 21.

14. At the time Welty was reviewing Warner's *A Garland of Straw* and *The Galantrys*, publishers were pressing Welty to revise the story "Delta Cousins" into a full-length novel. Reviews of her second collection of stories, *The Wide Net* (published 23 Sept. 1943), complained that technique obscured realism. For a discussion of Welty's difficulties with such critical challenges and how they probably drew her attention to stylistic weaknesses in the books she was reviewing, see Michael Kreyling, *Author and Agent: Eudora Welty and Diarmuid Russell* (New York: Farrar Straus Giroux, 1991) 100–15.

15. *Tomorrow* was a monthly magazine of essays, poetry, fiction, and book reviews owned and edited by Eileen J. Garrett and published by Creative Age Press in New York from 1941–51. Garrett states in her first editorial that she wishes "to know what each man who writes and dreams and creates, is thinking about, and by what structural process of thought he has arrived at building his own intellectual world . . . [her writers] will operate with truth and freedom within these pages" (September 1941: 2). Welty's story "At the Landing" was published in *Tomorrow*, April 1943. One of the editors, Katherine Woods, reviewed *The Wide Net* in the same issue as Welty's review of Warner's stories (54). A review of *The Best American Short Stories, 1943* follows Welty's review of *A Garland of Straw*, and Welty's story "Asphodel" is singled out as "a ballet of a story, gracefully choreographed, subtly costumed, tenuous and persistent as a dream." H. D. Vursell, the reviewer and a *Tomorrow* editor, writes that "Asphodel" "will remain all his life long with the reader who approaches it quietly" (November 1943: 53).

16. Francisco de Goya made a series of engravings depicting first-hand the Napoleonic invasions of Spain 1808–14 (*The Disasters of War*), illustrating the violence of the war with dramatic realism. Welty may be thinking specifically of the series of six small panels of "Capture of the Bandit Margarota [by the monk Pedro de Zaldivia]" that is in the permanent collection of the Art Institute of Chicago where Welty went often while she was a student at the University of

Wisconsin in the late 1920s. Welty also recalls seeing a Goya exhibition. It may have been the New York Metropolitan Museum of Art acquisition of twenty-nine drawings of *The Disasters* in 1935 or a 1955 exhibit of Goya's work shown in New York, Washington, and San Francisco. Welty says she traveled to New York for a week to ten days "every chance I got."

17. A comparison of the published review with the carbon typescript shows thirty-four substantive changes to delete superfluous description and amplification. Welty's original opening paragraph (deletions in italics) illustrates the typical compression of her review: "This is a disarming book, and a pleasure to read. It's The first-person story of a young hired man *living* on a farm in Alabama *about* twenty-some years ago, *and what everything about that was like. The* authenticity is worth something, and the pleasure [it takes] in life *in it* is worth more" (MDAH WC18, Marrs 68).

18. The following deletion from the end of this sentence reiterates Welty's criticism of authorial manipulation of characters and dialogue by praising Kroll's style: "because of the absence of any wish on the author's part to teach us anything or belabor us with psychology or morals. A more free-flowing and natural wisdom plays about the characters than any of that would call for" (MDAH WC18, Marrs 68).

19. Kroll's other novels are also about the South. *The Cabin in the Cotton* (1931) was the most successful, but it was probably *Rogues' Company: A Novel of John Murrell* (1943) that was interesting to Welty who had also fictionalized John Murrell in her 1942 story "A Still Moment." Her research for several historically-based stories qualifies her to judge authenticity in Kroll's novels.

20. Welty's first review of a significant author is twice as long as her nine previous ones and is placed a page or two earlier in the *Book Review*. It was deleted from the galleys of *The Eye of the Story: Selected Essays and Reviews*, probably to shorten the book (New York: Random House, 1978; hereafter cited as *Eye*). See MDAH WC16, Marrs 59–63. For a discussion of this review in relation to Welty's fiction, see Kreyling, *Author* 108–10.

21. As she was writing an introduction for a new printing of *To the Lighthouse*, Welty acknowledged her debt to Woolf: "I know, even though I couldn't show in my work, . . . the sense of what she has done certainly influenced me as an artist" (Prenshaw 325).

22. For an account of Welty's early pleasure in reading Perelman, see her review of his *Baby, It's Cold Inside*, *NYTBR* 30 August 1970: 1, 25.

23. "Dyak" or "Dayak" refers to the Indonesian people of the area of Borneo, and "Dyak-like tread" suggests, in the parlance of the times, an identification of Perelman's witty outrageousness with the "Wild Man of Borneo," a stock freak show figure.

24. Clifford Odets (1906–63) wrote social protest plays including *Waiting for Lefty* (1935) and *Awake and Sing* (1935).

25. For a discussion of Welty's use of a pseudonym, see introduction.

26. Welty often insists on truth and passion in fiction, and here, in art and in nonfiction.

27. Francisco de Goya (1746–1828, see note 16 for *A Garland of Straw*). In a passage not quoted in Welty's review, Biddle writes that he aspires to "create a mood, through color, line, and that indirect approach . . . which will supplement that particular episode of horror selected to illustrate the essence of war. Goya of course always had it." *Artist at War* (New York: Viking, 1944) 56.

28. In a 1978 interview, Welty said, "I remember reading that Goya had trained himself as an artist to see action, and when he drew a falling horse everyone said the figure was completely grotesque, but that was before the invention of photography, which proved that Goya's eyes saw everything absolutely right, the way a falling horse looked in mid air" (Prenshaw 263).

29. See Welty's review of *G. I. Sketch Book*, ed. Aimee Crane, *NYTBR* 29 October 1944: 20.

30. See also her next review of two more mystery story collections, *Sleep No More* and *Jumbee and Other Uncanny Tales*, *NYTBR* 24 September 1944: 5, 21.

31. *Weird Tales*, a genre magazine (1923–54) founded by H. P. Lovecraft, published many of the writers named in Welty's review.

32. "The Fireplace" is set at the Planter's Hotel, which burns to the ground in 1922 according to the story.

33. The term "Jumbee," Whitehead explains in the story "Black Tancrède," means "virtually any kind of ghost, apparition or *revenant*" in the West Indies (68).

34. In his history of the *New York Times*, Gay Talese explains that books by people from the *Times* "were nearly always given generous, if not extensive, treatment" (*The Kingdom and the Power* New York: World Publishing, 1969: 266). *Enjoy Your House Plants* might not have been reviewed except that Dorothy H. Jenkins was the garden editor of the *Times*. This relationship suggests another reason for the review's brevity and for the byline to be Welty's initials only.

35. According to William Hollingsworth's journal, the Municipal Art Gallery of Jackson, Mississippi, purchased a painting by Fredenthal in March or April 1943. See Jane Hollingsworth, ed., *Hollingsworth: The Man, the Artist, and His Work* (Jackson: U P of Mississippi, 1981) 61, 63. In her review, Welty does not mention Richard Wilcox's text, which takes the form of paragraphs describing each of Fredenthal's drawings. Wilcox, an associate editor for *Life*, had reported from several naval fronts.

36. A trade edition titled *Art in the Armed Forces* was published simultaneously by Hyperion Press and distributed by Scribner. It was nearly one hundred pages longer and was the book reviewed by most other journals. Both editions included brief biographies of the contributing artist-soldiers.

37. The correct title is *A Beleaguered City*.

38. *The Return* was first published in 1910, but it is the revised edition of 1922 that is reprinted in the Viking Portable collection that Welty reviewed.

39. *Portrait of Jennie* was published in 1940, not 1920.

40. Irving and his companions, Englishman Charles Joseph Latrobe and Swiss-Yankee Albert Pourtales, met with Judge Henry Leavitt Ellsworth at Fort Gibson. From there, Ellsworth was to supervise the 1830 Indian removal. Bean, whom Irving called Captain, was a ranger who hunted and protected the party on their tour.

41. *Prarie* is Irving's spelling. *A Tour of the Prairies* was published as part of *The Crayon Miscellany* (1835); however, the sample chapter included in *The Western Journals* is "The Creole Village," first published in 1837 in *The Magnolia*, then in *The Adventure of Captain Bonneville* (also 1837) and later in *Wolfert's Roost* (1855). "The Creole Village" was never in *A Tour of the Prairies* as McDermott (and Welty) suggest.

42. The following lines were cut at this point from Welty's typescript for the published review; they are not restored for *The Eye of the Story*: "—for instance, read his account of the bee hunt—he could be specific as well as splendid with vital detail. He could write with considerable pace when the need arose, and cover wide territory and fast action in one of his nimble, dash-filled paragraphs." (MDAH WC16, Marrs 54) See W. U. McDonald, Jr., "*The Eye of the Story*: Bibliographic Notes on the Contents," *Eudora Welty Newsletter* 2.2 (Summer 1978): 1–5 for brief notes on the variants between the reviews in *NYTBR* and *Eye*.

43. Welty's following quotation from the *Journals* was deleted from her typescript for the published review and not restored in *The Eye of the Story* version: "'Chief cook of Osage villages—a great dignitary—combining grand chamberlain, minister of state, master of ceremonies and town crier—has under-cooks. He tastes broth & c. When strangers arrive he goes about the village and makes proclamation— . . . a tall man painted-head decorated with feathers— —had an old greatcoat, with a wolf's tail dangling below.'" (MDAH WC16, Marrs 54).

44. *My Darling of the Lions* (Boston: Little, Brown, 1943).

45. Glenway Wescott had written eleven other books including poetry, novels, short stories, and essays before *Apartment in Athens*. That Wescott was a best-selling author is probably the reason for the page-one review. The other possible page-one book reviewed on that date was Richard Wright's *Black Boy* (4 March 1945: 3).

46. *Fireman Flower* (Hogarth Press, 1944). Welty reviewed the 1945 Vanguard Press (New York) edition which has the following blurb by her on the front flap of the dust jacket: "Hurrah for *Fireman Flower*. I read it with pleasure . . . The book is bound to prove exciting when you bring it out. Mr. Sansom makes one feel the powerful impression of an original mind at work—these are stories of compelling imagination and intensity. —Eudora Welty." The published review is a somewhat longer and slightly rearranged version of Welty's carbon typescript (MDAH WC18, Marrs 70).

47. Giorgio de Chirico (1888–1978) was a pioneer of metaphysical painting. His work was exhibited with the 1936 exhibit "Fantastic Art, Dada, and Surrealism"

(Museum of Modern Art). Other de Chirico works are in the New York Museum of Modern Art and the Art Institute of Chicago; see note 16 for *A Garland of Straw*.

48. *Storm* (New York: Random House, 1941), *Ordeal by Hunger; The Story of the Donner Party* (New York: H. Holt, 1936).

49. Welty's enjoyment of *Names on the Land* should not be confused with her interest in "place in fiction," although Stewart's book suggests answers to the questions Welty asks about a place: "Location is the crossroads of circumstance, the proving ground of 'What happened? Who's here? Who's coming?'" (*Eye* 118).

50. Undset's edition is based on stories collected by Norwegian folklorists Jørgen Moe and Peter Christian Asbjørnsen.

51. "Ahslad" in the *NYTBR*. "The Ashlad Who Made the Princess Say, 'You lie.'" *True and Untrue* 173–75.

52. Illustrated by Frederick T. Chapman.

53. Alexander Alexeieff.

54. Roman Jakobson provided the "folkloristic commentary."

55. Gustave Doré (1832–83).

56. The Federal Writers' Project, created in 1935 as part of Franklin Roosevelt's Works Progress Administration, sponsored guides for the forty-eight states. Lyle Saxon, State Supervisor, and Edward Dreyer, Assistant State Supervisor, directed the writing of *Louisiana: A Guide to the State* (1941). *Gumbo Ya-Ya* expands the "Folkways" chapter (83–93).

57. Perelman cartooned and wrote for *Judge*, a popular weekly humor magazine edited by Norman Anthony, from 1925–29. "High Jinks Travelogue" is Welty's first review after Van Gelder left the *Book Review* two and a half years earlier.

58. *Dawn Ginsbergh's Revenge* (New York: H. Liveright, 1929), *Strictly from Hunger* (New York: Random House, 1937), *The Dream Department* (New York: Random House, 1943), *Crazy Like a Fox* (New York: Random House, 1944, reviewed by Welty *NYTBR* 2 July 1944: 6), *Acres and Pains* (New York: Reynal and Hitchcock, 1947).

59. All twelve essays collected were previously published in *Holiday*, edited by Ted Patrick.

60. Bao Dai, "deposed Emperor of Annam in Indonesia" (59). The quotation is taken from the following passage: "Since he spoke almost no English, the interview was necessarily limited to pidgin and whatever pathetic scraps of French we could remember from Frazier and Square. To put him at ease, I inquired sociably whether the pen of his uncle was in the garden. Apparently the query was fraught with delicate political implications involving the conflict in Indo-China, for he shrugged evasively and buried his nose in his whiskey-and-soda" (*Westward Ha!* 60).

61. Macao, "the last remnant of Portuguese glory in China" is an island near Hong Kong (*Westward Ha!* 63).

62. In *Westward Ha!* Tungku Makhota is a Malaysian ruler (70).

63. *Young Man with a Horn* (Boston: Houghton Mifflin, 1938), Baker's first novel, is inspired by the life of jazz musician Leon Bismark (Bix) Beiderbecke (1903–31).

64. Welty may be thinking of Leslie Fiedler's essay "Come Back to the Raft Ag'in, Huck Honey!" a Freudian analysis (*Partisan Review* June 1948: 664–71).

65. In his review of *Intruder in the Dust*, "William Faulkner's Reply to the Civil-Rights Program" (*New Yorker* 23 October 1948: 120–28), Edmund Wilson charged that "Faulkner's weakness has also its origin in the antiquated community he inhabits, for it consists in his not having mastered . . . the discipline of the Joyces, Prousts, and Conrads. . . . Faulkner's provinciality, stubbornly cherished and turned into an asset, inevitably tempts him to be slipshod and has apparently made it impossible for him to acquire complete expertness in an art that demands of the artist the closest attention and care" (121–22). Welty responded to Wilson in a letter to the editors of the *New Yorker*, who printed it under "Department of Amplification," 1 January 1949: 50–51. She quoted Wilson and asked, "Could the simple, though superfluous, explanation not be that the recipient of the impact [of the south], Mr. Faulkner, is the different component here, possessing the brain as he does, and that the superiority of the work done lies in that brain?" (51). She also wrote to her friend John Robinson, "Faulkner is getting it from everywhere" (MDAH WC29, Marrs 176–77).

The *Hudson Review* had already bought Welty's story "Sir Rabbit" for the Spring 1949 issue, but perhaps the publication asked Welty to review *Intruder* for the Winter issue (January-February) 1949, after seeing her reply to Wilson in the *New Yorker*. In her review, Welty responds further to Wilson without naming him.

66. Wilson had complained, "This is one of the more snarled-up of Faulkner's books. It is not so bad as 'The Bear', which has pages that are almost opaque" (120).

67. Welty's review responds to Wilson's complaint that, "It would require a good deal of very diligent work and very nice calculation always to turn out the combinations of words that would do what Faulkner wants. His energy, his image-making genius get him where he wants to go about seventy per cent of the time, but when he misses it, he lands in a mess" (120). In an anonymously printed essay, "Place and Time: The Southern Writer's Inheritance" (*Times Literary Supplement*: *American Writing Today* 17 September 1954: xlviii), Welty wrote that Faulkner's "work is a whole that cannot be satisfactorily analyzed and accounted for, until it can be predicted—Lord save the day."

68. Arthur A. (Fritz) Peters's own breakdown occurred "about a year after his discharge from the Army, with which he was in Europe thirty-seven months as regimental stenographer, interpreter and translator, section general's secretary and claims officer," reported Hollis Alpert, "The Mind in Torment" *Saturday Review* September 17, 1949: 11. Welty was friends with Peters and his wife Mary Louise Aswell, who was Welty's editor at *Harper's Bazaar*.

69. Diarmuid Russell, literary agent for Welty and Peters, may have recommended Welty as a reader for the publisher, Farrar, Straus. The following blurb was published on the rear panel of the dust jacket for *The World Next Door*: "This book must be unique. It seems to reveal a world in a way and on a level which no other account of a like experience has either accomplished or attempted. Before our eyes this world *is* madness and pure logic and dream, produced in its changes—with much power, but as easily and objectively as bubbles from a pipe—simultaneously or one after the other in new combinations. It has the value of an honest and complete and new study of experience, brilliantly set down, and the excitement of some superior mystery or spy story—for it is the very material of suspense. Mr. Peters has done a thrilling piece of work, which this reader, once having begun it, could not put down" (3). Portions of Welty's comments were also printed on the publisher's invitation to read Peters's book and on the dust jacket of his next book *Finistère* (1951). Reproduced in George Bixby, "Blurbs: Welty on Fritz Peters," *Eudora Welty Newsletter* 4.1 (1980): 2–6; see also Noel Polk, *Eudora Welty: A Bibliography of Her Work* (Jackson: U P of Mississippi, 1993) 394.

70. In 1949, Welty visited San Lorenzo, Nice, and Siena, Italy. See Welty, *Photographs* (Jackson: U P of Mississippi, 1989) images 188–89, 195–98, and 213.

71. Welty contributed the following blurb that was printed on the rear panel of the dust jacket for *South*: "Mr. Sansom's writing is always interesting because it is always working . . . Like a microscope, a seismograph, an aerial, or a harp, it can pick up details and fluctuations the rest of us miss" (2). Reproduced in George Bixby, "Blurbs: Welty on William Sansom" *Eudora Welty Newsletter* 7.1 (1983): 1–3; Polk 394.

72. Welty reviewed Sansom's first story collection *Fireman Flower*, *Tomorrow* May 1945: 69–70. His other books were *Three* (London: Hogarth Press, 1946; New York: Reynal and Hitchcock, 1947) and *The Body* (London: Hogarth Press, 1949; New York: Harcourt, Brace, 1949).

73. This sentence is used on the rear panel of the dust jacket for Sansom's next book, *The Face of Innocence* (New York: Harcourt, Brace, 1951). Reproduced in Bixby, "Blurbs: Welty on William Sansom" (3); Polk 395.

74. Throughout the review, the author's name is misspelled "Macauley." It has been corrected here.

75. Macaulay had written twenty-one novels, three travel books, and some poetry and criticism, including *The Writings of E. M. Forster* (New York: Harcourt, Brace, 1938). During her travels to England and Ireland in 1949, Welty met Elizabeth Bowen and possibly Macaulay, who was Bowen's friend. Spencer Curtis Brown was literary agent for both Bowen and Macaulay.

76. Peter Breughel, the Elder, sixteenth century Flemish painter, painted rural peasant scenes such as *Wheat Harvest* or *August* (1565, New York Metropolitan

Museum of Art) and *Peasant Wedding Dance* (1566, Detroit Institute of Art) that contrast humankind with nature. See also note 2 for *Sweet Beulah Land.*

77. Janet Flanner's translation of *Cheri* is dated 1929.

78. Wescott wrote the "Introduction" for the collection.

79. The bracketed phrase, a line dropped from the printed review, is from Welty's carbon typescript of the review (MDAH WC18, Marrs 68).

80. Beginning around 1950, a sentence beneath a *NYTBR* review gave further identification of the reviewer. The following tag accompanies the Guareschi review: "Miss Welty, an American novelist and short-story writer who has spent much time in Italy, is the author most recently of *The Golden Apples*" (*NYTBR* 17 August 1952: 4). Welty traveled in Italy in 1949 and 1951.

81. *The Little World of Don Camillo* (New York: Farrar, Straus and Giroux, 1950).

82. Although it is not mentioned in the reviewer note, Welty visited Brighton, England, in summer 1951 (Kreyling, *Author* 155).

83. Patrick Hamilton (1904–62, British) wrote eight novels and three plays prior to *The West Pier* (1952) and its successor, *Mr. Stimpson and Mr. Gorse* (1953). Hamilton is best remembered for his plays *Rope* (1929) and *Gaslight* (1939) that were cast successfully into films by Alfred Hitchcock (1948) and George Cukor (1944) respectively.

84. Welty's opening paragraph written in a whimsical style to match the style of White's novel was deleted from the typescript for the *NYTBR*. Two other paragraphs of quotations from the novel were also cut, probably to shorten the review to fit onto the children's book pages. (The White review already required one page more than usually allotted for children's books.) More than twenty additional substantive changes were made from the typescript to the printed review, nearly all of them altering the style of Welty's review and changing the point of view from first to third person. Welty reportedly sent a copy of her typescript to White after the edited review was printed. She used her typescript for the setting copy of *The Eye of the Story.* Below are Welty's opening paragraph and a collation of a few other changes:

"If I had the qualifications (a set of spinnerets and the know-how), I'd put in tonight writing 'Adorable' across my web, to be visible Sunday morning hung with dew drops for my review of *Charlotte's Web.*" (*Eye* 203)

"varied, but not opposites" (*Eye* 204), "varied but not simple or opposites" (*NYTBR* 49); "for freedom" (*Eye* 204), "for complete freedom" (*NYTBR* 49); "When he was a baby the sun shone pink through his ears, endearing him" (*Eye* 204), "When he was a baby, he was a runt, but the sun shone pink through his ears, endearing him" (*NYTBR* 49); "they see what she's written for them—'Salutations!'" (*Eye* 204), "she says 'Salutations!'" (*NYTBR* 49); "earth, love and affection" (*Eye* 205), "earth, affection" (*NYTBR* 49); "night and day and seasons" (*Eye* 205), "pleasure and pain, and the passing of time" (*NYTBR* 49); "perfect, and perfectly effortless and magical, as far as I can see, in the doing" (*Eye* 205), "perfect and just about magical in the way it is done" (*NYTBR* 49).

85. The intent of this final paragraph is lost without Welty's original beginning (see note 84). The phrase "I will say" (not in the typescript) is added to the *Eye* version preceding "*Charlotte's Web* is an adorable book" for further clarification of the point of view (206).

86. The following sentence concludes this paragraph on the typescript: "Some of the stories themselves are Janus-like; and we may have seen so far, of his talent, only the face that looks back." (MDAH WC18, Marrs 69).

87. *The Catcher in the Rye* (Boston: Little, Brown, 1951).

88. The following sentence from the typescript is deleted here: "Very likely the short story is an especially happy form for such a talent to work in, because that medium's demands are higher and more special, and are difficult enough for his powers—and are thus a springboard." (MDAH WC18, Marrs 69).

89. *The Eye of the Story* review includes a quotation here to describe Battersea Rise, several sentences of additional quotation and description, and a rewritten final paragraph corresponding with the last two paragraphs of the *NYTBR* review. See *Eye* 221–26 and MDAH WC16, Marrs 58, 61.

90. Forster also appreciated Welty's writings. In 1947 he wrote to her, "I feel I should like to give myself the pleasure of writing you a line and telling you how much I enjoy your work *The Wide Net*. All the wild and lovely things it brings up have often been with and delighted me" (298). Quoted by Welty in "Writers' Panel" in *E. M. Forster: Centenary Revaluations*, eds. Judith Scherer Herz and Robert K. Martin (Toronto: U of Toronto P, 1982) 285–307. Welty and Forster met in Cambridge in 1954 (Prenshaw 34). Welty makes frequent reference to Forster in "The Reading and Writing of Short Stories" (1949), reprinted with revisions as "Looking at Short Stories" in *Eye*, 85–106.

91. Critical praise for *Rain on the Wind* (New York: Macmillan, 1950) and *The Bogman* (New York: Macmillan, 1952) appears on the rear dust jacket of *The Green Hills*.

92. Macken (1915–1967) was from Galway, Ireland. Descendants of thirteenth century ruler of the region, Richard de Burgh, became known as the tribes of Galway.

93. For Welty's revision in *The Eye of the Story*, this explanation of Dinesen's real name, the titles of Dinesen's previous books in paragraph two, and the rhetorical questions in paragraphs five and six are deleted. See *Eye* 260–63.

94. *Seven Gothic Tales* (New York: Modern Library, 1934), *Out of Africa* (New York: Random House, 1938), *Winter's Tales* (New York: Random House, 1942).

95. See also Welty's comments in *Isak Dinesen: A Memorial*, ed. Clara Svendsen (New York: Random House, 1965) 94–95.

96. The review in the *New York Herald Tribune* (9 October 1927) was titled "An

Essay in Criticism." Ernest Hemingway, *Men Without Women* (New York: Scribner's Sons, 1927).

97. Welty used her typescript rather than the *NYTBR* review as setting copy for *The Eye of the Story*. There are three substantive but minor differences between the *NYTBR* and *Eye* versions (21 September 1958: 6; *Eye* 190–92). For example, in the typescript and in *Eye*, this paragraph begins "This is published today in *Granite and Rainbow*" (MDAH WC16, Marrs 54, 57; *Eye* 190).

98. *The Common Reader* (1925), *The Common Reader: Second Series* (1932), *The Death of the Moth and Other Essays* (1942), *The Moment and Other Essays* (1947), *The Captain's Death Bed and Other Essays* (1950) were all published by Hogarth Press in England.

99. Dr. Mary Lyon and Miss Brownlee Jean Kirkpatrick.

100. Marie Corelli, pseudonym for Mary Mackay (1855–1924), wrote popular novels, but was greatly ridiculed toward the end of her life. Woolf's review of *Marie Corelli: The Life and Death of a Best Seller* by George Bullock (1940) begins "This is a depressing book" (*Granite* 212).

101. "Phases of Fiction" *Bookman* (April, May, June 1929).

102. The word "run" appears here in Welty's typescript and in the *NYTBR*, but the text of "Life and the Novelist" in *Granite and Rainbow* reads "rush" (MDAH WC16, Marrs 57; 41).

103. Welty crossed out *"To the Light House"* and interlined "it" on the typescript; she used Woolf's title in the closing paragraph (MDAH WC16, Marrs 57).

104. "The Jumblies," a nonsense poem by Edward Lear, was included in Welty's childhood encyclopedia, *Our Wonder World*, Vol. V, 268. (See note 173 for *Oxford Companion of Children's Literature*.) Welty refers to the refrain: "Far and few, far and few,/ Are the lands where the Jumblies live;/ Their heads are green, and their hands are blue,/ And they went to sea in a Sieve."

105. Welty cited the anecdotes about the Schrafft hostess, Mr. and Mrs. Mifflin, daughter Giselle Mifflin, and Pandemonium in her review of *Crazy Like a Fox* (*NYTBR* 2 July 1944: 6).

106. The *NYTBR* error of "hair" for "ear" is corrected (12 October 1958: 8). In conjunction with the final paragraph, the byline note for the review says, "Miss Welty's own ear for American speech has been revealed in such books as *A Curtain of Green*, *Delta Wedding*, and *The Ponder Heart*" (*NYTBR* 12 October 1958: 4).

107. Green wrote *Blindness* (1926) while he was a student at Eton. His novels, *Living* (1929), *Party Going* (1939), *Caught* (1943), *Loving* (1945), *Back* (1946), *Concluding* (1948), *Nothing* (1950), and *Doting* (1942) were published in the United States by Viking Press from 1949 to 1952. His autobiography, *Pack My Bag*, was published in 1940 and 1952 in London (Hogarth Press), and in 1993 in New York (New Directions). In 1960, the year prior to reviewing Russell's critical study of Green, Welty reread all of Green to write "Henry Green: Novelist of the Imagina-

tion" *Texas Quarterly* 4 (1961): 246–56, rpt. in *Eye* 14–29. The first paragraph in the *NYTBR* collates with the third paragraph of the carbon typescript. The first two paragraphs of the CTS are constructed of sentences found elsewhere in the review and in Welty's full essay (MDAH WC16, Marrs 58).

108. Macmillan, 1960.

109. Kingsley Weatherhead, *A Reading of Henry Green* (Seattle: University of Washington Press, 1961).

110. The Russell review was deleted from the setting copy of *The Eye of the Story* presumably to shorten the book and because Welty's essay on Green was already included. See Marrs 58, 62.

111. Welty reviewed *Last Tales* by Isak Dinesen, *NYTBR* 3 November 1957: 5.

112. A comparison of the carbon typescript with the published review shows ten substantive differences. Johannesson and Welty used the word "pervasive" to describe Dinesen's theme; the *NYTBR* printed "persuasion" in error (Johannesson v; MDAH WC18, Marrs 69; *NYTBR* 17 December 1961: 6).

113. The following paragraph was deleted from the carbon typescript for the *NYTBR* publication:

"He relates her work at once, and surely this is sound, to the stage. Miss Dinesen is indeed an old hand at theatricality; one might feel still more of a relationship with the film than with the stage itself. She uses the methods of film, its freedom to move into past and future, and at a remove; its lighting, its landscape and skies; she uses its kind of dream and fantasy, humor and shock, its kind of transitions, its telescoping and extending of time, its flashbacks and stories within the story." (MDAH WC18, Marrs 69).

114. The words "beyond what he is able to convey about himself" in the typescript are deleted for the *NYTBR* review. The words are also penciled in on Welty's photocopy of the published review (MDAH WC18, Marrs 69).

115. Reviewed by Welty, *Tomorrow* (May 1945): 69–70.

116. Six novels, two novellas, eight story collections including *South* (1950) reviewed by Welty (*Saturday Review* 23 September 1950: 16–17), two children's books, and four collections of nonfiction.

117. Corrected from "wound" in *NYTBR*. A carbon typescript and a photocopy of a typescript show numerous holograph changes made in blue ink (not confirmed as Welty's hand) that are not reflected in the *NYTBR* (MDAH WC18, Marrs 69).

118. The printed review includes two dozen substantive differences from the carbon typescript including mention that a chapter from the book would be collected in an Isak Dinesen memorial anthology (see note 95 for *Last Tales* and MDAH WC18, Marrs 69–70). Welty reviewed Dinesen's *Last Tales* (*NYTBR* 3 November 1957: 5) and another critical study, Eric Johannesson, *The World of Isak Dinesen* (*NYTBR* 17 December 1961: 6).

119. *Seven Gothic Tales* (London: Putnam, 1934), *Out of Africa* (London: Putnam,

1937), *Winter's Tales* (New York: Random House, 1942), *The Angelic Avengers* (London: Putnam, 1946), *Last Tales* (New York: Random House, 1957), *Anecdotes of Destiny* (New York: Random House, 1958), *Shadows on the Grass* (New York: Random House, 1960), *Ehrengard* (New York: Random House, 1963).

120. The following words are deleted from the typescript: "it may all be one long metaphor about her work" (MDAH WC18, Marrs 69–70).

121. Referring to the gods of a medieval people of northern and eastern Europe.

122. Narrator of *The Arabian Nights' Entertainment* who told stories to delay her death by the Sultan.

123. Isam Noguchi (1904–1988), U. S. sculptor and architectural designer.

124. At some point after appreciating each other's art, Graham and Welty became acquainted. In a tribute to Welty, Graham said, "Years ago my Company and I performed in Jackson. We were very nervous because we heard that Eudora Welty was in the audience. It puts you on edge knowing an eye, let alone a heart, like that is out front." *Shenandoah* 20 (Spring 1969): 36.

125. See Welty's story "Circe," *Collected Stories* 531–37.

126. Lehman Engel, a Jackson friend of Welty's, composed the music for "Ceremonials" (1932), "Ekstasis" (1933), "Transitions" (1934), "Marching Song" (1935), and "Imperial Gesture" (1935). Welty mentions Martha Graham, "Ceremonials," and "Ekstasis" several times in her newspaper review of Engel's career, "Jackson Composer Has Full Year Program," *Jackson State Tribune* 19 June 1933: 2.

127. The fourth review, of *No Flying in the House* by Betty Brock, was printed three weeks later (*NYTBR* 16 August 1970: 22). Welty's reviews are printed beneath the title of each book. The reviewer note mentions Welty's children's book, *The Shoe Bird* (New York: Harcourt, Brace & World, 1964).

128. *The Little Man* (New York: Knopf, 1966).

129. Welty's review is one of three reviews grouped under the headline "For Young Readers." Her name appears at the conclusion of her review.

130. Illustrated by Wallace Tripp. Welty normally includes a short statement about the illustrations; perhaps it was cut from the brief review. There is no extant typescript of the review.

131. See note 57 for *Westward Ha!*.

132. Reviewed by Welty, *NYTBR* 12 October 1958: 4, 14. Reviews of *The Most of S. J. Perelman* and *Baby, It's Cold Inside* are combined and slightly revised (deletion of repetition and additional quotations) in *Eye* 235–40.

133. *The Galton Case* (New York: Alfred A. Knopf, 1959), *The Chill* (New York: Alfred A. Knopf, 1964).

134. *Underground Man* put Kenneth Millar (aka Ross Macdonald) on the cover of *Time* with an eleven-column review by editor Raymond Sokolov who quoted Welty's review ("The Art of Murder," 22 Mar. 1971: 101–02). Welty's analysis of Mac-

donald's talent in the subgenre of detective fiction in her review is often cited in academic criticism of Macdonald's writing. See, for example, Bernard A. Schopen, *Ross Macdonald* (Boston: Twayne, 1990) 20.

135. In 1970, Welty told *NYTBR* editor Walter Clemons, "I've read all his books, I think. I once wrote Ross Macdonald a fan letter but I never mailed it. I was afraid he'd think it—icky" (Prenshaw 32). Macdonald read the interview and wrote to Welty, for he had been reading all *her* books. The following year, *NYTBR* editor John Leonard asked Welty for a page-one review of *The Underground Man*, and in the fall, he organized an "accidental" meeting for Welty and Macdonald in the elevator of the Algonquin Hotel (Leonard, "I Care Who Killed Roger Ackroyd," *Esquire* August 1975: 60–61, 120). Welty's review is collected in *Eye* (251–60) in a revised and expanded version.

136. *The Good Soldier* (New York: Knopf, 1951), *Parade's End* (New York: Knopf, 1950).

137. Welty was among the young writers whom Ford tried to help. Katherine Anne Porter introduced Welty's stories to Ford, and he tried (unsuccessfully) to find a British publisher for *A Curtain of Green* in 1938 and 1939. See correspondence from Ford (MDAH WC29, Marrs 164).

138. The review was reprinted in the *Jackson Daily News* with an Editor's Note: "Robert Benchley once said 'if you can't give a friend a good review, who can you?' The *New York Times* recently asked Eudora Welty to review an old friend's book: *Words With Music* (Macmillan, $7.95), by her fellow-Jacksonian and friend from childhood, Lehman Engel. . . ." ("Welty Reviews Engel's Book" 18 June 1972: 6F).

139. Neither Welty nor Engel mentions that Welty's 1954 novella *The Ponder Heart* was adapted for Broadway by Jerome Chodorov and Joseph Fields, although the reviewer tag notes that the adaptation "enjoyed a successful run" (*NYTBR* 28 May 1972: 7).

140. Clive Barnes, theater critic for the *New York Times* in the 1960s, 70s, and 80s.

141. *A Passage to India* (New York: Harcourt, Brace, 1924).

142. *E. M. Forster: A Life* 2 vols. (London: Secher and Warburg, 1977–78).

143. *The Novels of Jane Austen*, ed. R. W. Chapman, 6 vols. (Oxford: Oxford U P, 1933–69).

144. *Maurice* (New York: Norton, 1971).

145. *NYTBR* editors Nash K. Burger and John Leonard convinced Welty to review Dillard's book. Welty was reluctant because she had met Dillard previously at a conference (Burger, letter to the editor, 1991; Welty, interview with the editor, 1993). *Pilgrim at Tinker Creek* won the 1975 Pulitzer Prize for general non-fiction.

146. In 1971 Welty published her 1930s photographs, *One Time, One Place: Mississippi in the Depression, A Snapshot Album* (New York: Random House), although this is not noted in the reviewer tag.

147. *The Triumph of Will* (1935) and *Olympiad* (1938), Nazi propaganda film epics of noted artistic merit.

148. Eugene Atget (1857–1927), French photographer.

149. *The People of Moscow, Seen by Henri Cartier-Bresson* (New York: Simon and Schuster, 1955).

150. *NYTBR* printed "composition," but "competition" is penciled on Welty's photocopy of the published review and is used here (MDAH WC23, Marrs 194).

151. On her copy of the *NYTBR* review, Welty wrote "Use my original copy instead of this" (MDAH WC23, Marrs 195). The review in *The Eye of the Story* (269–76) includes six additional paragraphs, a different organization in three places, and numerous minor variations from the *NYTBR* piece (See also MDAH WC16, Marrs 59, 62).

152. Bowen and Welty met in 1949 in Ireland and began a lifelong friendship. See Peggy Whitman Prenshaw "The Antiphonies of Eudora Welty's *One Writer's Beginnings* and Elizabeth Bowen's *Pictures and Conversations*" in *Welty: A Life in Literature*, ed. Albert J. Devlin (Jackson: U P of Mississippi, 1987): 225–37.

153. *The Death of the Heart* (1938), *The Little Girls* (1964), *Eva Trout* (1968).

154. Patrick White (1912–1990), Australian novelist, winner of the 1973 Nobel Prize.

155. *Lady Ottoline's Album*, ed. Carolyn G. Heilbrun (New York: Knopf, 1976), a collection of Lady Ottoline Murrell's photographs, is given a brief review above a portion of Welty's review of *Letters* (*NYTBR* 14 November 1976: 12).

156. Perhaps Welty refers to the letter written April 17, 1916 (*Letters* 89–90).

157. In a brief remark under "Author's Authors" (*NYTBR* 5 December 1976: 4, 102–5), Welty names both the *Letters* and *Mrs. Dalloway's Party: A Short Story Sequence* by Virginia Woolf, ed. Stella McNichol (London: Hogarth Press, 1973) as interesting books she has read recently (102).

158. The review in *The Eye of the Story* includes a few variants from the *NYTBR* and additional quotations from the letters from Welty's typescript. Here, for example, she restores, "(There are a few brief explanatory notes to introduce some of the correspondents, and a good index, which will help you to find your place.)" (*Eye* 213 and 217–18 for additional letters quoted and MDAH WC16, Marrs 57, 61.)

159. Cartoonist Willie Gropper and journalist Paxton Hibben are among the protesters that Welty listed in her typescript (MDAH WC18, Marrs 70).

160. Lola Ridge (1871–1941) was a poet, whose novel *Firehead* (1929) was said to have been inspired by the Sacco-Vanzetti case.

161. In *Katherine Anne Porter: A Life* (London: Jonathon Cape, 1982), Joan Givner, points out that Welty is the only reviewer who notes the thematic link between Porter's fiction and her memoir of the Sacco-Vanzetti executions (193).

162. The majority were published first in the *New Yorker*, to which White started contributing in 1925, the year of its founding.

163. In the 1920s, Welty published a drawing and two poems in *St. Nicholas* (1873–1940), a monthly magazine for young readers (Polk 409).

164. In Coleridge's "Kubla Khan."

165. Prior to writing the review, Welty commented, "V. S. Pritchett's work has never stopped flowing from an original spring. In its abundance—the brilliant and unpredictable stories, the beautiful volumes of autobiography, the vigorous criticism, generous biographies—he seems to have written with the wisdom of experience and the freshness of youth. His relish of books and life is still undiminished" ("Writers' Writers" *NYTBR* 4 December 1977: 74). In a 1978 interview, also prior to receiving *Selected Stories* for review, Welty said that she regretted never writing about "P. G. Wodehouse, V. S. Pritchett, Edward Lear" (Prenshaw 231). See Welty's review of *The Oxford Companion to Children's Literature* (*NYTBR* 19 August 1981: 17) for her defense of Lear as a humorist.

166. Welty and Bowen became personally acquainted in 1949, although Bowen had reviewed Welty's first novel, *Delta Wedding*, two years earlier (*The Tatler and Bystander* 6 Aug. 1947: 182–83).

167. *Collected Stories of Eudora Welty* (New York: Harcourt, Brace, Jovanovich, 1980) published the previous year (1981), is noted beneath the review.

168. Iona and Peter Opie edited several books of children's folklore including *Oxford Dictionary of Nursery Rhymes* (1951) and *Oxford Book of Children's Verse* (1973).

169. *Alice's Adventures in Wonderland* (London: Macmillan, 1865).

170. Welty praised *The Catcher in the Rye* in her review of Salinger's *Nine Stories* (*NYTBR* 5 April 1953: 4).

171. See Welty's review of *Charlotte's Web* (*NYTBR* 19 October 1952: 49 and in *Eye* 203–06).

172. See notes 104 for *Granite and Rainbow* and 165 for *Selected Stories* by V. S. Pritchett.

173. Welty owned and read from the ten volumes of *Our Wonder World* (Chicago: Geo. L. Schuman, 1914); see *One Writer's Beginnings* (Cambridge: Harvard U P, 1984) 8–9 and "A Sweet Devouring" (*Eye* 279–85) for descriptions of her childhood reading.

Index

Index

Index

Index